THE BEST OF NORTHERN ITALIAN COOKING

HEDY GIUSTI-LANHAM
AND
ANDREA DODI

BARRON'S

First paperback edition 1994.
Published by Barron's Educational Series, Inc.
Previously published as *The Cuisine of Venice &
Surrounding Northern Regions*.

All inquiries should be addressed to:
Barron's Educational Series, Inc.
250 Wireless Boulevard
Hauppauge, New York 11788

Photographic Credits.

The color photographs in this book are by
Matthew Klein.

The black and white photographs are by
Leon J. Perer — Aries Studio.

Table settings are from
Ginori Fifth Avenue, 711 Fifth Avenue, New York City.

Cover design by Milton Glaser, Inc.

Library of Congress Catalog Card No. 94-14870

International Standard Book No. 0-8120-1122-8

Library of Congress Cataloging in Publication Data
Giusti-Lanham, Hedy.
   [Cuisine of Venice & surrounding northern regions]
   The best of northern Italian cooking / by Hedy Giusti-
Lanham and Andrea Dodi.
        p.   cm.
   Originally published: The cuisine of Venice & surround-
ing northern region. © 1978.
   Includes index.
   1. Cookery, Italian—Northern style.   I. Dodi, Andrea.
II. Title.
TX723.2.N65G58   1994
641.5945'31—dc20   94-14870
                                                  CIP

PRINTED IN HONG KONG BY WING KING TONG CO., LTD.

   45   130   98765

CONTENTS

ACKNOWLEDGMENTS

I would like to extend my gratitude to all the wonderful hostesses in the Veneto, from the Palazzi of Venice to the farms of Friuli.

I wish to express my special thanks to Marchese Roi of Vicenza and to Marialuisa Giacometti, not only for the great dinners I have enjoyed at their villas, but also for their generosity in sharing with me their priceless recipes.

And finally, I want to thank Professor John McAndrew, the most Venetian of all Americans, whose enjoyment of Venetian foods was a constant inspiration to me.

INTRODUCTION

This is by no means a *classic* Italian cookbook. It is the result of my experience as a hostess, first in Europe, then in various parts of the United States, with a very American husband and a wealth of American friends. I have learned to use the raw materials of this country, and I have discovered that there are some foods, including some vegetables, that are better here than in Europe. I try to use them as much as possible.

I have learned to adapt my style of cooking to the American style of living. For example, I try to avoid dishes that require the cook to be in the kitchen to the very last moment before eating. As both the cook and hostess, I enjoy having a glass of wine with my husband and guests before sitting down for a meal.

I have not, however, neglected the great classic dishes. When I have taken liberties with their ingredients or their preparations, I have clearly said so. The classic recipes for *Gnocchi alla Romana* or *Gnocchi di Semolino,* for example, are followed by a version of *Gnocchi alla Romana* made with hominy grits. Purists will hate me for it but only until they try it.

I have lived and cooked happily in this country for many years now and I have come to the conclusion that there is no Italian dish that cannot be duplicated with American ingredients or with ingredients available in this country. Some, like Parmesan cheese or *fontina,* have to be imported, but they are readily available in most parts of this country.

My recipes are strongly influenced by the region of Italy that ranges, roughly speaking, from Genoa and Turin to Trieste and the Austrian border. But they are most particularly of the region called *"Il Veneto,"* which ranges from the shores of Lake Garda to the Yugoslav border. I have made a few gastronomic excursions to the south of that region but the majority of the recipes have a strong Venetian flavor.

I have included a few recipes that some readers may consider "run of the mill." However, these recipes are part of the Italian cuisine, and what may be familiar to some may not be familiar to all.

There are relatively few pasta dishes included in this book. This is because in the Veneto there are relatively few devoted pasta eaters. (A pasta eater is a

person who cannot conceive of a meal, particularly a luncheon, that doesn't start with pasta.) It is also because most other books on Italian cooking contain a multitude of pasta dishes. But the reader will find a wealth of recipes for *risotto* in this book, ranging from the classic versions to the most recent and unusual variations. The reader will also be introduced to the glory that is *polenta* — that marvelous concoction made with cornmeal — and to the almost infinite varieties of using it.

I have put great emphasis on vegetables, a sadly neglected food in this country. They may be neglected because cooks are not aware of the many ways of preparing them. One might not like boiled (which is usually over-boiled) zucchini, but stuffed, sautéed, or grated zucchini are entirely different experiences. Nor do peas have to be boiled, with all their taste thrown out with the water in which they were boiled. The same is true of spinach; and eggplant doesn't *have* to be deep fried. The only rule to keep in mind when cooking vegetables is that they be in season. Hothouse vegetables, or produce that has been in cold storage too long, have little taste. Meat has always been somewhat of a luxury for a large section of Italy's population, with the result that a wonderful and tasty cuisine based on vegetables has developed. This cuisine is part of the daily diet of all Italians, regardless of their financial status.

It is inevitable that an Italian cookbook should be somewhat regional. The differences among the cuisines of the various regions are quite striking. This is a northern cookbook.

The differences between the cuisines of Venice and Turin, between that of Genoa and Verona make for great gastronomic variety. But there is one thing that these specialties from the different regions of Italy have in common: they are not overly complicated. If you enjoy cooking, you will be able to prepare them. And they won't take all your time.

I come from a very food conscious family. At the age of six I graduated from licking the spoon with the rest of the chocolate pudding to watching, spellbound, what the cook was doing. At the age of eighteen I was a hostess with a reputation for serving great food. Later on in postwar Berlin, as the wife of the *New York Times* correspondent, I managed to serve the best meals in the U.S. press community — or so I was told.

Some years ago, Andrea Dodi and I had the idea of creating an Italian cooking school in New York City. I chose the dishes to be prepared and explained their origins to the students. I also chose the wines. Andrea Dodi did the cooking. The school is still very much alive. Working at the school has convinced me that anyone who can cook, or even only wants to cook, can prepare a fine Italian meal. Italian cuisine at its best is relatively simple. All it requires is a little practice and a sensitive palate, since it is an extremely subtle cuisine. This last statement may come as a surprise to many who are used to

so-called Italian restaurants with their overuse of tomato sauce laced with an almost lethal dose of garlic.

Andrea Dodi is one of the really fine chefs I have met. At the school I learned some of his tricks: they are incorporated into the recipes in this book. In addition, the following recipes are exclusively Andrea Dodi's:

Gnocchi Verdi (Spinach Dumplings), page 141

Trancio di Pesce Spada or *Tonno alla Griglia* (Boston Scrod or Swordfish, Baked or Broiled), page 176

Petti di Pollo al Vermouth (Chicken Breasts with Vermouth), pages 194-95

Petti di Tacchino Cardinale (Turkey Breasts Cardinale), pages 198-99

Petto di Vitello Ripieno (Stuffed Veal Breast), pages 210-12

Polpettone di Manzo (Beef Meat Loaf), pages 244-45

Coscia di Agnello (Roast Leg of Lamb), pages 247-48

Pasticcio di Carne (Meat Loaf), pages 255-56

Rognoni d'Agnello (Lamb Kidneys), page 268

Lenticchie (Lentils), pages 288-89

Soffiato all'Arancio Rapido (Orange Soufflé), page 317

Torta di Cioccolata (Chocolate Cake), page 323

Sorbetto al Melone (Cantaloupe Sherbet), page 338

I have, at times, looked at a recipe and felt that it was just too much trouble. I hope that none of the recipes in this book will make you feel that way. I love to entertain and I frequently have no help, yet I manage to be with my guests before we sit down for dinner. All it takes is a little careful planning. Many dishes may be prepared in advance and require little, or no, last minute touches.

I have given instructions when food processors may be used because this new kitchen wonder has become part of so many people's standard equipment and it is making our lives a lot easier. Lastly, I have included menu suggestions as well as recommendations for appropriate wines to be served with each dish.

Eating should be a pleasure. I hope this book will make it so for you and your guests.

INGREDIENTS

Oil

Oil is one of the basic ingredients in Italian cuisine and many dishes are cooked in oil or in half oil, half butter. In our recipes, we have given the measurements for oil very carefully because too much oil, particularly in vegetables or salads, can destroy a dish.

For certain dishes olive oil is a must. This is true of all dishes in which the oil is uncooked, as in salads or in seasonings for raw vegetables. You have to *taste* the oil. When olive oil is essential for the recipe, we have indicated that in the listing of ingredients.

What olive oil you choose depends upon your personal taste. For sauces I prefer the greenish genuine oil of southern Italy; it has the taste of ripe olives. For salad dressings, on the other hand, the taste might be too strong. In that case, the refined oil (golden in color) of northern Italy is preferable. Lucca produces the best olive oil, but the oil of Imperia, on the northern seashore, is also very fine. The most important thing is to find genuine oil that hasn't been tampered with.

For frying, or deep frying, olive oil is not necessary. In fact, I sometimes prefer corn oil or similar oil to olive oil. The same is true for dishes where half oil, half butter is used. Even for basting broiled fish, I find corn oil satisfactory.

Fish soups are another matter, however. In a soup the oil adds flavor and should definitely be olive oil. Whether you use the hardy green oil of the south or the golden refined oil of the north is up to you; it is a question only your palate can answer.

Butter

The question of butter versus margarine is somewhat the same as that for oil. When the butter is an added taste in the dish it has to be butter, but if you

want to fry an egg and want to taste the egg rather than the fat it is fried in, there is no reason why you shouldn't use margarine.

We have tried margarine and found it not at all offensive. I don't think anyone could call it tasty because it has no taste (if it is good quality margarine, that is). The caloric content is the same for butter, but the cholesterol is much less.

Vinegar

Many of the recipes in this book use vinegar. We have only two rules for vinegar: that it be wine vinegar and that it be unflavored.

Rice

Americans are proud of their long grain rice and rightly so. It makes excellent steamed rice and superb Pilaf. But it also makes a rather unsatisfactory *risotto*. For a really great *risotto*, the short, thick grains of Italian rice are needed. The final result of a *risotto* — grains that are *al dente*, yet held together by a creamy substance — is only produced with Italian rice.

Italian rice, often sold in little canvas bags, is available in many specialty stores as well as in most Italian groceries.

Flour and Cornmeal

The recipes in this book use the all-purpose flour. This includes the recipes for pasta. Over the years I have heard many people say that pasta in this country can't compete with pasta made in Italy because the wheat is different. That is pure fiction. Most of the wheat used in Italy comes from the United States. The only difference between the pasta there and here is the skill in preparing it. If at first it doesn't work for you, keep trying.

Cornmeal is another important ingredient in this book, since it is used in *polenta*. Try to find the coarse cornmeal sold in Italian groceries. If you can't find it, then get the coarsest American variety. And if you use hominy grits for your *gnocchi*, get the medium coarse variety.

Cheese

When a certain cheese is given in a recipe but that cheese is not readily available, we often give an alternative. When *mozzarella* is listed, another bland

cheese that melts could easily take its place, provided it doesn't have a strong flavor. Bear in mind that the commercial *mozzarella* sold in this country is a far cry from the *mozzarella* in Italy. The U.S. variety is stringy and gets tough when it is cooked. If you live in a neighborhood where *mozzarella* is made fresh and stored in water (without wrapping), you will be able to tell the difference. The fresh *mozzarella* is soft, almost saltless, and coats food gently when it is cooked. The commercial variety tends to make a thick layer that toughens when it is cooked and gets tougher as the food cools. The alternative to fresh *mozzarella* is to cut the commercial variety very thin if you intend to place it in *lasagne* or over a slice of meat. A domestic Swiss cheese (less flavorful than the imported variety) might also give you less trouble.

There are two Italian cheeses for which there is no substitute: *fontina* and *Parmigiano*. The real *fontina* has a gray-brown rind and comes from the Piedmont. There is also a *fontina* with a red rind on the market, but this is not made in Italy and has very little resemblance to the real thing.

Fontina has a nutty but mild flavor, unlike any other cheese. The perfume is not mild, however, and might lead one to believe that the cheese is very strong. It isn't; it melts gently, without lumps and without getting stringy. It is a must for any kind of *fonduta*, whether it be the Piedmontese type made with *fontina* and milk, or the *Fonduta di Lugano*, made with white wine. If you can't buy *fontina*, don't attempt a recipe that calls for it. It is irreplaceable.

The other cheese that has no substitute is *Parmigiano*, or Parmesan cheese. *Romano* or *pecorino* have their places in some dishes but when Parmesan cheese is called for, you have to use it. And it should always be freshly grated.

There are various types of Parmesan cheese and several are available in the United States. Keep in mind that Parmesan cheese should be light yellow and not chalky or white. It should be well aged before it is sold in one of those enormous black wheels. When it is cut open it should be moist. It will keep for a while if wrapped in aluminum foil, then placed in an airtight plastic box and stored in the refrigerator. When you are ready to use it, chip off chunks with a sharp knife (there is a special Parmesan cutter for this purpose) and feed the chunks into your food processor or cheese grater. Don't throw away your leftover crusts: scrape off the black rind and drop the crusts into the broth for a *minestrone* or cook them in a *risotto* to add extra flavor to the dish.

A cheese of Italian origin but made in this country is *ricotta*. There is a whole milk and a skim milk variety. The skim milk *ricotta* comes closer to the type we find in Italy. *Ricotta* is sold in plastic containers and is available in most supermarkets. When the container is opened, there is usually some liquid on top. There are two ways to dry the *ricotta*: empty the container onto a paper towel, place another paper towel on top, and let it stand for a few minutes. The paper will have absorbed most of the moisture. Or, if you want a really

dry *ricotta*, place the cheese in a piece of cheesecloth, make a loop with the ends of the cloth and hang it from the faucet of your sink to drip.

There is one other cheese that fits into the category of the "irreplaceable ones" although it is less well known and less widely used than Parmesan or *fontina*. It is the green-gold Gorgonzola. There is a sauce that can be made with Gorgonzola and this sauce cannot be made with a substitute. But it is at its best raw, eaten with pears or apples.

A cheese we never encountered in Europe is Muenster — at least the kind of Muenster we know in this country. We have used it in the recipe for *formaggio fresco*, instead of the Italian version. The Muenster is a very acceptable substitute.

Vegetables

That fresh vegetables are preferable to frozen or canned ones is obvious, provided the fresh ones are ripe and truly fresh. If they are neither, the frozen (and sometimes even the canned) vegetables might be a better choice.

Artichokes are often a problem. They are among my favorite vegetables when they are firm and green, without brown edges. Often I see them in markets out of season and they look as if they have been stored for a long time. They can't be eaten raw or boiled or baked. In fact, they can't be eaten at all. Artichokes must be eaten in the spring. Frozen artichokes may be used in egg dishes or cooked together with meats that will lend some flavor. Canned artichokes, if properly rinsed of the sour brine in which they are packed, may be stuffed or covered with *besciamella* and used as a garnish around a meat dish.

Green beans can also be a problem. If they don't snap smartly when broken, then you are probably better off with a frozen package of beans. Do not use canned, however, because canned beans, no matter what brand, have a peculiar taste.

Peas, on the other hand, take canning well. Unless you grow your own peas or have a market where you can buy tender young peas, the small canned peas have more taste than the larger fresh ones. If you do use canned peas, use the water the peas are packed in as well; it adds flavor.

I find American cabbage a little tougher than the Italian variety and I have, at times, replaced it with kale, particularly in *minestrone*. Broccoli rapa and knob celery are both available in this country but are sadly neglected by the average cook. All that is needed is for the cook to get to know them better. We have included some recipes for a start.

Carrots in this country are marvelous, provided you stay away from the

very large ones that tend to be wooden. Small carrots freeze well and I have even found good canned carrots.

I have tried frozen zucchini and have decided that it is better to go without zucchini altogether if the fresh ones are not available.

In my opinion, the prime offender is the pale, watery, mealy tomato. When a sauce calls for juicy ripe tomatoes and they are not available, whole canned tomatoes (principally the imported variety) might be a better choice. And don't discard the canning juice. If it is not needed in the sauce, it might be added to a broth or a *minestrone*.

As for the dried beans used in these recipes, bear in mind that most beans available here may be used for the dishes. Brown beans are good for *Sopa de Fasoi*, as are cranberry beans. The only type I have difficulty finding are the white beans. They are slightly flatter than other beans and somewhat larger. They are available in many Italian grocery stores.

Herbs and Spices

Fresh herbs are, of course, preferable to dried ones. The trouble is that people who live in cities find them hard to find in markets. I once suggested to a lady that she try to grow some herbs on the windowsill of her kitchen. "What windowsill?" she asked. Some kitchens don't have a window, let alone a sill. The situation is not as hopeless as it sounds. Some dried herbs are perfectly acceptable.

Oregano is good as a dried herb. Pretty though the plant is, if you have a garden in which you can grow it, dried oregano is flavorful. In fact, it is so flavorful that I sometimes object to it when too much of it is used either in salads or in sauces.

Nothing quite takes the place of a sprig of fresh rosemary tucked under the wings of a chicken or tied to a roast of veal, but a sprinkling of dried rosemary leaves does add flavor as well.

The same thing is true of sage. There is a world of difference between a sprig of fresh sage and the dried variety, but the dried leaves don't lose that flavor completely, particularly if you rub them between your fingers to break them before using. Don't rely on the powdered variety.

Thyme and tarragon are not greatly used in Italian cooking, but I find both quite acceptable in their dried form.

Dried parsley on the other hand is strictly a waste of time. I have tried whole dried leaves as well as flakes and have never been able to extract any flavor from them. Parsley is almost always readily available in markets and is also easy to grow. All parsley needs is a little light and a little moisture.

Dried basil is equally unsatisfactory. It tastes of almost nothing and only serves to make me homesick for Italy's marvelous strongly scented *basilico*. A bunch in the kitchen can make a whole apartment smell like spring. For some reason, American basil has a milder flavor and scent. You just have to use more of it than of the Italian variety.

Basil can be preserved in salt. Place the fresh leaves in a container, cover with coarse salt, and continue to layer with basil and salt. The basil will lose its color during storage, but not its taste. Don't freeze basil; just refrigerate it. And don't ever expect to use it as a garnish; the leaves will darken and go limp, although the flavor will remain.

Many of the recipes in this book use coarse salt, and for these I suggest using kosher salt. What pepper you use is a matter of personal taste, but it should be freshly grated for each recipe.

The following is a recipe for Italian Spices — *Spezie all'Italiana*. In old recipes, you often find the ingredients include a *pizzico di odori*, or a pinch of spices. Here are instructions for making these spices.

2 tablespoons nutmeg, freshly grated
2 tablespoons cinnamon
5 bay leaves
1 teaspoon ground white pepper
1 teaspoon ground cloves
1 teaspoon dried thyme

Prepare the spices either in a mortar and pestle or in a food processor. If you are making the spices by hand, place all ingredients in the mortar and pulverize with the pestle. Strain ingredients through the finest sieve.

If you are using a food processor, place all ingredients in the bowl and run the motor for 20 seconds, using the sharp blade.

Place the spices in a metal box with a tight-fitting lid. The spices will keep their aroma for several weeks.

Bear in mind that commonly available dried bay leaves and *alloro* (fresh bay laurel) are not the same thing. If you are lucky enough to have fresh laurel within reach, pick the leaves when they are dark green and glossy. Dry them in the sun. Commercial, dried bay leaves will do, but they are a poor substitute.

BASIC SAUCES

For Pasta

It is my firm belief that sauces are at their best when they don't cook too long. We all know that parsley should only cook for seconds because it turns bitter. We also know that fresh basil loses its taste when cooked too long. But even tomatoes (fresh ones, of course) should not be cooked so long that they lose their bright red color.

Who has not been served a so-called *Salsa di Pomodoro,* or tomato sauce, which is thick and brown and almost inedible? The only taste it had was a sharpness, owing to an overdose of hot pepper. The fact that it was probably made with canned tomatoes (or even tomato paste) is not the real problem. When properly handled, they can give very good results. What really destroys these sauces is the length of cooking time. They sit on the stove until they have lost their freshness, their taste, and even their looks.

So here are a few recipes that take very little time, give excellent results, and ask only one thing: that the ingredients be good.

 # Salsa Aglio e Olio

Garlic and oil sauce

Serves 4

8 tablespoons olive oil
4 cloves garlic, finely chopped
Salt and freshly ground black pepper
3 tablespoons parsley, finely chopped
½ cup Parmesan cheese, freshly
   grated (optional)

Heat the oil in a skillet, add the garlic, and cook until the garlic is blonde. Don't allow the garlic to burn or even to get dark.

Add the salt and pepper to taste. Stir and add parsley; cook for just a minute more (never allow parsley to cook for more than a minute). Pour the sauce over very hot *pasta* (spaghetti, noodles, or whatever your fancy is). Mix very well so that each piece of *pasta* is well coated. Add Parmesan if you wish. Real garlic lovers prefer not to. They enjoy the taste of garlic unmolested by other tastes.

Salsa con le Acciughe

Sauce with anchovies

Serves 4

1 clove garlic
8 tablespoons olive oil
2 anchovy filets
Black pepper, freshly ground
Pinch of hot red pepper
3 tablespoons parsley, finely chopped

Rub your skillet with a clove of garlic and then discard the garlic. Heat the oil over low heat. Or, if you want a stronger taste of garlic, heat the oil, add the garlic, and then discard the garlic when it gets blonde.

Chop the anchovies and add to the oil. Crush the anchovy pieces with a wooden spoon until they are practically disintegrated. Add the black pepper and the red pepper. When the oil has absorbed the anchovies, add the parsley, mix briefly, and pour over hot *pasta*.

This sauce is particularly good for spaghetti, but do not add Parmesan; fish and cheese just don't mix.

Salsa con Tonno e Piselli

Sauce with tuna and peas

Serves 6

½ cup olive oil
1 can (6½ oz.) tuna packed in oil
½ cup small fresh peas or 1 can (7 oz.) peas

3 tablespoons broth
2 anchovy filets (optional)
Salt
2 tablespoons chopped parsley

Heat the oil in a skillet and add the tuna, breaking up the tuna with a fork. If you are using fresh peas, lower the heat and add the broth and peas. Cover for about 5 minutes, stirring frequently. Add more broth if needed and cook until the peas are tender.

If you are using canned peas, add the peas along with the liquid, then add the broth, adjusting the amount to compensate for the canning liquid. Do not reduce the heat but rather cook the mixture for a couple of minutes, stirring carefully to avoid crushing any peas.

If you are adding anchovies, chop them then add them to the skillet. Mix with the tuna, using a wooden spoon, until the filets are almost disintegrated.

Taste the mixture and add salt if needed. Reduce heat and simmer until the sauce is the consistency you wish. Add the parsley and cook a minute longer.

Pour this sauce over very hot pasta but don't add Parmesan cheese.

Salsa di Fegatini e Pomodori

Chicken liver and tomato sauce

Serves 6

¾ pound chicken livers
3 tablespoons olive oil
3 tablespoons butter
1 clove garlic, chopped
½ cup dry white wine
½ teaspoon rosemary and marjoram, mixed
   together
1 pound tomato purée

Clean the chicken livers and remove any filaments or tendon. Chop well but don't purée them (if you use a food processor, turn the motor on and off immediately for a quick chopping action).

Heat the oil and butter in a medium-sized saucepan. Add the garlic but don't let it brown. Add the chopped chicken livers to the butter-oil mixture and sauce. Add the white wine and spices and mix well. Lastly, add the tomato

purée and cook the mixture for a couple of minutes. If the sauce appears too thick, add a couple of spoonfuls of water or broth to thin it.

Pour the sauce over spaghetti, *tagliatelle,* or macaroni.

NOTE

Please keep in mind that the recipe calls for tomato purée, not for tomato paste.

# Salsa di Gorgonzola

Gorgonzola sauce

Serves 6

1 pint heavy cream
½ pound Gorgonzola cheese
½ cup Parmesan cheese, freshly grated

Heat the cream in a saucepan but don't let it boil. When the cream is hot, add the Gorgonzola and, over very low heat, slowly melt the cheese, stirring it with a wooden spoon.

When the Gorgonzola is dissolved, pour the sauce over *pasta* or *gnocchi.* Sprinkle with Parmesan cheese and, if the *pasta* is served in an ovenproof dish, place the dish briefly in the broiler.

NOTE

Don't try to replace the Gorgonzola with another similar cheese: it won't work. The sauce will be lumpy and will look rough. With the Gorgonzola, it will be smooth and shiny.

# Pesto

Sweet basil sauce, Genoa style

This is one of Genoa's great contributions to gastronomy. It is a most difficult recipe to duplicate in this country but no cookbook would be complete without it. The basic difficulty is that basil in this country and Italian

basil are two different things. This has already been discussed in the chapter on ingredients. However, there is also a big difference between the basil I grow on my window sill in the city and the basil a friend grows in the country. The leaves of my plant are small and fairly fragrant, but his are large, glossy, and also fragrant. How does one give the quantity of leaves to use in the recipe? In Italian we have a great way to say a *"manciata,"* meaning a handful. There is also a question of personal taste — I like a lot of basil, but some people might find it too pungent.

There is one other problem. *Pesto* requires *formaggio Sardo,* a sheep's cheese from Sardinia. It is not available in this country and the closest we come to it is *pecorino Toscano,* sheep's cheese from Tuscany. And that too is very hard to find. *Pecorino Romano,* however, is readily available, but it is much sharper than the Sardinian variety. The answer is to use much less of the *pecorino Romano,* lest it overpower the Parmesan.

At this point, one might ask, why bother? Please bother; it is worth it. Here are two recipes — one made the old-fashioned way in a mortar, the second in a food processor. However, I do not recommend making *pesto* in a blender because it purées the basil too much.

Serves 6 to 7

3 cups fresh basil leaves
1 clove garlic
3 tablespoons pine nuts (pignoli nuts)
½ cup Parmesan cheese, freshly grated
2 tablespoons pecorino cheese, freshly grated (if
   using Tuscan pecorino, use 3 tablespoons)
¾ cup olive oil
Salt

Chop the basil leaves and place them in a mortar (earthenware is preferred to wooden). Chop the garlic and add, then add the pine nuts. Work the mixture with a pestle until you have a coarse paste.

Place the mixture in a bowl, add some of the cheeses. When the mixture becomes too solid to handle, start adding the oil a little at a time. Continue adding cheese, alternating it with the oil. Taste, and add salt to taste. Keep mixing until all the oil has been added.

If you have a food processor, use the same proportions but place the basil leaves, the garlic, and the pine nuts in the bowl. Using the sharp blade, run the motor for 3 seconds. Put the mixture into a bowl and set aside.

Place the chunks of Parmesan and *pecorino* in the bowl of the food processor and run the motor for 5 seconds, according to the age of the cheese. If the Parmesan is very hard, you might need a couple of seconds longer. Add the cheeses to the basil mixture and start pouring the oil into the bowl in a

steady thin stream as you would for a mayonnaise. *Pesto,* however, should be thicker than a mayonnaise.

The classic Genoese dish is *Trenette col Pesto,* a special size of *pasta,* but it may be used for any kind of *pasta,* provided you add a couple of tablespoons of the water in which the *pasta* has cooked.

NOTE

If you don't use the pesto right away, it will keep in the refrigerator for a couple of days. It might also be frozen, although it loses some of its fragrance.

 ## Salsa di Pomodoro

Tomato sauce

Yields 2 cups

4 large ripe tomatoes, peeled and seeded
3 tablespoons olive oil
1 small onion, finely chopped
1 clove garlic, crushed
Salt and freshly ground black pepper
1 tablespoon butter

Purée the tomatoes in a food mill or a blender. Heat the oil in a skillet, then add the onion and garlic. When the onion is transparent, add the tomatoes and simmer gently. Taste and add salt and pepper.

Remove the garlic and add the butter. Continue stirring until there are no watery edges around the sauce; this should take about 20 minutes.

Serve this sauce very hot.

NOTE

This sauce could also be used with boiled meats.

Salsa di Pomodoro Friulana

Tomato sauce, Friuli style

Yields 3 cups

4 large ripe tomatoes, peeled and seeded
3 tablespoons butter
2 tablespoons chopped onion

2 tablespoons very fine breadcrumbs
½ cup lean broth, either chicken or beef
1 teaspoon salt
1 teaspoon sugar (optional)

Chop the tomatoes coarsely but don't discard any of their water. Purée
them in a food mill or push them through a sieve.
In a small saucepan, heat the butter and add the onion. Cook until the
onion is wilted, then add the tomatoes. Cook, stirring for a couple of minutes.
Add the breadcrumbs and then the broth a little at a time until the sauce is the
thickness you desire.

NOTE

This sauce is used over hot polenta as well as with boiled meats, particularly boiled
beef.

Uncooked Tomato Sauce

Yields 2 cups

3 large ripe tomatoes or the equivalent of canned
   tomatoes
1 clove garlic
Pinch of salt
1 tablespoon capers, finely chopped
2 tablespoons parsley, finely chopped
8 large olives, either black or green,
   finely chopped
8 tablespoons olive oil

Peel the tomatoes and discard the seeds. Chop the flesh finer than you
would for a normal sauce.
Place the clove of garlic in a bowl, preferably porcelain, glass, or
earthenware. Add the tomato pieces and the salt; stir so that the salt dissolves
completely. Add the capers and the parsley. Add the chopped olives and stir
so that all ingredients are well mixed.
Add the oil to the top of the mixture so that the mixture is almost
submerged. Let it stand for 24 hours, then remove the garlic. Pour the sauce
over very hot pasta and mix well.

NOTE

There is no rule that forbids the addition of Parmesan cheese to this sauce, but it is so flavorful that it really isn't necessary.

If possible, use the type of olives that are sold loose, rather than those from a jar.

My Favorite Tomato Sauce

Yields 2 cups

1 clove garlic
8 tablespoons very fine olive oil
3 large ripe tomatoes, or the equivalent of
  canned, peeled, seeded, and chopped
Salt and freshly ground black pepper
5 or 6 leaves fresh basil, chopped, or ½ teaspoon dried

Rub the inside of your skillet with the clove of garlic, then discard the garlic. Heat the olive oil and, when it is very hot, add the tomato pieces. Add the salt, pepper, and basil and stir the ingredients with a wooden spoon. Once the mixture has begun to cook, simmer it for 5 or 6 minutes, but no longer. If the tomatoes aren't quite ripe, they will take a little longer to lose their raw appearance, but by all means don't allow the sauce to cook so long that it gets brown.

Serve this sauce very hot over the pasta of your choice, then sprinkle with ½ cup Parmesan cheese, freshly grated.

NOTE

If you use dried basil, you don't chop it, of course. Whereas the dried will add some flavor to your sauce, it does not compare to the taste of fresh basil.

For Meats or Fowl

Besciamella or Balsamella

White sauce

Yields 1½ cups

2 tablespoons butter
2 tablespoons flour

1 cup milk, at room temperature
Pinch of nutmeg, freshly grated
Salt

Melt the butter in a sturdy saucepan that will permit you to use both hands to prepare the sauce.

As soon as the butter foams (before it gets brown) add the flour and reduce the heat. Begin to beat steadily with a wire whisk. When the mixture is smooth, add the milk and continue beating with the whisk. There must be no lumps. Cook for about 2 to 3 minutes, then add nutmeg if desired and salt to taste.

NOTE

Everyone knows that the Marquis Louis Nointel de Béchamel gave this sauce its name during the time of Louis XIV. Not many people know that the ladies of Bologna, with their keen interest in food, spoke of a sauce called balsamella *before they knew that the Marquis existed.*

 Salsa Verde

Green sauce

Yields 2 cups

2 slices white bread
⅓ cup + ½ teaspoon vinegar
2 anchovy filets, chopped
1 teaspoon capers, chopped
1 slice garlic (about ¹/₅ of a clove), chopped
½ cup olive oil
Salt
3 tablespoons parsley, finely chopped

Cut off and discard the crusts of the bread slices. Moisten the remainder with ½ teaspoon of vinegar. Pass the moistened bread through a sieve.

Place the bread particles in a bowl with the anchovies, capers, and garlic slice. Add the remaining vinegar and the oil to the ingredients, slowly working it as you would a mayonnaise and adding a little oil at a time until the consistency is thick but light. (The quantities given for the vinegar and oil may be altered to suit personal taste.)

Taste the sauce and add salt. Add parsley just before serving. This is the classic sauce served in Italy with boiled meats.

NOTE

This sauce should not be made in a blender or food processor because the ingredients should not be puréed.

 # Salsa di Rafano

Horseradish sauce

Yields 1½ cups

½ cup grated fresh horseradish or 4 tablespoons
   prepared
4 tablespoons breadcrumbs
1 tablespoon olive oil
½ cup broth, either chicken or beef
½ teaspoon dry mustard (optional)

Place the horseradish in a small bowl and add the breadcrumbs and oil. Begin adding the broth 1 spoonful at a time until the mixture has the consistency of a paste. Let the ingredients stand for a few minutes to allow the breadcrumbs to absorb the liquid. If the mixture seems too thick, add a little more broth.

Add the mustard, if desired, then mix and serve with boiled beef, boiled chicken, or cold ham.

NOTE

If you are using prepared horseradish, you might prefer to omit the mustard because the prepared horseradish usually contains spices.

 # Salsa allo Scalogno

Sauce with shallots

Yields 1½ cups

2 shallots, finely chopped
1 teaspoon parsley, finely chopped

1 tablespoon water
1 egg yolk
½ cup mayonnaise

Place the shallots and parsley in a blender. Add the water and the egg yolk. Run the blender at high speed for 30 seconds, then add the mayonnaise. Run the blender for another 10 seconds.
Serve this sauce with cold meats.

 Salsa al Dragoncello

Tarragon sauce

Yields 1 cup

1 tablespoon fresh tarragon, finely chopped
½ cup mayonnaise
1 egg yolk
1 teaspoon dry white wine

Place all the ingredients in a shallow bowl. Mix with a hand beater or an electric mixer for 1 minute or until the ingredients are well blended. Serve this sauce with cold fish or fowl.

 La Pearà

Serves 6

2 tablespoons beef marrow
2 tablespoons butter
2 cups breadcrumbs
2 cups strong beef broth
1 tablespoon black pepper, freshly ground
½ teaspoon salt

Melt the marrow and butter in a saucepan, stirring with a wooden spoon. Add the breadcrumbs and stir until the bread has absorbed all the fat.
Add the broth a little at a time, stirring constantly, until the sauce has the

consistency of a thick mayonnaise. Add the pepper, reduce the heat, and simmer (in Venetian, the word is *pipar*) for about 2 hours. Stir occasionally and add more broth if the sauce begins to thicken too much.

Taste the sauce and add salt and more pepper if necessary. The sauce should be very peppery and, depending upon the pepper used, 1 tablespoon might not suffice.

Serve this sauce with bland meats or fowl.

NOTE

Recipes for this sauce have been found in medieval manuscripts. It is said that it came to Venice from the Orient. The word pearà *means "the peppery one" in Venetian. When you try this sauce, the reason for the name becomes obvious.*

 Salsa Magnonese

Yields 2 to 2½ cups

2 egg yolks
1 teaspoon salt
Juice of 1 lemon
¾ cup olive oil
3 tablespoons wine vinegar

In an enamel saucepan, mix the egg yolks with the salt using a wooden spoon. When the salt is completely absorbed, add the lemon juice a little at a time. Beating either with the wooden spoon or a wire whisk, start adding the oil a few drops at a time. Be careful always to mix in the same direction; if you start turning from the left to the right, you should continue to do so.

As the sauce begins to thicken place the saucepan on the lowest possible setting of your stove and continue mixing, adding the vinegar a few drops at a time. Remove the pan from the heat and taste the sauce shortly after you have added the first spoonful of vinegar. It may be that you prefer the taste of the sauce with less vinegar. If not, add the remaining vinegar for a sharper taste.

Serve this sauce warm with fish or boiled meats.

NOTE

The most important thing in preparing this sauce is not to let the sauce come to a boil or the egg will be cooked.

The resemblance, both in name and ingredients, to a mayonnaise is obvious. I have been unable to trace the origins of this sauce, which is quite popular in the Veneto. All that I have discovered is that it appears in cookbooks of the late 19th century.

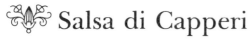

Salsa di Capperi

Sauce of capers and anchovies

Serves 6

4 anchovy filets
½ cup wine vinegar
3 tablespoons capers (packed in vinegar),
  chopped
½ cup olive oil
Salt (optional)
2 tablespoons parsley, finely chopped

Place the anchovy filets and the vinegar in a blender and run the motor for 20 seconds. Transfer the mixture to a saucepan.
    Add the chopped capers to the saucepan. Boil the mixture for 5 minutes with the pan covered.
    Place the contents of the saucepan in a bowl. Add the oil and beat with a wire whisk until smooth. Taste and add salt if desired. Add the parsley, mix again, and serve, hot or cold, with meats.

My Salad Dressing

Yields 1 cup

2 teaspoons Dijon mustard
½ teaspoon salt
2 teaspoons wine vinegar
1 tablespoon capers, chopped
⅓ cup olive oil

Place the mustard in the bottom of a glass or porcelain salad bowl. In a separate small bowl dissolve the salt in the vinegar and then add this to the mustard. Mix, then add the pepper. Mix again, then add the capers and blend in.

My own system is to add the salad greens at this point but some people like to add them at the end. Mix the salad greens with the vinegar mixture. Add the oil and toss well.

This dressing is rather sharp but it is particularly good with bland meats such as cold turkey or cold roast of veal.

Appetizers
Antipasti

In Italian restaurants in this country I have frequently been asked by the waiter or the owner, "How about a little *antipasto* to begin with?" I have sometimes ordered it out of sheer curiosity.

The "*antipasto*" is invariably a small plate containing a slice of *prosciutto,* a slice of *provolone* cheese, and a slice of *coppa,* that fattish meat that falls somewhere between salami and *prosciutto.* You always get a small stalk of celery and three olives: sometimes there are two black ones and one green, sometimes it's the other way around. You might also be served a piece of pimento and an anchovy. By and large, the contents of the plate never vary, unless the waiter suggests an *antipasto caldo;* a hot *antipasto,* that is (*hot,* as in warm; not *hot,* as in spicy).

If you order it, it will invariably consist of a stuffed mushroom, a piece or two of hot zucchini stuffed with meat, and maybe a small stuffed tomato.

Where did all this start? And especially, why?

Antipasto means literally "before meal." I have nothing against those little plates that get set before me every now and then, but does a slice of sharp *provolone* really belong before a meal?

I enjoy watching a familiar scene in restaurants in Italy: an elegant couple may be seated in a restaurant in Venice, in Milan, or in Verona. They are studying the menu and have decided to skip the *antipasti* because they are going to have *risotto* and one has to watch one's calories.

He nibbles on a few *grissini,* those very thin breadsticks that are irresistible, and ogles *il carrello degli antipasti,* that seductive cart of appetizers that the waiter always seems to place in the line of vision of a client who has decided to skip them. He turns to the lady: "The *risotto* will take 20 minutes. How about a little *antipasto?* Veeery little . . . ." She shrugs, he orders.

"Now let's see. Give me a slice of *prosciutto;* a stuffed egg; maybe one sardine, but a very small one . . . ah, and a few *gambaretti.* No, that's too many." (The waiter removes one tiny shrimp.) "That's all, except maybe a taste of celery salad and a small artichoke or two."

The plate in front of him groans. So does his wife.

"Do you want a taste, dear?" He asks, hoping that she won't but she will — only to prevent him from eating too much, of course. She makes that quite clear by chewing sadly.

Those "before meals" can be turned into whole meals with great success, if you duplicate them at home. Suppose you are giving an after theatre party. You will be coming home with your guests.

Before going out, place on a buffet a dozen or so small bowls or rectangular dishes containing slices of Italian salami, rolled up slices of *prosciutto,* celery root salad, and some other dishes included in this chapter. Place a stack of small plates at the end of your buffet table, accompanied by small forks. Some of the dishes will have to remain in the refrigerator until you come home but it won't take but a minute to put them on the buffet.

Try this for an after theatre party, but also consider it for a Sunday lunch; held indoors or outdoors, it will be equally successful.

Keep one detail in mind: make sure nothing requires knives unless you have either a lot of tables or very few guests. Cut the slices of *prosciutto* in half and make little cornucopias out of the salami. It makes it easier to pick them up with a fork.

 # Bresaola

4 slices per person

Bresaola is to beef what *prosciutto* is to pork. It comes from the Valtellina, a region in the north of Lombardy, a name my readers will encounter frequently in this book because I am an ardent admirer of its wines.

My admiration for *bresaola* is equally ardent. In fact it is a sort of rite with me: every time I go to Italy my first meal starts with *bresaola.*

A canned version is available in this country; I don't advocate it. *Bresaola* should be sliced very thin — if possible, even thinner than *prosciutto.* For some reason, the canned version is sliced fairly thick and is packed in oil. There is also a fresh *bresaola* available. It is hard to come by and is quite dry, whereas the *bresaola* we get in Italy is quite moist. There is, however, a Swiss filet of beef that comes close to the original in both taste and texture. It is called *grison.*

The slices should be placed on a platter (or on individual plates) so that only the edges overlap. They should be cut so thin that they would stick together were they piled on top of each other.

Count 4 slices of *grison* per person, squeeze a little lemon juice on each slice, and follow by dripping on a little olive oil (about ½ teaspoon per slice), then sprinkle a little finely chopped parsley on top. Add a little freshly grated pepper if desired.

The addition of parsley was the idea of Orio Vergani, the unforgettable founder of the Accademia Italiana della Cucina, the prestigious Italian gourmet society. *Bresaola* lovers have adopted it with joy and their *bresaolas* are the better for it.

 ## Carpaccio

Serves 6

1 pound very lean raw beef
1 tablespoon Worcestershire sauce
1 cup homemade mayonnaise
½ teaspoon Tabasco
½ teaspoon dry mustard
⅓ cup beef stock, very strong

Meat should be very pink, very lean, and very tender. Use either filet or London broil and slice the meat as thin as possible. (One way of obtaining very thin slices is to freeze the meat slightly — not as hard as a rock, but so that it may be sliced with an electric knife. However, what you gain in thinness you lose in flavor.) Slices should be about 3 inches wide and 1½ inches high.

Place the meat slices on individual plates, 4 slices per person. Add the Worcestershire sauce to the homemade mayonnaise and beat with a wire whisk. Add the Tabasco and dry mustard and beat until all ingredients are totally mixed.

Add the beef stock a little at a time until you get the consistency of a very thick soup. Coat the meat slices with this mixture but don't cover them completely. Some of the bright red of the meat should be visible; it is the combination of the 2 colors that gives the dish its name: Vittore Carpaccio was a Venetian painter known for his use of brilliant reds and whites.

NOTE

This is, of course, not a classic dish. It is the invention of one of the world's greatest restaurateurs: Cipriani. Few people who have been to one of his restaurants — located in Venice, on the island of Torcello, in Asolo, or in Treviso — would question my definition of him. But even fewer would question my statement that it is more difficult to get a recipe out of Signor Cipriani than it is to prevent Venice from being flooded. I got this recipe by questioning waiters for many years. Even then, I got one ingredient from one of them and a few others from another waiter. I have tried making various versions of Carpaccio over the years. This one works.

 # Carpaccio alla Verona Antica

Carpaccio the Old Verona way

Serves 6

1 pound very lean raw beef
1 tablespoon Worcestershire sauce
1 cup homemade mayonnaise
½ teaspoon Tabasco
1 tablespoon Cognac
⅓ cup whipped cream

Prepare the meat slices as described in the preceding recipe. Blend the Worcestershire sauce with the mayonnaise, add the Tabasco and beat until all ingredients are totally mixed.

Add the Cognac, then the whipped cream a little at a time until you get the consistency of a very thick soup. Coat the meat slices with this mixture but don't cover them completely.

NOTE

This is a different version of Carpaccio as tasted in one of the most delightful restaurants we have recently discovered. Verona Antica is located in Verona on a winding street behind the famous Hotel Due Torri.

We ordered Carpaccio and found it delicious although somewhat different from the original version. We inquired and the recipe was readily given. This version makes for a very smooth sauce and the Cognac adds a welcome touch.

The meat at Verona Antica was sliced paper thin and here too the chef admitted that, in order to achieve these thin slices, the meat had to be a little stiff with cold, although not quite frozen.

 # Pasticcio di Fegatini di Pollo

Chicken liver paté

Serves 10

1 pound chicken livers
1 cup brandy
1 stick + 2 tablespoons butter
Salt

(continued)

Baked Polenta with Sausage

Black pepper, freshly ground
Pinch of sage
6 slices bread

Place the chicken livers in a bowl and cover with brandy. Let them stand in a cool place for a couple of hours but don't refrigerate.

After 2 hours, remove the livers from the brandy. Heat 2 tablespoons of butter in a skillet, add the chicken livers, salt, pepper, and sage. Sauté the livers until done, stirring frequently to avoid sticking. Turn the livers so that all sides cook evenly — no blood should be visible. The cooking time is about 6 to 8 minutes. Let cool. Place the livers with their juice in a blender, then add the stick of butter. Run the blender at low speed for about ½ minute. Add the brandy and run again at high speed for another ½ minute. Pour the mixture into a shallow bowl and refrigerate it for 24 hours.

Cut each slice of bread into 4 triangles and toast in the oven until golden. Unmold the *pasticcio* onto a platter. If the surface of the *pasticcio* should look a little uneven, use a rubber spatula to straighten it out. Serve surrounded by toasted triangles.

This is a very rich dish.

 # Rotoli di Salmone Affumicato

Rolled smoked salmon

Serves 4

½ cup heavy cream, whipped
1 teaspoon horseradish, freshly grated
3 tablespoons red caviar
8 slices smoked salmon, about 4" by 2"

The cream should be whipped until very stiff. Add the fresh horseradish and mix well. (Prepared horseradish may be used but all the liquid should be removed. Drain the prepared horseradish on a paper towel until all the liquid has been absorbed.)

Add the caviar to the mixture, mixing lightly. The "beads" of caviar should not be crushed.

Place as much of the mixture in the center of each slice of salmon as it will

take. Fold the sides over the center. The mixture should not ooze out. Place 2 "rolled salmon slices" on each plate, folded side down.

NOTE

This is a very rich dish and 2 rolls per person are ample. Italians use Rheinlachs instead of Nova Scotia salmon. It is slightly more salty and more smoky than the salmon we are used to. If you use Nova Scotia you might want to add a little pepper to the cream mixture. Don't sprinkle it on top of the salmon: it destroys its pink perfection.

I don't have to add that this is not an ancient recipe. It was developed quite recently by the chef of one of Venice's best-known restaurants.

 # Fettine di Salame al Parmigiano

Slices of salami with Parmesan

Serves 10

1 pound Genoa salami
1 cup Parmesan cheese, freshly grated

Have your grocer remove the skin from 1 pound of Genoa salami and slice it on the machine, as thin as possible.
Place the slices on a baking sheet, without overlapping. Sprinkle them with the Parmesan, as evenly as possible. Place in the broiler for about 2 to 3 minutes. Watch them carefully because they burn easily. When they are crisp, remove the sheet from the broiler and slide the salami slices onto a paper towel to absorb excess fat. Place another baking sheet of slices in the broiler and move the broiled slices to a hot platter. Continue to broil until all slices are done. They should be crisp enough to be picked up with the fingers.

 # Fondi di Carciofi al Limone

Artichoke hearts with lemon juice

Serves 6

Juice of 1 large lemon
4 artichokes
1 clove garlic, finely chopped

(continued)

1 tablespoon parsley, finely chopped
Salt and freshly ground black pepper
⅓ cup olive oil

Squeeze the juice from 1 large lemon. Don't discard the peels. Remove stem and hard outer leaves from 4 firm artichokes. Rub the artichokes with the inside of the lemon peel to prevent them from turning black.

Place the artichokes in a saucepan, cover them with water, and add half the lemon juice. Cook briskly for about 10 minutes or until the centers of the artichokes can be pierced easily with a fork. The exact cooking time depends on the age of the artichokes. When finished, remove them from the water and let cool.

Slice the artichokes coarsely, remove the thorny centers, and place them in a bowl (glass, porcelain, or stainless steel). Add the garlic, parsley, salt, and pepper and mix well. Beat the oil and other half of lemon juice together and pour this over the artichokes. Allow to stand for 5 minutes before serving, either as an appetizer or with cold meat.

Serve without wine because artichokes destroy the flavor of wine.

 # Carciofi al Forno

Baked artichokes

Serves 6

6 medium-sized artichokes
1 lemon
1 clove garlic, finely chopped
3 tablespoons finely chopped parsley
½ cup breadcrumbs
3 tablespoons capers
Salt and freshly ground black pepper
1 cup olive oil

Preheat the oven to 375°. Artichokes should be in season. Pick nice fresh green ones without brown spots or discolored tips. Remove the stems but don't discard. Remove the tips of the leaves and discard, as well as the tough outer leaves. Cut the lemon in half and, while you trim the artichokes, rub the bottoms and sides with 1 lemon half to keep them from turning black.

Using your fingers, open the centers (after having cut off the thorns of the center leaves) and remove the choke with the help of a pointed spoon. Place the other half of the lemon in a pan of water and add the artichokes after you have trimmed them. Keep them floating in the water with the lemon while you work on the rest of the artichokes and while you prepare their stuffing.

Add the garlic to the chopped parsley and breadcrumbs. If the capers are preserved in salt, rinse and chop them, then add to the parsley and garlic. Add salt and pepper to taste, moisten with a little oil, and fill the centers of the artichokes with the mixture. With your fingers, open some of the tightly closed leaves and stick a bit of the mixture between the leaves.

Oil a baking dish large enough to hold the 6 artichokes but not so large that they will topple over. They should stand upright. Pour the remaining oil over the artichokes. Clean and peel the stems and place them in the dish around the artichokes. Place the dish, uncovered, in the center of the oven. Bake until the tops are slightly crisp. Baste frequently with the juices from the dish.

Serve at room temperature. Just before serving, place artichokes either on a platter or on individual dishes, and baste the artichokes again with their juices.

No wine should be served with artichokes. They play a funny trick on your tastebuds and make all wines taste sweet. Serve these artichokes as a first course and start serving wine with the second course.

NOTE

These artichokes have a variety of names. The French call them "à la diable" (though they admit that it is an Italian way of preparing them). In Italy we call them "alla Giudea" or "all'Inferno." I refuse to call them "alla Romana" because only small tender artichokes deserve that name. At their best they can actually be eaten in one bit. We can, at times, find small artichokes in Italian stores but they are not the same thing.

The stems are too good to be discarded. If you think that they don't look elegant enough to be placed on the platter next to the artichokes, then eat them in the kitchen when no one is looking.

 Involtini di Prosciutto e Asparagi

Asparagus tips wrapped in prosciutto

Serves 6

1 pound thin green asparagus
Salt
8 slices lean prosciutto

Clean the asparagus and boil in salted water. If available, use an asparagus cooker so that the asparagus remains firm. Drain well. Discard the tough parts of the asparagus and cut the tender parts into about 2½-inch lengths. Cut each slice of *prosciutto* into 3 pieces and wrap each piece around 2 or 3 asparagus tips, according to the thickness of asparagus.

If served with drinks, secure the rolls with toothpicks. If served as a first course, allow 4 "bundles" per person. Serve on small individual plates, on a lettuce leaf, if desired.

 # Asparagi con Salsa di Uova Sode

Asparagus with hard-boiled egg sauce

Serves 4

Water
2 pounds very fresh asparagus
4 whole eggs
Juice of ½ lemon (more, if desired)
Salt and freshly ground black pepper

Bring the water to a boil in an asparagus cooker. Clean the asparagus and remove thorny bits on stems. Remove the hard part of the stems leaving just enough stem to pick them up easily. If you use a cooker in which the asparagus must lay flat, don't put them in the water; they should cook over steam.

When they are done (slightly *al dente* and not mushy), divide them into 4 portions and place on individual dishes to cool.

Hard boil 4 eggs. Break up the eggs with a fork and chop them very well. Add the oil and lemon juice (using as much lemon juice as your palate desires). Add salt. Pour a little of the sauce over each portion and add black pepper — just a sprinkling. Serve cold.

NOTE

If you have a food processor, chop eggs using the sharp blade for about 5 seconds, then add the oil and lemon juice for another 5 seconds. Taste and add the salt. Run 1 additional second.

 # Fagioli Lessi con Tonno

Boiled beans with tuna

Serves 4 to 6

1 pound white beans (navy beans)
Salt
1 large white onion
1 can (6½ oz.) tuna, packed in oil
½ cup olive oil
3 tablespoons wine vinegar
Black pepper, freshly ground

Soak the beans overnight. Drain and place in a saucepan. Cover with water, add a pinch of salt, and cook, uncovered, until done. They should not be raw but don't allow them to get mushy. Cooking time is about ½ hour, varying somewhat with the quality of the beans.

While the beans are cooking, remove the outer skin from the onion and let it stand under cold running water for at least 15 minutes. Slice the onion as thinly as possible. Drain the tuna, and add it to the onion, breaking the tuna with a fork.

As soon as beans are cooked, place them in a bowl and season them immediately with oil, vinegar, salt, and pepper. This should be done while the beans are still warm. Add the onion and tuna and then toss.

NOTE

The reason why the tuna should be drained of its oil is that the oil is too fishy. Use only fresh oil for seasoning.

This is not a dish for tender stomachs. For those who can't take the raw onion, there is a version that replaces the onion with hard-boiled eggs.

 # Insalata di Pollo e Granoturco

Chicken and corn salad

Serves 4

6 ears of corn
Water
Salt

(continued)

2 whole chicken breasts
1 cup fresh mushrooms, peeled and sliced
½ cup fontina or Swiss cheese, slivered
1 teaspoon black pepper, freshly ground

For the dressing:
1 teaspoon salt
3 tablespoons red wine vinegar
½ cup olive oil

Choose the ears of corn carefully: they should not be too young but also not too old. Their color should be bright yellow, not orange.

Bring the water to a vigorous boil. Add salt. Cook the corn *al dente*, dropping it into the water, then letting it cook for 2 or 3 minutes. Remove from the water and let cool.

Remove the skin from the chicken breasts. Bring the water to a boil in a small saucepan, then add the chicken breasts. Cook over medium heat until done. Let the chicken cool in the broth. Remove and cut the meat into ½-inch cubes. (Don't discard the broth. Use it for a *minestrone* or for *risotto*.)

With a very sharp knife, cut the kernels off the cobs, being careful not to cut into the cob. You should have about 3 cups of corn.

Place the mushrooms, cheese, corn, and chicken cubes into a bowl and keep cool (but not refrigerated) until ready to serve.

To prepare the dressing, place the salt and the vinegar in a small bowl. Dissolve the salt in the vinegar, then add the oil and beat well with a fork. Just before serving, pour this dressing over the chicken-corn-mushroom mixture. Add pepper and toss.

NOTE

Of course, this is not a classic dish. In fact, the corn shows a definite American influence. But I tasted it for the first time in the home of a Venetian friend and have prepared it several times since, with great success. Some days I have also added a few tablespoons of chopped capers or a couple of chopped olives and even 2 stalks of celery, finely chopped. All these ingredients add a little flavor but I don't really recommend the olives because they make the salad look dark (if you use the proper oily olives, that is). If you are in the mood for a treat, add a small white truffle, sliced very thin. Even a canned truffle adds immensely to the salad.

Sedano di Verona in Insalata

Celery root salad

Serves 4

2 medium-sized celery roots
1 lemon
⅓ cup olive oil
Salt and freshly ground black pepper

Peel the celery roots and remove all the dark spots. Rub them with half a lemon. Slice the roots as thinly as possible, using the "slicer" on the side of your cheese grater. While slicing, continue to rub with lemon to keep the slices from getting too dark.

Place the slices in a glass or porcelain bowl and toss with oil, salt, and pepper.

NOTE

This is the Italian version of the French Celery Remoulade.

 # Uova Sode col Pesto

Hard-boiled eggs with pesto

Serves 6

6 hard-boiled eggs
½ cup pesto (see pages 18-20)
12 capers (optional)

Slice the eggs in half lengthwise. Remove the yolks and add 3 of the yolks to the *pesto* and mix well. Reserve the other 3 yolks for another recipe. Fill the egg-white shells with the *pesto* mixture as you would if you were to use mayonnaise or mustard. If you wish, place a caper in center of each egg.

If you serve the eggs with drinks and people will be picking them up with their fingers, don't dilute the *pesto* with additional oil. However, if you use the eggs as appetizers on individual dishes with lettuce, add a trickle of olive oil on top and scatter a few capers around the eggs.

 # Insalata di Melanzane

Eggplant salad

Serves 6

4 medium-sized eggplants
Salt
½ cup olive oil
1 clove garlic
Black pepper, freshly ground
½ cup wine vinegar

The eggplants should be firm, glossy, and not more than 6 or 7 inches long. Wash the eggplants and remove the green tops. Don't peel. Cut into slices lengthwise. The slices should be about ⅓-inch thick.

Place the slices on a sieve or on a double thickness of paper towels. Sprinkle liberally with salt (coarse salt is better than fine; in this country, kosher salt is the best). Let stand for about 30 minutes. The eggplants should shed a lot of water and, with it, their bitter taste.

Pour the oil into a small bowl. Add the garlic. Let stand while the eggplants drip. When ready, remove the garlic from the oil and discard.

If you have a grill, prepare the coals. If not, heat the pan you use to grill bacon or steaks. Pat the eggplant slices dry and brush them with olive oil on one side. Place the slices on the grill, oiled side down. Sprinkle pepper on top. Brush the top side with oil and turn the slices. Cook on the other side. When the eggplants have lost their green tint and the edges are curled, they are done.

Make a layer of eggplant on a long platter. Sprinkle with vinegar. Make another layer on top. Sprinkle with more vinegar and let stand in a cool place. The eggplant slices should be well moistened with vinegar but not drowned. Serve as an appetizer.

 # Teste di Funghi Ripieni

Stuffed mushroom caps

Serves 4

1 pound fresh mushrooms, as large as possible
½ cup Parmesan cheese, freshly grated
2 tablespoons butter

2 tablespoons fine breadcrumbs
Salt and freshly ground black pepper
1 tablespoon parsley, finely chopped
Pinch of nutmeg, freshly grated
1 tablespoon olive oil

From 1 pound of fresh mushrooms choose the 12 largest and whitest caps (count 3 to 4 caps per person). Wipe each with a wet paper towel. Cut off the dirty parts of the stems and discard. Chop the stems and some of the smaller and less good-looking mushrooms. If you have a food processor, use the sharp blade and run the motor for about 5 seconds. The mushrooms should be almost puréed. If you don't own a processor, chop with a *mezzaluna,* a moon-shaped knife. Add the Parmesan cheese to the mushrooms along with 1 tablespoon of butter at room temperature. Mix well. Add the breadcrumbs, salt, pepper, and parsley. Add the nutmeg and mix until all ingredients are well blended.

With the other tablespoon of butter, coat a baking dish that will hold all the mushroom caps without touching each other.

Make a little heap of chopped mushroom mixture in each cap. Shape of mushrooms should be almost round. Place the stuffed mushrooms in the baking dish, leaving even spaces between them. Drop a few drops of oil on each cap. Place in the broiler for about 10 to 12 minutes, depending on the size of the caps, and be careful not to place them too close to the heat. They should be cooked but not burned; the distance from the heat should be about 8 inches.

These mushroom caps are best when served hot. Place them on a slice of toast, if desired. They may also be served cold with drinks, but I feel that they lose a little of their taste when they are cold. Hot or cold, they are a far cry from the standard "stuffed mushrooms" you get, alas, in many restaurants. Those are usually redolent of breadcrumbs, garlic, and oil until the taste of mushroom has been all but killed.

 # Insalata di Funghi, Sedano, e Formaggio con Tartufo

Mushroom, celery, and cheese salad with truffles

Serves 4

2 cups fresh mushrooms, sliced
2 innermost hearts of celery

(continued)

1 cup Parmesan cheese, slivered
Salt
Black pepper, freshly ground
½ cup olive oil
Juice of ½ lemon (optional)
1 white truffle, fresh or canned

Clean the mushrooms and slice both the caps and stems if they are very fresh and white. Remove all the sandy parts from the stems and peel the caps if necessary.

Remove all outer stalks of celery and keep these for other uses. Slice the pale yellow center of the celery as finely as possible.

If you can find a really fine Parmesan cheese, which is yellowish and slightly moist, cut it into slivers. If this is unavailable, you could substitute Swiss cheese.

Mix the mushrooms, cheese, and celery in your most beautiful glass or porcelain bowl. Season the mix with salt, pepper, and oil, and add lemon juice, if desired.

If you are the happy owner of a white truffle, one the size of a walnut will be plenty for this recipe. Don't wash it. Scrape the sand off (if there is any) with a very sharp small knife, taking off a little of the surface as you scrape. You don't want to actually peel the truffle because you might take off more than necessary. The truffle should be pinkish gray. Slice the truffle, either with a truffle slicer or with a cheese slicer, by holding it over the mushroom mixture and sliver the truffle on top of it.

NOTE

This is the utmost of all first courses. In Italy, it is made with "ovuli," mushrooms that are the size and shape of an egg and are white inside and orange-colored outside. They scare foreigners half to death but they are delicious and harmless. They are found only in the fall, as are truffles. In fact, some people go to Italy because of the truffle season.

 # Insalata di Cipolle con Acciughe

Onion salad with anchovies

Serves 8

1 pound young onions
6 anchovy filets (if possible, use the kind that are
   preserved in salt. If those are not available,
   anchovies packed in olive oil may be used)

---

3 tablespoons wine vinegar
Pinch of salt
½ cup olive oil
Black pepper, freshly ground (optional)

I t is very important that the onions be really fresh and small otherwise this dish becomes somewhat overwhelming. Peel off the outer skin of onions as well as the second skin. Keep the little onions under running cold water for about ½ hour. Pat dry and slice very thin, either with a sharp knife or with a slicer.

If you are using anchovies packed in salt, rinse these well under running water, remove the spines, and chop coarsely. If you are using anchovies preserved in oil, remove these from the can, drain, and chop. Sprinkle the chopped anchovies over the onions and mix. In a small bowl beat together the vinegar, salt, and olive oil. Sprinkle with pepper. Pour mixture over onions and let stand for an hour before serving. Don't refrigerate; just keep in a cool place.

Serve as appetizer or in addition to a green salad. A small helping goes a long way, but is delicious!

 Ravanelli con Tonno

Radishes with tuna

Serves 4 to 5

1 bunch fresh radishes
1 can (6½ oz.) tuna packed in oil
4 hard-boiled eggs
Salt
½ cup olive oil
Juice of 1 lemon (optional)
Black pepper, freshly ground
2 tablespoons parsley, finely chopped

W ash radishes, remove stems and leaves, and slice as thinly as possible, using the slicer on the side of your cheese grater.
Drain the tuna and break it up with a fork. Add to radish slices. Slice eggs or chop coarsely and add to radishes. Add salt to taste, and mix well

in a glass or porcelain bowl. Add oil and toss. Taste to see if you want to add lemon juice. Personally, I like to add the lemon juice.

Let stand for 10 minutes (longer if you wish). Just before serving, grate a little black pepper on top and sprinkle parsley over everything at the last minute.

NOTE

This is a popular appetizer in Milan, where radishes are called "remolazzitt." It is particularly good in this country where radishes, when in season, are as beautiful as anywhere in the world. This dish may be prepared ahead of time, placed on individual dishes, and served as first course for an informal meal.

Antipasto di Pomodori e Acciughe

Appetizer of tomatoes and anchovies

Serves 6 to 8

5 large ripe tomatoes without blemishes
1 teaspoon salt
2 teaspoons dried oregano (or 3 teaspoons, if you
   are lucky enough to have fresh oregano)
10 anchovy filets
½ cup olive oil

This dish should be prepared only when tomatoes are in season. Avoid making it with mealy tomatoes that have been kept in storage.

Wash and dry the tomatoes but don't peel them. Remove any touches of green where the stems had been. Cut into slices of approximately ¼-inch thickness. Place these on a platter and spread them out as much as possible. Sprinkle salt over them and let them stand for at least ½ hour. Pour off the liquid.

In a shallow bowl make a layer of the tomato slices, and sprinkle a little oregano over them. Chop a couple of filets of anchovies coarsely (each filet should be cut into about 4 or 5 pieces). Sprinkle these anchovy pieces over the tomatoes and then pour a little oil over them. Continue with a layer of tomatoes, oregano, and anchovies until all ingredients have been used. Let this stand in a cool place for at least 3 hours (6 hours is better).

Serve as first course for a summer luncheon, or place on a buffet table.

NOTE

This dish may be prepared by alternating layers of tomatoes with layers of boiled zucchini. Zucchini should be carefully washed and sandy parts scraped off but should not be peeled. They should be placed in vigorously boiling water and cooked for 5 or 6 minutes, then sliced and salted liberally and allowed to stand for at least ½ hour; excess water should be drained off.

Antipasto di Pomodori e Basilico

Appetizer of tomatoes and sweet basil

Serves 6 to 8

5 large ripe tomatoes
1 teaspoon salt
1 cup fresh basil
½ cup olive oil

Wash and slice tomatoes as in the preceding recipe. Salt and let stand for ½ hour. Pour off the water.

Make a layer in a bowl. Chop the basil very fine, leaving 4 or 5 leaves unchopped for later use. Sprinkle a little of the chopped basil over the tomatoes, pour a little olive oil over them, and continue with layers of tomatoes and sprinklings of basil, adding a little oil after each layer. When all the ingredients are used up, let stand in a cool place (not in the refrigerator) for at least 3 hours.

Before serving, coarsely chop the remaining basil leaves and sprinkle over the top of the salad.

NOTE

This dish should be prepared only when fresh basil is in season. Dried basil will not do. The reason for reserving a few leaves of basil for the last moment is that basil, once it is chopped, tends to get dark and doesn't look so well. Its taste, however, lasts for many hours.

 # Pomodori col Pesto

Tomatoes with pesto

Serves 6

6 ripe tomatoes (all the same size if possible)
Salt
1 cup pesto (see pages 18-20)
3 tablespoons olive oil

Remove any green parts of the tomatoes where stems had been but be careful not to cut too deeply into the flesh. Cut the tomatoes in half horizontally and sprinkle liberally with salt. Turn them upside down and let them stand for about ½ hour. They have to shed a lot of their liquid and seeds. Don't remove all seeds because it would produce more of a cavity than you want.

Spread a little *pesto* over the surface of each tomato. Some of it will sink in; when it does, add a little more. The *pesto* should form a thin layer over each tomato. Just at the moment of serving them, pour a trickle of olive oil over each. Place the halves on a bed of lettuce. Serve at room temperature.

Formaggio Fresco Fritto

Fresh cheese, fried

20 slices

½ pound Muenster cheese, or 1 package (8 oz.)
  of commercial mozzarella
1 whole egg
1 cup yellow cornmeal
Vegetable shortening, such as Crisco
Salt

Muenster cheese is available in various packages: sliced, round, and in a long brick about 2½" by 1½". Buy the latter. If it is unavailable, try *mozzarella*.

Cut the cheese into slices about ½-inch thick. Beat the egg well with a fork. Spread the cornmeal on a paper towel. Heat the shortening in a fairly

deep saucepan. When a couple drops of water sprinkled on the surface sizzle and fume, the fat is hot enough. Don't let it get brown.

The cheese should be at room temperature. Dip the slices into the beaten egg and coat them well. Then dip them into the cornmeal, making sure all sides are equally well coated. Use a fork to drop them into the hot fat, no more than two slices at a time. Turn them with a slotted spoon and watch them get golden. Remove the cheese slices with the slotted spoon and place them on a paper towel. Sprinkle a little salt on them while they are still very hot.

NOTE

Every region of Italy has its own formaggio fresco. They are cheeses without any name except fresco because they are freshly made almost daily. They vary quite a bit because some are made with cow's milk and some with sheep's, or a mixture of both. The Formaggio Fritto comes from the Friuli where the formaggio fresco is slightly acidulous. Muenster comes close to it in taste but it is a richer cheese. If there is a Spanish grocery in your neighborhood, look for cheso blanco; it is a Spanish version of formaggio fresco and lends itself admirably.

One of the advantages of this appetizer, which creates quite a sensation at cocktail parties, is that you may dip it in egg and cornmeal well ahead of time and then fry it at the last moment. It takes about 2 minutes to fry. And, if you have a well-ventilated kitchen, you can do it in the presence of your guests in a deep chafing dish.

Crostini di Polenta al Gorgonzola

Polenta and Gorgonzola cheese appetizers

Serves 15 to 20

2 quarts water
1 teaspoon salt
1 pound yellow cornmeal
2 tablespoons butter
1 teaspoon Worcestershire sauce
¼ pound Gorgonzola cheese
2 tablespoons shortening, such as Crisco

Prepare the *polenta*, following the basic instructions on pages 82-83, and keeping it rather solid. When *polenta* is done, pour it onto a wet tablecloth or onto a wet marble-top table. Using either the back of a knife or the back of a spoon dipped in hot water, flatten the *polenta* to a ½-inch thickness. Let it cool.

Have the butter and Gorgonzola cheese at room temperature and mix them together, mashing both well with a fork. Add the Worcestershire sauce and mix until totally blended.

When the *polenta* is cold, cut it into strips of desired width, using a wooden spatula or the sharp edge of a rubber spatula. Melt the shortening in an iron skillet and deep-fry the strips until quite crisp. Fry a few at a time, so they don't overlap in the skillet. As they are done, place them on a paper towel but keep them hot. At the moment of serving, spread the butter-and-Gorgonzola mixture on the *polenta* and serve hot with drinks.

NOTE

If desired, sprinkle a little paprika over the surface of the appetizers. If no Gorgonzola is available, grated Swiss cheese may be used. In this case, strips should be placed briefly under the broiler before serving to allow the cheese to melt. Do not substitute with blue cheese.

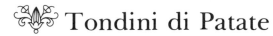 Tondini di Patate

Potato rounds

Serves 6

1 pound large old potatoes
½ teaspoon salt
1 tablespoon butter
3 tablespoons Parmesan cheese, freshly grated
1 egg
Black pepper, freshly ground
Pinch of nutmeg, freshly grated
¼ pound fontina cheese
¼ pound lean prosciutto

Preheat the oven to 350°. Peel the potatoes and slice them. Boil in salted water for about 10 minutes, or until quite done. Drain the potatoes and place them in a pan over very low heat. Mash them with a potato masher while they are cooking, in order to get rid of excess water. Remove from the heat.

Add the butter, Parmesan cheese, egg, pepper, and nutmeg and beat with a wire whisk until the butter is melted and all the ingredients are well blended. Take heaping tablespoons of the mixture and form little balls. Place

the balls on a buttered baking sheet and flatten the top of the rounds. Bake the rounds in the preheated oven for 15 minutes.

Cut the *fontina* into slivers and cut the *prosciutto* into pieces more or less the size of the potato rounds. Remove the rounds from the oven and cover each one with a small slice of *prosciutto,* top with *fontina,* and place again in the oven for 1 minute, or until the cheese has melted.

NOTE

Potato rounds may be prepared ahead of time and placed in the oven at the last minute. If fontina is not available, Swiss cheese might be used instead but the flavor of fontina is irreplaceable, and no other cheese will produce quite the same result.

Ricotta Appetitosa

Ricotta appetizer

Serves 20

1 container (15 oz.) skim milk ricotta
2 teaspoons salt
2 shallots
2 teaspoons black pepper, freshly ground

Empty the container of *ricotta* onto a paper towel. Pat it dry with a second paper towel. You will be surprised how much liquid the towels will absorb.

Place the *ricotta* in a bowl, add salt, and mix very well so that the salt is evenly distributed. Peel the shallots and place them in a food processor, if you own one. Using the sharp blade, run the motor for about 10 seconds. The shallots are evenly absorbed. Add shallots to the ricotta. Add half the pepper and mix. Place the mixture in a serving bowl and sprinkle the remaining pepper on top, both for taste and for looks. Serve with whole wheat crackers or raw vegetables.

NOTE

I have tried to add ½ cup (tightly packed) chopped watercress to the mix and have found it good. But it must be eaten almost immediately because watercress gets a wilted taste after a while.

There is an Italian restaurant on the coast of the south of France where this ricotta appetizer is served automatically while you order your dinner or your luncheon — the way bread and butter are served in this country.

 Pizzette Finte

Fake miniature pizzas

Serves 10

10 slices white bread
1 can (16 oz.) whole tomatoes
6 anchovy filets
1 teaspoon oregano
⅓ cup olive oil

The bread should be firm, not the very soft and fluffy type. Cut the slices into quarters without removing the crust. Put these quarters on a baking sheet and place in broiler for 2 or 3 minutes, or until slightly golden.

Place the tomatoes in a sieve and allow to drain. When all the liquid is gone, remove the seeds. Turn the bread squares over so that the uncooked sides face you. Place a small piece of tomato in the center of each square, place a small piece of anchovy on top, sprinkle with oregano, and add a few drops of oil. Place these again in broiler for 2 or 3 minutes or until the edges are golden. Serve very hot.

Scaloppine Fritte in Miniatura

Miniature fried veal cutlets

Serves 10

8 slices veal scaloppine (approximately 2
* pounds)*
1 stick butter
1 whole egg
1 cup very fine breadcrumbs
Salt and freshly ground black pepper
1 tablespoon large capers
Juice of 1 lemon

Remove all the fat and bits of skin from the *scaloppine*. Place these between 2 layers of wax paper (top paper moistened) and beat well with a cleaver or a rolling pin. The meat should be very thin. Cut each slice into bite-sized pieces (about 1½″ by 1″).

Heat the butter in a skillet until golden, but don't allow it to brown. Beat the egg lightly in a deep dish. Coat the pieces of meat with the egg and then with the breadcrumbs. Sauté the meat in the butter on one side, turn with a spatula, and sauté on the other side. The veal should be golden — approximately 2 minutes on each side. Place the pieces on a paper towel and sprinkle them with salt and pepper while they are still hot.

At the moment of serving, place a caper on each little slice, stick a toothpick through the caper into the meat and sprinkle a bit of lemon juice on each piece. Serve hot or cold.

Minestre in Brodo

Minestra is a first course. When you order a meal in an Italian restaurant, particularly an old-fashioned one, the waiter or host, or whoever takes your order, will ask, *"e come minestra?"* — "As for the first course?"

Minestre may be *in brodo* or *asciutte:* in broth, like *Tortellini in brodo,* or dry, like pasta, *risotto,* or *polenta. Minestre in brodo* are gentle broths with either small pasta or rice cooked in them. The base might be either chicken or beef stock or a combination of both. To prove how gentle the dish is it is frequently referred to as *"minestrina in brodo,"* meaning a small *minestra.*

As children we used to dread it and pretend to be feeling fine even if we had overeaten the day before or had the beginning of a cold because mother's order was automatically that what we needed was a *minestrina in brodo.* In other words: the Italian *minestrine* are to Italian cuisine what the chicken soup is to Jewish cooking.

If a well-known customer of a restaurant says that he feels like skipping the first course because he doesn't feel hungry the owner will immediately suggest a *minestrina in brodo* which will do wonders for an unenthusiastic stomach. Since adults can defend themselves (whereas children can't), they might choose to order or not to order one. And if they do choose, they might make the broth more interesting by ordering it with rice and chicken livers or with asparagus tips.

Why mothers think (or used to think) that only the blandest broth without Parmesan or other amenities would do the trick is beyond me. Maybe it is because the threat of it prevented us from faking illnesses that were more due to exams than to our health. The strange thing is that, whereas tomatoes and beets, which I hated as a child, have become for me well-liked vegetables, *minestrine in brodo* still make me feel puny.

Minestrone

Minestrone literally means "the big first course." And that it is! Big, filling, and delicious.

There are almost as many ways to make a *minestrone* as there are people who make them. Not only does every region of Italy have at least one *minestrone "tipico"* which it claims as its very own, but every cook has his or her own way of making it.

There is one thing they all have in common: they don't *plan* a *minestrone*. They look into their refrigerators and find that they have the makings of a *minestrone* and then they buy perhaps a few additional items.

I remember being a weekend guest of friends when the hostess said to me, "There is absolutely nothing in the fridge . . . let's go marketing." I know that fridge: there is always something in it. I looked and found a small piece of leftover pot roast, a couple of carrots, an onion, a few potatoes, a venerable crust of Parmesan, and even a piece of Polish sausage. I scraped the fat off the pot roast, added a little oil, and browned the onion in it. I brought two quarts of water to a boil, scraped the black rind off the Parmesan, and added it to the water, along with the onion, the carrots (diced), the potato (peeled but left whole), and the piece of meat. And, most unorthodox, I added a few cubes of Polish sausage. I left it all simmering, well covered, over a very low flame. *Then* we went marketing. When we got back, I added a few vegetables, particularly a few ripe tomatoes, seeded, peeled and cut into chunks. I tasted it: it needed very little salt, but it did need a few herbs and, of course, at the very end, ½ cup of Parmesan. Just to show off, I also added ½ cup of dry red wine.

My *minestrone* kept simmering while I prepared an elaborate second course. I might have spared myself the trouble. The *minestrone* disappeared to the last drop but no one was able to do justice to the rest of the meal.

Whichever recipe for *minestrone* you choose to make, keep in mind that you must use your judgment in selecting the vegetables. If the recipe calls for zucchini (summer squash) and they are old and soft, replace the zucchini with another vegetable. If tomatoes are not in season, you might use canned tomatoes (the equivalent amount will be given in the recipes). The same goes for peas, green beans, etc. In some cases, frozen or canned vegetables could be used if fresh ones are not available. But when a recipe calls for *fresh* sweet basil and basil is not in season, wait for the spring. Dried sweet basil cannot take the place of the fresh.

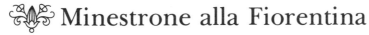

Minestrone alla Fiorentina

Minestrone, Florence style

Serves 6

½ cup pancetta, diced (if unavailable, use ½
    boiled ham, ½ salt pork)

(continued)

2 carrots, medium size, washed and scraped
1 stalk of celery
1 small onion, thinly sliced
1 clove garlic, finely chopped
1 teaspoon fresh rosemary or ½ teaspoon dried
1 tablespoon fresh basil, chopped, or 1 teaspoon
   dried
3 large ripe tomatoes, coarsely chopped and
   seeded (if unavailable, use 3 peeled canned
   tomatoes)
½ cup olive oil
4 cups water
2 cups fresh white beans, shelled (if unavailable,
   dried beans may be used)
½ head of cabbage (or kale, if preferred)
Salt and freshly ground black pepper to taste
1 cup elbow macaroni or any other small pasta
1 tablespoon parsley, finely chopped

If you are substituting ham and salt pork for the *pancetta,* wipe the salt off the salt pork before dicing it. Chop the carrots and celery; the pieces should not be larger than ½ inch and not smaller than ⅓ inch, but they need not be evenly chopped.

Place the *pancetta* or ham and salt pork in a large saucepan. Add the carrots, celery, onion slices, garlic, rosemary, and basil. Sauté quickly until the onion is wilted, then add the tomatoes and then the oil. Continue to sauté for 10 minutes, stirring the ingredients now and then.

In a separate saucepan boil the beans in the water until they are tender but not overcooked (about 20 minutes). If dried beans are used, the beans must first be soaked overnight. Drain the cooked beans but don't discard the water. Place half the beans in a food processor and purée with the sharp blade, running the motor for about 30 seconds. Add this purée to the vegetables, then add the rest of the cooked beans and the cabbage or kale, cut into thin strips. Add the water reserved from cooking the beans and then season to taste with salt and pepper. Cover and simmer for at least 2 hours. Check the broth now and then. If it seems to be too thick, add a little water or broth. When finished, allow to sit.

About 10 minutes before serving, bring the soup to a strong boil and add the macaroni. Stir and add the chopped parsley (the parsley is added at this late stage because it does not improve with cooking; it gets bitter).

Cook the macaroni with the broth and vegetables for 6 to 10 minutes,

according to the quality of the pasta. The only way to tell if it is done is to bite into a small piece. It should, of course, be *al dente,* or bitable but not mushy.

Pour the *minestrone* either into a tureen and serve to your guests at the table or ladle the soup into individual deep dishes or bowls.

NOTE

I believe that minestrone is best if cooked a day before serving, kept in a cool place (never in the refrigerator) overnight, and then reheated the day it is to be eaten.

Although kale is certainly not an Italian vegetable, I find that it is preferable for this particular use to cabbage grown in this country. And tradition wants that no grated Parmesan be added to this version of minestrone. I don't know why and I have always added a liberal sprinkling of freshly grated Parmesan to mine anyway.

Minestrone alla Genovese

Minestrone, Genoa style

Serves 6

2 quarts water
1 cup fresh cranberry beans, shelled
2 ripe tomatoes, or 2 whole canned tomatoes
2 medium-sized potatoes
2 carrots, washed and scraped
2 medium-sized zucchini
2 stalks of celery
1 small head of escarole
2 medium-sized scallions
6 tablespoons olive oil
1 cup pasta (penne, small rigatoni, or ziti)
10 leaves fresh basil
Salt to taste
½ cup Parmesan cheese, freshly grated

Bring the water to a boil in a large saucepan. Add the beans, reduce the heat, and simmer while you peel the tomatoes, removing the seeds and cutting them into chunks. Add the tomato chunks to the water.

Peel the potatoes, then cube and add them to the pot. Dice the carrots and add them also. Then dice the zucchini and celery, chop the escarole and scallions coarsely, and add these to the pot as well. Pour 4 tablespoons of olive oil over the vegetables, cover and simmer for about 2 hours.

Add the pasta, mix well, and let cook for about 15 minutes uncovered. Chop the basil leaves rather fine and, just before removing the *minestrone* from the stove, taste and add salt, basil, the remaining 2 tablespoons of oil, and the cheese. Serve very hot.

Minestrone alla Milanese

Minestrone, the Milanese way

Serves 6

2 quarts broth, either chicken or beef or a
   mixture of both (if you have no broth handy,
   cubes may be used)
2 pounds assorted vegetables, chosen according
   to season (see note)
2 slices salt pork or unsmoked bacon
1 clove garlic, finely chopped
2 tablespoons parsley, finely chopped
3 tablespoons olive oil
1 cup Parmesan cheese, freshly grated
Salt and freshly ground black pepper
1 cup rice, preferably Italian rice

Bring the broth to a boil and add the vegetables, starting with the ones that take the longest time to cook: celery, carrots, cabbage, and so on. Decrease the heat and simmer.

Chop the pork fat and fry in a small skillet. Add the garlic and cook for about 10 minutes, then add to the vegetables. Cover and simmer for at least 2 hours; the longer the better.

About 20 minutes before serving time, add the oil and 2 tablespoons of Parmesan cheese plus the parsley. Taste the soup and add salt and pepper if needed. Bring the soup to a strong boil and add the rice. Stir, let cook, uncovered, for 20 minutes or until the rice is done.

Pour the *minestrone* into a large tureen and serve with a ladle or fill small soup dishes and serve each person individually. Serve the rest of the Parmesan cheese in a separate bowl, for each person to sprinkle over his or her own dish.

NOTE

Celery, carrots, potatoes, onions, peas (frozen or fresh) are available all year. The zucchini might be left out and replaced with another vegetable. Spinach, kale, or cabbage are usually available, as are cranberry beans. Green beans, if fresh ones aren't available, may be replaced with frozen ones. If ripe tomatoes are out of season, replace with whole canned tomatoes. The important thing is that no one vegetable should dominate. If you have ½ cup of diced carrots, use ½ cup of diced celery and ½ cup of green beans, etc. Use no more than 1 large ripe tomato. Vegetables should not be shredded but rather cut into pieces at least ½-inch long.

A minestrone is best if prepared the day before it is to be served. If this is what you intend to do with this particular minestrone, keep the rice very much al dente or undercooked. In Milan, the soup is frequently served at room temperature, and it is called semi-freddo, *meaning "half-cold." Under no circumstances should a minestrone be refrigerated. If you wish to keep it overnight, cover it and keep it at room temperature.*

My Own Minestrone

Serves 6

1 pound (approximately) beef short ribs
2 quarts water
2 large ripe tomatoes (if not in season, 2
    tablespoons of tomato paste)
2 carrots
2 stalks of celery
1 cup fresh green beans, cut into ½-inch pieces
1 cup fresh green peas (if not in season, frozen
    may be used)
1 small head of escarole, shredded
1 cup fresh spinach, stems removed and leaves
    shredded
3 medium-sized zucchini, diced
2 medium-sized potatoes
Salt and freshly ground black pepper
1 teaspoon oregano
¾ cup Parmesan cheese, freshly grated
10 leaves fresh basil (if not in season, omit)

Remove as much of the fat from the meat as possible, but don't discard the bones. Bring the water to a boil and add the meat. Peel the tomatoes, remove the seeds, and cut into chunks. Add to the water. Scrape the carrots, dice (about ½-inch thick), and add to the pot. Dice the celery and add. Chop the beans and add them to the pot, then put in the peas, shredded greens, and diced zucchini. Peel the potatoes but leave them whole and add them to the pot. Cover and simmer over low heat for 1 hour.

Taste and add salt and pepper as desired. Add the oregano and simmer for another hour.

Remove the meat. At this point, the bones can easily be detached. Discard the bones and gristle and cut the meat into bite-sized pieces, then place back in the broth. If the potatoes are not yet disintegrated, mash them with a fork or a potato masher while in the broth. Add the basil then half the Parmesan cheese and taste. If the carrots and tomatoes have made the broth slightly too sweet, add 1 tablespoon of wine vinegar. Simmer a few minutes longer. Serve with rest of the cheese in a bowl, to be sprinkled over the *minestrone* by each guest.

NOTE

Vegetables may be substituted according to personal taste. Instead of 2 carrots, 1 carrot and 1 turnip might be used. Escarole may be replaced with cabbage (which gives a heavier taste) or kale. The quantity of vegetables should remain the same.

If possible, prepare the minestrone 1 day before serving. Don't refrigerate it. Let it stand, covered, in a cool place, then reheat it before serving. The 24-hour rest will greatly improve its taste.

 # Minestrone con Cotiche di Maiale

Minestrone with pork skins

Serves 6

½ *cup salt pork, diced*
2 *medium-sized carrots, washed and scraped*
1 *small onion*
2 *stalks of celery*
1 *pound Italian (or pear) tomatoes*
½ *pound pork skins*

2 quarts water
2 large potatoes (the mealy type)
1 cup fresh white beans or cranberry beans (if
    fresh beans are not available, dried white
    beans may be used but first they must be
    soaked in water overnight)
2 cabbage leaves (taken from the center of the
    head), coarsely chopped
Salt and freshly ground black pepper
2 medium-sized zucchini, coarsely chopped
1 cup fresh green peas, shelled
¾ cup rice
3 tablespoons parsley, coarsely chopped
6 fresh basil leaves (or ½ teaspoon dried)
¾ cup Parmesan cheese, freshly grated

Sauté diced salt pork over high heat in a skillet. Chop the carrots, onion, and celery. Add these to the pork fat and allow the vegetables to wilt. Peel the tomatoes, remove the seeds, chop coarsely, and add to the pork fat. Scrape the tough outside of the pork skins and cut the skins into strips about ⅓-inch wide.

Place the sautéed vegetables in a large saucepan, add the pork skins, and then add the water. Bring to a boil. Peel the potatoes but don't cut them up; add them whole to the vegetables, then follow by adding the beans. Cook over medium heat, covered, for about 1 hour. Uncover and, if too much liquid has evaporated, add a little water or broth. Taste broth and add salt and pepper to taste. With a potato masher, crush the potatoes without removing them from the pan. Add the remaining vegetables (cabbage and zucchini) then add the rice and simmer over low heat, cooking the rice until it is done. Add the peas to the *minestrone*. Then add the parsley and basil just before removing the pot from the heat. Pour the *minestrone* into a tureen or into individual dishes, and sprinkle liberally with Parmesan cheese.

NOTE

The vegetables indicated in the ingredients listing may be varied slightly; you may use 1 carrot and 1 turnip; cabbage may be replaced with kale. The only necessities are the potatoes, the tomatoes, and, in my opinion, the zucchini. The total quantity of vegetables you use should be the same as given in the recipe.

 # Minestrone con le Cotiche Freddo

Minestrone with pork skins, at room temperature

Serves 6

The preparation for this recipe is more or less the same as for the previous recipe. There are only 2 differences: after the pork skins have been sautéed with the vegetables, they are removed and are not simmered with the soup. In addition, the rice is kept a little underdone.

While the soup cooks, the pork skins are cut into thin strips and placed at the bottom of deep individual soup dishes. When the *minestrone* is done, pour it into the dishes, being careful not to disturb the strips of pork skin. The dishes of soup are then allowed to stand, covered with wax paper, in a cool place for several hours.

At the moment of serving, a plate is placed over each deep dish and turned upside down. The *minestrone* comes out quite solid and makes an attractive mound on each plate, with the strips of pork skin forming a decoration on top. The dish is sprinkled with Parmesan cheese at the moment of serving.

 # Brodo di Pollo con Asparagi

Chicken broth with asparagus

Serves 4

1 quart chicken broth, preferably homemade
6 to 8 fresh asparagus stalks
Salt
Pinch of nutmeg, freshly grated (optional)
2 tablespoons parsley, finely chopped
½ cup Parmesan cheese, freshly grated

Italians don't remove the fat from chicken broth because chickens in Italy are leaner than they are in this country. That, at least, is the way it was. Now Italian chickens also are getting their meals served to them to make them fat and shiny, so they no longer run around looking for food; it was that

running around that kept them lean and tasty. If your chicken broth seems quite fatty, remove some of the fat and leave just a few round spots of fat on the surface. Bring it to a boil.

Remove all thorny tips from the asparagus stalks; wash them well under cold water. Cut off and discard all the tough lower parts; cut the tender portions into bite-sized pieces. Add these to the broth and cook until quite tender but not mushy. Taste and add salt; add nutmeg if desired.

When the asparagus is cooked, ladle the broth into individual dishes, sprinkle a little parsley over each and serve with the Parmesan cheese in a separate bowl. Some purists don't add any additional flavoring to asparagus, not even Parmesan cheese.

NOTE

When buying a bunch of asparagus, you'll always find that there are a few stalks that aren't as straight or as thick as the others. Use them for this broth, but make sure you use only the tender parts.

 # Brodo con Riso e Fegatini

Chicken broth with rice and chicken livers

Serves 6

1 quart chicken broth, preferably homemade
1 cup rice, preferably Italian
¼ pound chicken livers
2 tablespoons butter
2 sage leaves, fresh, or ¼ teaspoon dried
Salt
Black pepper, freshly ground (optional)
2 tablespoons parsley, finely chopped
½ cup Parmesan cheese, freshly grated

Chicken broth should be of excellent quality, not made from cubes. Bring the broth to a boil, add the rice and stir. Reduce the heat and stir now and then.

While the rice cooks, clean the chicken livers; remove the whitish membrane and chop coarsely. Melt the butter in a skillet, then add the livers and the sage leaves. Cook until well done but not hard. Add salt to taste and

pepper if desired. If fresh sage is used, discard the leaves. Add the livers to the broth. Taste a grain of rice to see if it has reached desired doneness. Add the chopped parsley, and then remove the broth from the heat.

Pour the broth into a tureen (or into individual deep dishes) and sprinkle Parmesan cheese on top.

Minestrina di Spinaci e Riso in Brodo di Pollo

Spinach and rice in chicken broth

Serves 4

2 pounds fresh spinach
3 tablespoons butter
1 small clove garlic
6 cups chicken broth
Salt and freshly ground black pepper
½ cup rice
3 tablespoons Parmesan cheese, freshly grated

Wash the spinach repeatedly in lukewarm water, remove the hardest parts of the stems, then cook for about 10 to 12 minutes. You can cook the spinach either by boiling it in a large amount of water or by steaming it in the water that clings to the leaves. When done, it must be squeezed dry with your hands, a little at a time. Chop the cooked spinach fine but don't purée it. If you use a food processor, use the sharp blade and run the motor for 1 second.

Melt the butter in a fairly large saucepan, but don't allow it to brown. Add the garlic whole and brown it lightly. When it is golden, remove and discard. Add the chopped spinach and cook for 3 to 4 minutes. Add broth, then the salt and pepper to taste.

Bring the broth to a vigorous boil and add the rice. Stir frequently and cook over medium heat for about 20 minutes, or until rice is done *al dente,* meaning "bitable."

Serve the soup in individual dishes, sprinkling a little Parmesan cheese over each dish. Or, if you prefer, serve it in a tureen and ladle it out at the table. Serve the Parmesan separately; each guest can sprinkle the desired amount over his or her individual dish.

Minestra di Scarola al Latte

Escarole soup with milk

Serves 4

1 medium-sized head of escarole
2 cups chicken or beef broth
1 cup milk
⅜ cup Parmesan cheese, freshly grated
Salt
2 tablespoons olive oil (optional)

Remove the tough outer leaves of the escarole as well as any wilted looking leaf tips. Keep the center with its very tender leaves (about the size of a carnation) for use in a salad. This leaves you with about 15 healthy leaves. Shred these to bite size.

Bring the broth to a boil and add the escarole. Turn the heat very low, cover, and simmer for about 20 minutes. Add the milk. Taste and add Parmesan cheese, reserving about 2 tablespoons to sprinkle over the soup just before serving. Taste again and add salt if needed.

Soup may be served after being simmered for about 30 to 40 minutes. But, if you give it a little more time, it will only get better; in fact it is at its best the next day.

If you like a richer soup, turn off heat, pour the olive oil over the top, mix vigorously, and serve. Sprinkle the remaining Parmesan cheese over the top at the moment of serving. *Polpettone di Manzo* (see pages 244-45) would be a most appropriate second course.

 ## Scarola e Pastina in Brodo

Escarole and little pasta in broth

Serves 6

1 medium-sized head of escarole
2 quarts broth, chicken or beef
Salt
⅓ cup olive oil
½ cup dry small pasta (semi di melone or
   stelline)

(continued)

½ cup Parmesan cheese, freshly grated
Black pepper, freshly grated
2 tablespoons parsley, finely chopped (optional)

Wash the escarole and remove the dark outer leaves. Coarsely chop the rest; pieces should be about 1 or 1½ inches long.

Bring the broth to a boil and add escarole and salt. Cover and simmer for about 30 minutes. The escarole should be cooked a little more than you would cook it if you were to serve it as a vegetable.

Add the oil and bring the broth to a strong boil. Add the pasta and stir the broth with a wooden spoon. Continue to cook for about 5 minutes. Try 1 little piece of pasta; if it is still bitable but not mushy, then it is done.

Remove the pot from the heat, add the pepper, and stir. Sprinkle the parsley on top if desired. Serve the soup in individual bowls or in a tureen. Present the Parmesan cheese in a separate bowl, for each person to sprinkle over his or her individual dish.

NOTE

Canned broth may be used but Italians would prefer to make this dish when they have the broth, after having prepared a boiled chicken or boiled beef.

 # Paparot

Spinach and cornmeal soup, Friuli style

Serves 6

2 pounds fresh spinach (if necessary, substitute 2
   packages of frozen chopped spinach)
2 tablespoons butter
2 tablespoons olive oil
1 clove garlic
2 quarts broth, chicken or beef
Salt and freshly ground black pepper
1 cup yellow cornmeal
½ cup sifted all-purpose flour

Risotto with Fresh Asparagus

If you use fresh spinach, wash it several times in a lot of lukewarm water. Either cook it for 10 to 12 minutes in a large amount of water, or steam it for 8 minutes in only the water that clings to the leaves. The important thing is that it should have all the water squeezed out of it after it is cooled. Chop the cooked spinach finely. If you have a food processor, use the sharp blade and run motor for 10 seconds.

Melt the butter in a pot, add the oil and the garlic. As soon as the garlic becomes golden, remove and discard it. Add the spinach and broth to the butter-oil mixture. Simmer over low heat. Add salt and pepper to taste.

Sift the cornmeal with the flour. Using a ladle, remove about 1 cup of broth from pot. Let it cool for a couple of minutes then add it to dry mixture. Stir vigorously until there are no lumps. Add the mixture to the broth and stir so soup is smooth. Simmer over a very low heat for 30 minutes. Pour hot into individual bowls, or serve in an earthenware tureen. Nothing looks more inviting on a cold winter evening than the sight of a hostess ladling out this soup to her guests. In Italy the serving is done by the hostess, not by the host.

NOTE

In Friuli, this soup is eaten without grated cheese. If you are one of those people who can't conceive of a soup without a touch of Parmesan cheese, there is no rule against adding it.

 # Stracciatella

Serves 6

6 cups homemade broth, beef or chicken or a
   mixture of both
4 whole eggs
3 tablespoons breadcrumbs, very fine and made
   only from white bread
½ cup Parmesan cheese, freshly grated
Salt and freshly ground black pepper
½ teaspoon nutmeg, freshly grated

Bring the broth to a boil in a steady saucepan (you will need both hands for the preparation of this dish and won't be able to hold the saucepan if it is uneven). While the broth heats up, break the eggs into a bowl and whip with a wire whisk. Add the breadcrumbs and the Parmesan cheese very little at a time, beating constantly until all ingredients are blended. Add a little salt and freshly ground black pepper (gauge the salt according to how salty the broth is). Add the nutmeg.

Turn the heat to medium.

The egg mixture should have the thickness of a rather solid mayonnaise. Hold a colander in one hand, over the boiling broth. Pour the egg mixture through the holes and into the broth. Keep mixing the soup with the wire whisk and simmer for 5 minutes. The egg mixture will form floating little strands. Serve in a tureen or in individual soup bowls.

Personally I feel that the soup should be followed by a chicken dish, if it was made with chicken broth, and by beef, if the broth was a beef broth. Actually, *Stracciatella* has a personality of its own and may be served as first course of any meal.

NOTE

The important thing about this soup is that the broth be very good; canned broth should be avoided. This soup is both light and nourishing. When I was a child it was given to me when I was thought to look peaked. I tried to look peaked in order to get it.

Zuppe

Zuppa is a thick soup that has bread in it. Bread doesn't have to be a main ingredient: 1 slice of stale toasted bread, placed in the center of a deep dish over which the liquid part of the soup is poured, makes it a *zuppa. Minestrone* on the other hand, thick as it is, is no *zuppa,* no matter how hard it tries. *Minestrone* might contain pasta or rice, but it still remains a *minestrone.*

Zuppa di Pesce (pages 167-68), made almost entirely of fish, with just 1 slice of bread per person, is definitely a *zuppa.* The only exception is *Sopa* (or *Zuppa*) *di Fasoi,* a specialty of the Veneto and Friuli. It has no bread in it and has been a *zuppa* for centuries. It still is.

 # Pancotto alla Casalinga

Bread soup, Family style

Serves 6

½ loaf stale Italian bread
4 cups broth or 4 bouillon cubes and 4 cups water

(continued)

6 tablespoons olive oil
Salt and freshly ground black pepper
2 tablespoons thick tomato paste
½ cup Parmesan cheese, freshly grated
1 teaspoon oregano

Cut the bread into chunks without removing the crust. Pour the water or broth into a saucepan large enough to hold 8 to 10 cups. Add the bread chunks to the liquid and let them soak for 30 minutes. When bread is quite soft, break it up with a fork.

Cover the saucepan and bring to a boil. Reduce the heat and add the broth, oil, salt, and pepper and simmer, uncovered, stirring frequently to make sure mixture doesn't stick to bottom of the saucepan. If you have old crusts of Parmesan cheese, scrape off the black rind and add the cheese rinds to the bread mixture. (Be sure to remove the crusts before serving. They can be quite hard if they are old enough.)

After 30 minutes, add the tomato paste and the oregano and mix well. Continue to simmer. Add half of the Parmesan cheese. Mix and continue to cook for another hour. If you have the time, allow the soup to stand for an hour before serving.

When you are ready to serve, reheat then pour the soup into a tureen or into individual dishes. Sprinkle the rest of the Parmesan cheese over the soup and serve hot. This soup should be so thick that you almost want to eat it with a fork.

NOTE

I call this dish Bread Soup Family Style because it is a dish I remember from my childhood. It can't be found in any cookbook and was, probably, the invention of a cook in my family. A real pancotto is a sturdy dish and makes almost a meal in itself. On a winter Sunday it is an ideal luncheon dish, followed by nothing but a salad and fruit.

 Pancotto Ligure

Bread soup, Ligurian style

Serves 6

½ loaf stale Italian bread
4 cups water

6 tablespoons olive oil
Salt and freshly ground black pepper
1 teaspoon oregano
1 clove garlic
½ cup Parmesan cheese, freshly grated

D on't remove the crust from the bread, but cut it into chunks of about 2 to 3 inches. Soak the bread in lukewarm water in a saucepan. When bread is soft, break it up with a fork until it is quite mushy. Bring the water to a boil and simmer over very low heat, covered. After a few minutes, add oil, salt and pepper, and oregano. Continue to simmer uncovered for at least 1 hour, stirring every now and then to make sure the bread doesn't stick to the bottom of the saucepan. If the mixture dries out too much, add a little more water. The consistency should be that of a very thick soup. *Pancotto* is actually better the next day.

If you wish to serve the soup from a tureen, rub the inside of the tureen with a clove of garlic, then pour the soup into the tureen. If you wish to serve it in individual dishes, rub each dish with the garlic. Just before ladling the soup, add half of the Parmesan cheese and mix well. Sprinkle the rest of the cheese over the soup in the serving dish.

NOTE

Pancotto should really be called "Pane cotto," meaning cooked bread, but over the centuries it has become 1 word. It is one of the best known, and tastiest, dishes of what is known as Cucina Povera, the poor man's cuisine (although it cannot be considered that today, considering the prices of Parmesan and olive oil). It used to be served when there was leftover bread that would otherwise have been thrown out or made into breadcrumbs. But this dish is so delicious that people let bread get stale in order to prepare it.

 ## Pancotto alla Parma

Bread soup, Parma style

Serves 6

½ loaf stale Italian white bread
2 quarts good broth, chicken or beef or a mixture
 of both (canned or homemade, but not with
 cubes)

(continued)

Salt and freshly ground black pepper
3 tablespoons butter
3 tablespoons olive oil
Pinch of nutmeg, freshly grated
¾ cup Parmesan cheese, freshly grated

Cut the bread into slices. Or, if it is too stale, break it into chunks, but don't remove the crust.
Bring the broth to a boil and add the bread. Cook, uncovered, over low heat, for at least 30 minutes. Taste and add salt and pepper if needed. Add the butter, oil, and nutmeg and continue cooking for another 30 minutes.

Before removing the pot from the heat, add half the Parmesan cheese and serve remaining cheese in a separate bowl, for each person to sprinkle over his or her individual dish.

NOTE

This used to be considered a delicious and most inexpensive dish. With the current price of Parmesan cheese (and it has to be the best), it is no longer inexpensive. It is, however, still delicious.

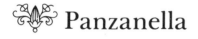 ## Panzanella

Serves 6 to 8

1 loaf of stale Italian bread (average size), cut
  into chunks
Water
½ cup olive oil
2 tablespoons wine vinegar
¼ cup sweet basil, finely chopped
¼ cup chives, finely chopped
2 large ripe tomatoes, peeled and coarsely chopped
Salt and freshly ground black pepper
½ cup Parmesan cheese, freshly grated

If you don't have a loaf of stale bread, place a fresh loaf in a medium oven (300°) for about 40 minutes. Let it cool and break it into chunks.
Place the bread chunks in a saucepan and add enough water to cover. Let it stand until the bread has absorbed all the water. If parts of the bread

still seem dry, add a little more water to the saucepan. When the bread is a complete mush, place the saucepan over very low heat and bring it to a simmer.

Add the oil, vinegar, basil, and chives, stirring almost constantly to prevent the mush from sticking to the bottom of the pan. Add the tomatoes. Taste and add salt and pepper. Simmer uncovered and stir frequently until the mixture becomes a creamy substance.

Remove the saucepan from the heat and cool completely. Don't refrigerate it but keep it in a cool place for up to 24 hours. Transfer the soup to a tureen or to individual bowls and sprinkle Parmesan cheese over the top. Serve with additional grated Parmesan cheese in a separate bowl, if desired.

NOTE

This is a very old recipe that had been forgotten for a long time. Perhaps it is because of the high price of meat or because of a return to the cuisine of simpler times, but now Panzanella has become very popular at summer parties in Italy. People speak about Panzanella Parties as they do about una spaghettata, *meaning spaghetti parties. Panzanella has the advantage of being able to be prepared ahead of time; when served cold, it is ideal for a hot summer luncheon.*

Some people prefer to use onions rather than chives and they add the onion (finely chopped) after the mixture has been cooked and has cooled. Personally, I find that the raw onion is a bit too much.

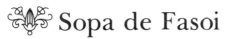 Sopa de Fasoi

Venetian bean soup

Serves 6

2 cups pinto beans, dried or fresh
8 cups water
½ cup salt pork, chopped, salt scraped off
⅓ cup olive oil
1 medium-sized onion, thinly sliced
Salt and freshly ground black pepper
1 tablespoon heavy cream (optional)

All types of small beans may be used for this dish. If dried beans are used, soak them in water overnight. Then drain and cook in fresh water very slowly, stirring frequently, so that the beans don't stick to the bottom of the pot. When the beans are done (approximately 1 hour

cooking time), take half of them and purée through a sieve. Add puréed beans to the pot with the rest of the beans.

Heat the chopped salt pork in a skillet, add the oil, let it get very hot, then add the onion. Sauté the onion until it is transparent; don't let it get brown. Add this onion and oil-salt pork mixture to the soup. Taste and add salt and pepper as desired. Simmer uncovered for about 30 minutes. Add a little water if too much liquid has cooked away. Add the cream at the last moment if desired.

The classic way of serving *Sopa de Fasoi* is in individual earthenware bowls. A small pinch of fresh pepper is placed in the bottom of each bowl, and a trickle of oil is added, in the shape of a cross. The soup is poured over it.

NOTE

Some people like their soup really thick. They add a large potato, peeled but raw, at the very beginning. The potato should dissolve completely. If small chunks are left they may be mashed with a potato masher, without removing them from the soup.

 Sopa di Riso e Fasoi

Rice and bean soup

Serves 6

1 cup white beans
¼ pound salt pork
2 stalks of celery
1 small white onion
4 bay leaves
2 quarts broth, chicken or beef or a combination
  of both
1 cup rice, preferably Italian
Salt and freshly ground black pepper
½ cup Parmesan cheese, freshly grated

Soak the beans overnight in water. Drain.
Scrape the salt off the salt pork, dice and place in a large pot. Chop the celery and onion moderately coarsely (if you use a food processor, chop with the steel blade for about 2 seconds).

Heat the salt pork over high heat but don't allow it to brown. Add the celery, onion, and bay leaves and sauté. Add the beans, stir, and add the broth. Reduce heat, cover, and cook over low heat for about 2 hours. Check every now and then to make sure the broth doesn't evaporate.

When beans are done, add the rice and, if needed, a little additional broth or water. The rice will absorb quite a bit of liquid as it cooks. Increase the heat and stir constantly while the rice is cooking. After 20 minutes try a grain. The rice should be "bitable" and not mushy. Add salt and pepper, remove the bay leaves, then pour the soup into a tureen or into individual bowls. Serve the Parmesan cheese separately.

NOTE

As mentioned in the introduction to this section, a zuppa (sopa is the Venetian and Friuli word for zuppa) is a soup with bread in it. However, Sopa di Fasoi has no bread in it but is also called a "sopa."

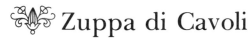 Zuppa di Cavoli

Cabbage soup

Serves 6

1 medium-sized cabbage
2 quarts broth, preferably beef broth and, of
    course, preferably homemade, but canned may
    be used
Salt and freshly ground black pepper
3 tablespoons chopped pancetta or the equivalent
    amount of salt pork
1 clove garlic
6 tablespoons butter
10 or 12 slices of French or Italian bread
¾ cup Parmesan cheese, freshly grated

Preheat the oven to 350°. Remove the outer leaves of the cabbage. Also remove the tough bottom part of the inner leaves. Shred the cabbage coarsely. Bring the broth to a boil and add the cabbage, salt, and pepper.

Place the *pancetta* in a skillet and heat, but don't allow it to brown. Chop the garlic and add it to the skillet. Remove the cabbage from the broth and

add it to the *pancetta;* coat the pieces well but don't continue cooking. Keep the cabbage warm. In a large skillet, melt butter and fry the bread slices until golden.

Make a layer of fried bread at the bottom of a large casserole, sprinkle it with Parmesan cheese, make a layer of cabbage, and then sprinkle the cabbage with Parmesan cheese. Continue until all ingredients have been used. Pour the soup over the layers, and sprinkle with the remaining Parmesan.

Bake the soup in the preheated oven for about 30 minutes. Serve the soup with a ladle into individual soup bowls or deep soup dishes. If desired, serve some additional Parmesan cheese alongside in a bowl, for each person to sprinkle over his or her individual dishes.

NOTE

I find the cabbage in this country to be tougher and less flavorful than the smaller Italian version. I have tried this soup with kale instead of cabbage, with excellent results. It is, of course, totally unorthodox but the taste is good.

I say "French or Italian bread" because I find very little difference in taste between those long loaves normally sold in supermarkets that say either French or Italian bread. In my opinion they are neither, and those sesame seeds that are sometimes added certainly don't make them more Italian!

La Zuppa del Povero

The poor man's soup

Serves 6

1 pound broccoli rapa (wild broccoli or mustard
  greens)
2 quarts water or broth
Salt and freshly ground black pepper
6 tablespoons olive oil
6 tablespoons Parmesan cheese, freshly grated
6 slices of stale Italian bread

Preheat the oven to 350°. Wash the wild broccoli. If the stems are very tough, cut off the hardest parts; if they are too long, cut them into pieces 4 to 5 inches long. Bring the water or broth to a boil and add the broccoli and a little salt. Cook covered over medium heat for at least 1 hour. Add oil and pepper, if desired. Cook for another 10 minutes and add the Parmesan cheese, leaving 2 tablespoons for later use.

Place the slices of bread in the preheated oven until golden. Place 1 slice of toasted bread at the bottom of each individual soup dish or in a tureen. Ladle the soup over the bread and sprinkle the rest of the Parmesan cheese over it. Serve very hot.

NOTE

This is a very old recipe of unknown origin. In view of the liberal use of olive oil it is probably Tuscan where olive oil is cheap (or at least was cheap, when the name Poor Man's Soup was created). No matter what your bank account is, this is a delicious dish for a cold winter luncheon.

Minestre Asciutte

Minestre asciutte, translated literally, means Dry First Courses; that is exactly what they are. We have mentioned that all first courses are *minestre*. A *minestra asciutta* is a first course you eat with a fork and not with a spoon. Some *zuppe* are so thick that you almost have to use a fork, but it is the *almost* that prevents them from being considered *minestre asciutte*.

On the other hand, all pasta dishes, *risottos*, and *polentas* are *asciutte*. In this section, we have included many recipes for *polenta* and *risotto* particularly, but you will also find some intriguing pasta and *gnocchi* dishes as well.

Polenta

In some parts of northern Italy, *polenta* is as much a part of the daily diet as bread; in fact, it replaces bread. In some restaurants of the Veneto or the Friuli, you will see that your check reads *"coperto e polenta."* In other parts of Italy it would read *"coperto e pane."* It is usually a small amount and, if you watch the amount of *polenta* (or bread) some Italians eat, the restaurateur seems to have the right to charge for it.

Polenta is a mush made of cornmeal. But, unlike the spoon bread of the southern United States, it is made of coarser ground cornmeal, cooked until it gets quite solid and eaten either instead of bread, briefly put on the *gratticola* (gridiron), or made into dozens of different dishes, with the addition of cheeses, meats, sausages, mushrooms, or ragouts.

The Italians of the north are known to love their *polenta* so much that their southern Italian brethern like to refer to them as *polentoni*. And in Bergamo, one of the most beautiful towns of the region, just a little to the north of the *autostrada* that leads from Milan to Venice, there still exists the "Feast of the *Polenta*," when the king of the *polenta* gets elected. Whether he is crowned because he eats the most, or whether it is because he cooks the best, is not quite clear.

My longtime friend, author of many cookbooks and of a food column signed "Falstaff," Vincenzo Buonassisi, has made a study of the origins of our

polenta. It is well known that Christopher Columbus, when he landed on an island he called *Hispaniola,* was introduced to bright yellow grains he called *mahiz,* spelling the name as best he could after hearing the local population pronounce it. Columbus undoubtedly brought some *mahiz* (or *mais*) to Europe. But Mr. Buonassisi found evidence of cornmeal, or *polenta,* in northern Italy long before Columbus.

It seems that the first cornmeal the Italians encountered came from Persia. The fact that it is, to this day, called *granoturco,* or Turkish grain, would prove him right as Persia, in the 14th century, was dominated by the Turks.

Whatever its origin, we bless the day on which the Italians were introduced to it. In the Veneto, and the Friuli particularly, it is part of life.

No country home, be it the farmer's or the landowner's, was without an enormous fireplace in the kitchen, large enough to hold a bench on either side on which the family sat on cold winter nights. Between them hung the traditional *paiolo,* the huge copper kettle, suspended from a thick chain, in which the *polenta* was cooked.

It takes 1 hour for the *polenta* to be done (and another 30 minutes to be perfect, the real connoisseurs of *polenta* say). So, while the hostess was stirring with all her strength, the rest of the family was exchanging the news of the day; sipping a glass of local wine, of course. This is the equivalent of the "cocktail hour" in the old Friuli. And in some old homes of today's Friuli, too. *Polenta*-cooking is a rite and you can still find country restaurants where the old tradition remains unchanged.

When I was married, my nurse, who was a Friulana, came to the wedding, an honored guest. She presented me with a *paiolo,* the copper gleaming from years and years of polishing. I thanked her with a hug and asked: "Do you think I could find a smaller one somewhere?" She looked at me with a mixture of pity and contempt. "They don't come smaller," she said and our relationship was never the same again. What would she say if she saw me cook *polenta* over gas in a stainless steel pot? She didn't live to see it.

And she was not the only one who wouldn't compromise. On a recent visit to Vicenza, one of the most elegant cities of northern Italy, I went to a hardware store: a magnificent emporium of everything a cook and a hostess can dream of. There was china and flatware from the traditional to the most modern design, mixers, blenders, ice buckets and cutlery of all shapes and sizes. And there, in a room by itself, was "the corner of the *polenta.*" Copper kettles, chains to hang them from, and enormous hooks to be attached to the ceiling, from which to hang the chains. And *bastoni,* of course, the wooden sticks about 3 feet long, with which the *polenta* used to be stirred. I say "used to be" because with a bow to modern times, there were also some equally long wooden spoons. It does make life easier!

The reason for the unusual length of sticks, spoons, or spatulas is that *polenta*, when it gets thick, "spits" when it bubbles. Whoever does the stirring is likely to suffer a series of tiny burns on hands and forearms if he or she is standing too close to the kettle.

I have tried to protect myself by wearing a barbecue mit. No good. Your grip on the spoon isn't firm enough for the vigorous stirring. And vigorous it must be. And constant. And always in the same direction. If you pour the cornmeal with your left hand (pouring ever so slowly), keep stirring clockwise with your right hand. As the saying goes: after 1 hour the *polenta* is done; after 1½ hours it's perfect.

Later on in the recipes, I shall give modern versions of *polenta*-cooking and even some shortcuts. But right now, picture the ritual of making *polenta*. It was, and in many families still is, the highlight of the day. *Polenta* is more than food; it is a way of life.

First comes the choice of the cornmeal — yellow or white, coarsely ground or fine — according to your taste, to the kind of dish you wish to prepare, and to what is available.

The salted water has come to a strong boil in the large kettle, and there is a second kettle with boiling water; it's the "standby-kettle." Slowly, slowly the maker of *polenta* pours the cornmeal into the boiling water. (One rapid gesture and too much cornmeal drops into the water all at once, lowering the temperature of the water suddenly and making the cornmeal one big lump. Disaster! You have to throw it out.) Stirring, stirring . . . the cornmeal thickens, the smooth surface glistens. Now it is thicker than you want it; that is where the "standby-water" comes in. You add a little of it to the kettle in which the *polenta* is cooking. You continue stirring until you have the desired consistency.

The true *polenta* experts say that it is precisely this alternating thickening and thinning that makes for a perfect *polenta*.

Once it is done to your liking, place a pristine tablecloth on the kitchen table, moisten it lightly, turn your kettle upside down and allow the golden contents to flow onto the tablecloth. This has to be done right away while the *polenta* is hot. As soon as it cools, it will harden. Scrape the sides and bottom of the kettle with a wooden spatula. The *polenta* should make a beautiful mound.

If you want to eat the *polenta* with a ragout, or with butter and cheese, don't let it cool. Spoon it, still very hot, onto a platter or onto individual dishes and add one of the many condiments in the following recipes.

If you want to use it instead of bread, or if you intend to fry it, allow it to cool and cut it into the desired thickness, using a string for cutting.

In times gone by, *polenta* used to be cut only with a musical string. Now any string strong enough to do the cutting is permissible. Even a wooden knife or spatula is acceptable. But never, under any circumstances, use metal!

Not even if it were gold. The taste of metal destroys *polenta,* or so we have been told. Obviously this was before stainless steel. I remember eating *polenta* with a wooden spoon. Now we use forks, made of silver or even stainless steel. It doesn't seem to harm the *polenta.* As for cutting it into slices or strips, I still use either a string or a wooden utensil. Habit, maybe. Or prejudice.

 # Polenta

Basic recipe

Serves 6 to 8

2 quarts water
1 teaspoon salt
1 pound yellow cornmeal (coarsely ground, if
  available)
Kettle of boiling water in reserve

See Illustrated Techniques, page 349

Bring 2 quarts of water to a strong boil using a sturdy kettle you don't have to hold: you must have both hands free. Add the salt. With your left hand, start pouring the cornmeal into the boiling water while you start stirring with your right hand. Pour as slowly as possible (*a pioggia,* we say in Italian: "like a gentle rain") and stir as rapidly as possible, using a long wooden spoon or stick. As the cornmeal mush thickens, you will stir more slowly because *polenta* requires quite a bit of strength.

After 30 minutes, the cornmeal should no longer cling to the sides of the kettle and should seem thick enough to eat. It isn't. It may be *cooked* but it isn't *done.* At this point, add a ladle of the boiling water you have in reserve and continue stirring. Purists say that *polenta* should cook for 1 hour and 30 minutes; I feel that 1 hour suffices even for the coarsest cornmeal.

If you have a marble-top table, wet it lightly. Lift your kettle with both hands, tilt it, and allow the golden mush to flow onto it. If you don't have a marble top, place a tablecloth on your table, wet it slightly, and pour the *polenta* onto the cloth.

 Polenta

Basic recipe for our times

Serves 6 to 8

2 quarts water
1 teaspoon salt
1 pound yellow or white cornmeal
Kettle of boiling water in reserve

See Illustrated Techniques, page 349

See Illustrated Techniques, page 349

Bring 2 quarts of water to a strong boil and add the salt. Use a sturdy kettle that doesn't need holding on to: you must have both hands free. Pour the cornmeal *very* slowly into the boiling water while stirring constantly. Stir clockwise, without ever turning the other way and without ever stopping. Use a wooden spoon with the longest handle you can find and wear an old dress with long sleeves to avoid those tiny burns a boiling *polenta* can produce.

After 30 minutes, the cornmeal mush should be thick enough and should also no longer cling to the sides of the kettle. Purists say that it should cook for 1 hour more. Actually 30 minutes more suffices. If it is too thick to continue stirring, add a little of the water you have in reserve, 1 ladle at a time. It may be that all you need is 1 ladle to continue cooking. Only you can judge how much additional water you want to use, depending upon the use you want to make of the *polenta*. If you intend to let the *polenta* cool — cutting it into slices (about 1-inch thick), frying it on the gridiron, and eating it instead of bread — then you want a solid *polenta*. If you want to use it for one of the many following dishes, you'd better keep it slightly soft.

The choice of cornmeal also depends upon the use you want to make of the *polenta*. A coarse cornmeal, sold in bulk, is available in many Italian markets. It is the best for *polenta*, eaten sliced, either broiled or fried, with or without cheese. For many of the following *polenta* dishes, however, a finer *polenta* is preferable. Quaker cornmeal may be used, though in my opinion it cooks too fast. You get the desired consistency but you don't get the flavor of *polenta*. If you use it with many condiments, as many of the following recipes call for, it will do — either yellow or white.

Once your *polenta* is done, place a pristine tablecloth on the kitchen table, turn your kettle upside down, and allow the contents to flow onto the tablecloth. Scrape the sides and bottom of your pot with your wooden spoon. *Polenta* should make a beautiful mound.

If you want it to cool, let the *polenta* stand without touching it. When the time comes to cut it, you may use a wooden spatula if you have one, but a

stainless steel knife will also do. Do not use any metal other than stainless steel, however, because the taste of metal will destroy the taste of *polenta*.

If you want to use it right away, accompanied by one of the many condiments, don't allow it to cool but, rather, spoon it, very hot, onto a platter or onto individual dishes. Cover the *polenta* with melted butter and cheese, a ragout, hot sausage, etc.

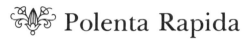

Polenta Rapida

Quick polenta

Serves 6

4 cups water
1 teaspoon salt
1 cup yellow cornmeal (coarsely ground, if
  available)

Add salt to the cold water. Add the cornmeal and mix thoroughly until no lumps are left. Place the mixture over low heat and stir until it thickens — about 10 minutes.

Wet a large piece of double-layer cheesecloth. With the help of a spatula, pour the *polenta* onto the cheesecloth. Tie the ends loosely and place it in a sieve (choose a pot large enough to suspend the sieve). Fill the pot halfway with water. Place the sieve with cheesecloth over it. *The water must not touch the cornmeal mixture.* Cover the sieve with aluminum foil and place a lid on top of that.

Bring the water to a boil and allow the *polenta* to cook over steam for 1 hour. Check every now and then to make sure the water doesn't boil so vigorously that it touches the cornmeal. After an hour, turn off heat and let the *polenta* stand, uncovered, for 5 minutes. Wet a marble-top table lightly (or place a wet tablecloth over a wooden surface) and turn sieve upside down onto the wet surface. Remove the sieve, and also carefully remove the cheesecloth. The mound of *polenta* is ready for all of the following recipes.

NOTE

I wish I could say that the results from this version are the same as those you get by stirring, stirring, stirring. I can't. This recipe makes a perfectly acceptable polenta, but not for polenta fans. It lacks subtlety. It compares to the hard-earned polenta the way a wig compares to a head of luscious hair.

Polenta Valdostana

Polenta, Piedmont style

Serves 8

2 *quarts skim milk*
1 *teaspoon salt*
1 *pound yellow cornmeal*
½ *pound fontina cheese, slivered (if*
  unavailable, Swiss cheese)
¼ *stick butter*

Bring the milk to a boil and add the salt. Use a large kettle because the milk tends to boil over easier than does water. Pour the cornmeal into the boiling milk, stirring constantly with a wooden stick or long wooden spoon (see page 81).

When the *polenta* is half done (about 25 minutes), add the cheese slivers and mix thoroughly until the cheese is completely melted. Continue cooking, and stirring, until the *polenta* is done (about 50 minutes).

Melt the butter in a small saucepan until golden. Pour the *polenta* into a serving bowl, pour the butter over the whole surface and serve very hot.

A very sturdy wine is urgently needed with this *polenta*. The Piedmont is blessed with many: either a Barolo or a Gattinara will hold their own with this formidable dish.

NOTE

The quantity of cornmeal and liquid used are the same as in other polenta recipes. I say "serves 8" instead of 6 because this is the richest polenta of them all. The 8 people will be lucky if they can move after having enjoyed it. I suggest using skim milk because it reduces the richness of the dish somewhat, although in the Piedmont, no one has heard of skim milk. I have also slightly reduced the quantity of butter. In the Piedmont, a cook would not measure the butter: she would simply inundate the polenta.

This dish is called Piedmont style because fontina is a typical cheese from the Piedmont. If you have to replace it with Swiss cheese, the flavor will be slightly different.

 # Polenta con Besciamella al Forno

Baked polenta with white sauce

Serves 6 to 8

2 *quarts water*
1 *teaspoon salt*

1 pound cornmeal
2 cups besciamella, medium thick (see pages 22-23)
1 cup Parmesan cheese, freshly grated
2 tablespoons butter

Prepare a *polenta*, following the basic instructions on pages 81-83. If you have a marble-top table, wet it lightly and pour the *polenta* over it as soon as it is done. Smooth the surface with the wet blade of a knife and flatten to a 1-inch thickness. If you have no marble top, spread a tablecloth over your kitchen table and wet it lightly. Pour the *polenta* over the cloth and flatten it. Let it cool.

Preheat the oven to 375°. Prepare a *besciamella* (white sauce) and cover the bottom of an 8-inch ovenproof dish (choose one with rather high 3- to 4-inch sides). When the *polenta* is cold, cut it with a wooden spatula or a piece of string. The size and shape of the slices depend on the shape of your dish. Make a layer of *polenta* on top of the *besciamella*, sprinkle with Parmesan, make another layer of *polenta*, followed by a layer of *besciamella* and so on. The last layer should be *polenta*, liberally dotted with butter and sprinkled with Parmesan.

Place the dish in the center of the preheated oven and bake for about 40 minutes. Remove and serve.

This *polenta* dish should be served with a red wine such as a Valpolicella.

Polenta al Forno con Fontina

Baked polenta with fontina cheese

Serves 6

2 quarts water
1 tablespoon salt
3 cups yellow cornmeal (coarsely ground, if available)
½ pound fontina cheese
⅓ cup Parmesan cheese, freshly grated
6 tablespoons butter

Prepare the *pölenta* following the basic instructions on pages 81-83. Wet a marble-top table (or a large cookie sheet) with cold water and pour the *polenta* onto it. Flatten it with the blade of a wet knife and let it cool completely. Butter a rectangular baking dish, making sure that the sides

and bottom are well coated. The dish should be pretty enough to come to the table.

Preheat the oven to 400°. Make a layer of *polenta* (about ¼-inch thick) on the bottom of the dish. Cut the *polenta* either with a wooden knife or a fine string, held very tightly. Cut the *fontina* into slivers, using the "slicer" on your cheese grater. Cover the *polenta* with the *fontina*. Make another layer of *polenta* and continue until the *polenta* and *fontina* have been used up. The last layer should be of *polenta*. Sprinkle the Parmesan cheese on top, dot with butter, and place in a preheated oven. Bake for about 30 minutes or until the top is golden.

Serve a red wine from the Piedmont with this: a sturdy Barbera or a more elegant Gattinara. And don't make any plans for the rest of the evening. You will be spending it in a glow of well-fed laziness.

NOTE

There are replacements for most cheeses. There is none for fontina. If you can't find any, don't try this dish. And make sure the cheese is Italian fontina. There is a perfectly good cheese around called Scandinavian fontina. It is not the same thing. It will do for an after-dinner cheese, but it will not do for this recipe. The two are easily distinguishable: the fontina from the Piedmont has a brownish rind that looks almost like the bark of a tree. The Scandinavian one has a red rind.

One night, in a beautiful country villa in the hills over Biella (in the Piedmont), I was served a variation of this dish. The polenta was cooked in half milk, half cream. The top was flooded with brown homemade butter. The dish was placed in the oven ever so briefly. It all had a creamy, dreamy texture. I couldn't eat for 3 days, but it was worth it!

 Polenta al Parmigiano

Polenta with Parmesan cheese

Serves 8

2 quarts milk
1 teaspoon salt
1 pound yellow cornmeal
2 tablespoons butter
3 eggs, separated
¾ cup Parmesan cheese, freshly grated
1 tablespoon breadcrumbs

Bring the milk to a boil, add the salt, and pour in the cornmeal, adding it ever so slowly. Stir constantly with the other hand, using a long wooden stick or a wooden spoon. After about 15 minutes, add 1 tablespoon of butter. Continue cooking for another 15 minutes; *polenta* should be quite soft. If it seems too solid, add a little boiling milk or boiling water.

Preheat the oven to 400°. Allow the *polenta* to cool a little while you beat the egg whites until stiff. Add the egg yolks, one at a time, allowing the first one to be absorbed before adding the next. Add half the grated cheese and then all the egg whites, folding them in gently. Butter an 8-inch ovenproof dish and coat it with breadcrumbs. Spoon the *polenta* into the dish, leveling the surface with the blade of a wet knife. Cover with the rest of the Parmesan and place the dish into the hot (400°) oven for about 20 minutes. Check after about 10 minutes: if top seems too brown, lower the heat.

This is a very rich dish that will easily serve 8. It requires a very solid red wine: a Barolo, if you want to make it festive; a Barbera or a Barbaresco if these are your daily wines.

NOTE

A dish like this is obviously both a first course and a main course. It may be followed by Insalata Mista Cotta (see pages 307-8) but most people would be happy with a dessert of fresh fruit.

 ## Polenta Pasticciata con Ricotta

Baked polenta with ricotta

Serves 6

2 quarts water
1 teaspoon salt
1 pound yellow cornmeal
1 container (15 oz.) skim milk ricotta
Salt and freshly ground black pepper
¾ cup Parmesan cheese, freshly grated
2 tablespoons butter

Bring the water to a boil, add the salt, and then the cornmeal, following the basic instructions on pages 81-83. Allow the *polenta* to cool. Preheat the oven to 375°. Place the *ricotta* in a bowl, add salt and pepper to taste, and work it with a wooden spoon until smooth. Butter an ovenproof

dish (about 3- to 4-inches deep). Cut the *polenta* into slices about ½-inch thick. Place a layer of *polenta* at the bottom of dish, spread a layer of *ricotta* (about ¼-inch thick) over the *polenta*, and sprinkle with Parmesan. Continue with another layer of *polenta*, then another layer of *ricotta* until all the ingredients have been used. The last layer should be *polenta*, liberally dotted with butter and sprinkled with Parmesan.

Place the dish in the preheated oven. Bake the *polenta* for about 30 minutes or until the top is golden. Serve very hot.

This is a very rich dish that requires a sturdy red wine. On a cold winter evening a Barbera would go well.

NOTE

This baked polenta is a meal in itself, with fresh fruit as dessert.

 # Polenta Arrostita con Uova Sode

Baked polenta with hard-boiled eggs

Serves 6

2 quarts water
1 teaspoon salt
1 pound yellow cornmeal
2 tablespoons butter
6 hard-boiled eggs
⅓ cup olive oil
½ cup Parmesan cheese, freshly grated

Prepare a rather solid *polenta,* following the instructions on pages 81-83, and let cool.

Preheat the oven to 400°. With a piece of string or a wooden spatula, cut slices about ¾-inch thick. Coat a shallow baking dish with 2 tablespoons of butter. Make a layer of *polenta,* cover with a layer of hard-boiled eggs, make another layer of *polenta,* then pour the olive oil over the surface. Sprinkle with Parmesan and bake in a hot oven (400°) for about 30 minutes. The crust should be quite crisp.

Serve as a first course, with *Spinaci all'Olio* (see pages 293-94), or with a salad. The wine to drink with this *Polenta Arrostita* is a Merlot from Friuli. If

not available, a dry red wine, not overpowering but also not too light, may be substituted.

NOTE

This polenta may be cooled slightly, cut into wedges, and served with drinks as an appetizer. A small paper napkin should be wrapped around one end of each wedge.

 # Polenta Cortina d'Ampezzo

Baked polenta with sausage

Serves 6 to 8

2 tablespoons shortening, such as Crisco
1 cup sweet sausage, diced
2 quarts water
1 teaspoon salt
1 pound cornmeal
3 whole eggs
Salt and freshly ground black pepper
½ cup Parmesan cheese, freshly grated

Melt the shortening in a skillet and add the diced sausage. Stir, browning the cubes. Drain the sausage and reserve both meat and fat. Set aside and keep warm.

Prepare the *polenta*, following the basic instructions on pages 81-83, and keep it rather soft. Add the sausage and mix well. Beat the eggs lightly and add them to the *polenta* after you have removed it from the heat. Add salt and pepper.

Preheat the oven to 400°. Pour half the fat into an ovenproof bowl (preferably glazed earthenware). Pour the *polenta* into it. Smooth the top with the blade of a knife or the back of a spoon dipped in hot water. When the top is level, pour the rest of the fat over it; top with grated Parmesan and bake in the oven (400°) for about 20 minutes, or until the top is golden. Serve immediately.

A dry red wine should be served with this: a Merlot, if available, or a Chianti.

NOTE

I call this dish Polenta Cortina d'Ampezzo after the ski resort in the Dolomites where I first tasted it. Even after a morning of skiing it was a meal in itself. I remember biting into an ice-cold apple for dessert. Some of us managed to nibble on a piece of Parmesan with the fruit.

 # Polenta Pasticciata con Funghi

Baked polenta with mushrooms

Serves 6

2 quarts water
1 teaspoon salt
1 pound yellow cornmeal
½ cup imported dried mushrooms
¼ pound salt pork
1 small onion
1 carrot
1 stalk celery
1 pound ripe tomatoes, peeled, seeded, and
  coarsely chopped
Salt and freshly ground black pepper
1 stick butter
½ cup Parmesan cheese, freshly grated

Prepare a rather soft *polenta*, following the basic instructions on pages 81-83.
Soak the mushrooms in lukewarm water. Scrape the salt off the salt pork, chop, and place in a saucepan over medium heat. Chop the onion, carrot, and celery and add to the fat. When all of the ingredients are lightly colored, add the tomatoes. Stir the vegetables with a wooden spoon and cook over low heat until the liquid from the tomatoes has almost completely evaporated. Squeeze the mushrooms dry and chop them but don't discard the water. Add the mushrooms to the tomatoes and taste before adding salt and pepper. If the pork fat is quite salty, very little additional salt is needed. Add the water in which the mushrooms have soaked (it shouldn't be more than ½ cup). Cook the mixture until quite thick.

Preheat the oven to 375°. Coat a deep ovenproof dish with plenty of butter. The sides of the dish should be about 4 inches high. Cut the *polenta* into slices about ½-inch thick. Make a layer of *polenta* at the bottom of the dish, cover with the tomato-mushroom mixture, dot with butter, and sprinkle with

Parmesan. Make another layer of *polenta*, followed by one of sauce, butter, and Parmesan. Continue until all ingredients are used. The last layer should be *polenta*, dotted with butter and sprinkled with Parmesan.

Bake the *polenta* for about 45 minutes or until the top is golden. Some people like to place it briefly under the broiler to get a darker crust. Serve very hot.

A good red wine, like a Merlot from the Friuli region, should be served with this dish.

NOTE

Polenta Pasticciata should be served by itself. It is a sturdy main course. If you wish to serve it as a first course, a salad may be served afterwards, followed by fruit and cheese.

Polenta Misteriosa

Mysterious polenta

Serves 6 to 8

2 quarts water
1 teaspoon salt
1 pound yellow cornmeal
1 stick butter
5 large ripe tomatoes (if out of season, use 1
    pound whole canned tomatoes)
3 tablespoons olive oil
5 leaves fresh basil (optional)
Salt and freshly ground black pepper
1 small onion, finely chopped
5 whole eggs

Prepare a fairly solid *polenta*, following the basic instructions on pages 81-83. Let it cool completely (*polenta* may be prepared a day ahead). Have the butter at room temperature. With your hands, break the *polenta* into chunks and place the chunks in a bowl. Add the butter, a little at a time, and, with a fork, mix well until the *polenta* has the consistency of dough. (If you have a food processor it's child's play: place a few chunks of *polenta* and a couple tablespoons of butter in the machine, run the motor for about 30 to 40 seconds, empty, and repeat with the rest of the *polenta*.)

Butter a rectangular baking dish (12-inch by 8-inch, or any other shape you like) and line it with *polenta*, being careful that both bottom and sides of dish are equally lined.

If fresh tomatoes are used, dip them briefly in boiling water and peel. Cut the tomatoes into chunks, remove seeds, and place in a saucepan. Add the oil, chopped basil, salt, and pepper (*polenta* is bland, therefore the mixture requires quite a bit of both salt and pepper). Add the onion and simmer over medium heat, stirring frequently so the mixture won't stick to the bottom of the saucepan. Cook until all the water from the tomatoes has been absorbed and the mixture is the consistency of a thick sauce.

Preheat the oven to 350°. Beat the eggs with a hand mixer until the whites and yolks are well blended. When the tomato mixture stops bubbling add it to the eggs and mix well; add half the Parmesan cheese and mix again. Pour the tomato mixture into the *polenta*.

Place the dish in the preheated oven. After about 15 minutes, remove from the oven and, with the prongs of a fork, make a little pattern into the edges of the *polenta*. The edge should be crimped neatly and in a regular pattern. Bake for additional 20 minutes or a total of 35 minutes.

Let stand for 5 minutes before serving or until the filling has stopped bubbling. Serve without unmolding, with the rest of the Parmesan in a separate dish.

A dry red wine, like a Bardolino or a Valpolicella, goes well with this.

NOTE

I call this dish "mysterious" because the friend who gave me the recipe had challenged all her guests to guess what the filling was and no one was able to.

This dish takes a little time to prepare. Polenta and butter have to be mixed well and the tomato-egg mixture should be really smooth before pouring it into the polenta shell. But it is a most effective dish and well worth your trouble.

Crochette di Polenta con Salsa di Pomodoro

Polenta croquettes with tomato sauce

Serves 6 as a first course,
8 as accompaniment

2 quarts water
1 teaspoon salt
1 pound yellow cornmeal

1 cup besciamella (see pages 22-23)
5 egg yolks
Salt and freshly ground black pepper
2 whole eggs, beaten lightly
2 tablespoons flour
Shortening for deep-frying, such as Crisco
Parmesan cheese, freshly grated (optional)
2 cups salsa di pomodoro (see page 21)
   (optional)

Prepare the *polenta*, following the basic instructions on pages 81-83. As soon as the *polenta* is done, remove from heat and, stirring rapidly, incorporate the *besciamella* and the egg yolks, one at a time. Taste, and season with salt and pepper. This part of the croquettes should be prepared ahead of time. If you prepare it *far* ahead (for example, in the morning to finish cooking in the evening), cover the *polenta* with a wet cloth.

When the time comes to make your croquettes, wet a marble-top table if you have one. If you don't have one, then spread wax paper over your table and wet it lightly. With the aid of a tablespoon, shape the croquettes, one at a time. Dip the croquettes in the beaten egg, then in the flour. Heat the shortening. The fat is ready when you drop a few drops of water on the surface and they sizzle. At that point, drop the croquettes in, one at a time and deep-fry. When they are golden, remove using a slotted spoon and place on a hot serving platter. If desired, sprinkle the croquettes with freshly grated Parmesan cheese.

Crochette may be served as a first course, with tomato sauce served on the side so *crochette* stay crisp, or as an accompaniment to a roast instead of potato croquettes.

If the *crochette* are served as a course by themselves they should be accompanied by a red wine. Choose one not too heavy: something like a Valpolicella or a Bardolino. If they are served as an accompaniment, the choice of wine is dictated by the meat they accompany. With a roast of veal, many will prefer a white wine and I recommend a fruity wine: a Tocai from the Friuli (no resemblance to the Hungarian Tokay) or a white wine from Tuscany.

___

NOTE

Purists will behead me, but I once found myself out of cornmeal and my heart set on making these crochette. I used coarse hominy grits. I don't say that the result was exactly the same but, in a pinch, the substitute will do.

Rice

Rice, for northern Italians, is almost as important as bread. This is particularly true for the people of Lombardy, the home of the famous *Risotto alla Milanese.*

"I didn't know that one could actually be homesick for a dish," said a Milanese friend of mine, after spending a couple of months in New York. I cooked a *risotto* for him. He was happy!

Risotto is different from any rice dish of other nations. It is called *"risotto all'onda"* (with waves) because, whereas each grain should be separate, they should be held together by a creamy substance, made of broth, butter, and quantities of Parmesan cheese. This creamy substance, which gives *risotto* its unique flavor, however, easily overcooks the rice. Real *risotto* lovers say that, at a dinner for 8, the last person served will find his *risotto* less perfect than the first.

Restaurants in Lombardy, which pride themselves on their *risotto,* used to have 4 or 5 pots cooking at once around lunch time. Each contained *risotto,* and each was started about 10 minutes later than the previous one. Since a *risotto* takes between 25 and 30 minutes to cook (the time varies a little according to the quality of the rice), no customer had to wait too long. I am told that some restaurants still use this system, and I hope it's true. Leftover *risotto* is immediately removed from the stove and used for *Risotto al Salto,* which we will describe later.

However, *risotto* is not the only way Italians eat rice. They also eat *Riso in Bianco* (literally, white rice), which is steamed rice with butter added and sometimes sprinkled with Parmesan cheese. A recipe for the perfect fluffy rice cooked *al dente* is given, as well as a selection of many *risottos.*

Italian rice, usually sold in small canvas bags, is always preferable to other types of rice. But for *Riso in Bianco* and a few other rice recipes, long grain rice may be used. For *risotto,* however, Italian rice is a must. The long grain variety just doesn't seem to produce the creamy substance that is the basis of a real *risotto.*

Although we have indicated that Italian rice is usually sold in small canvas bags, we recently bought it in cardboard boxes of 1 pound or 2 pounds each. The explanation was that the canvas bags are more expensive, or more difficult to pack and that they will eventually be replaced by the cardboard boxes. Although the rice was equally good, the boxes didn't seem as friendly as the canvas bags.

 # Risotto

Serves 6

1 pound Italian rice
2 quarts broth, chicken or beef or a mixture of
    both
¼ stick + 1 tablespoon butter
1 cup + 3 tablespoons Parmesan cheese, freshly
    grated
Salt and freshly ground black pepper

See Illustrated Techniques, page 350

Clean the rice but don't wash it. If, for some reason, you feel that you want to wash it, dry it carefully before using it. Bring the broth to a boil. As soon as it is boiling, melt the butter in a separate deep pot and add the rice. Stir with a wooden spoon over high heat until rice is well coated with butter and glistening. Lower the heat to a simmer and add the boiling broth, 1 ladle at a time, stirring constantly. As soon as the broth is absorbed, add another ladle. The rice should be covered with broth but not submerged. Cook for 10 minutes, then add the cup of grated cheese, salt, and pepper. If you have crusts of Parmesan cheese, soak them in water overnight and add them to the rice as soon as you start your *risotto*. Remove the crusts before serving. They don't replace the grated cheese but they add flavor.

The average cooking time for *risotto* is 25 minutes but it varies slightly according to the quality of the rice. The only way to test it is to take a spoonful, blow on it because nothing is hotter than *risotto*, then try it. Grains should be "bitable" but not hard.

When the rice is done, add the tablespoon of butter, mix well, and spoon onto a warm platter. Cover with the remaining cheese. Serve immediately.

Risotto is a sturdy dish and can take a sturdy wine. It reacts well to a Chianti.

NOTE

Some cooks have the theory that the liquid (broth) should be 4 times the amount of rice. That is misleading. Some types of rice absorb more liquid than others and I prefer to have a little broth left over rather than to run out of it.

A slight variation is to add an onion, sliced thin, to the butter in the pot before adding the rice. The onion should be allowed to get transparent, but not to brown. There are those who feel that the onion is indispensable. I don't agree. If the broth is flavorful and the Parmesan of good quality, the taste of onion detracts rather than adds to the flavor of the risotto.

Risotto Mantovano

Risotto, Mantua style

Serves 6

1 quart milk
1 quart water
1 pound Italian rice
Salt and freshly ground black pepper
½ cup heavy cream
1 cup chicken livers
4 tablespoons butter
5 or 6 leaves fresh sage, or 1 teaspoon dried
Pinch of nutmeg, freshly grated
1 cup Parmesan cheese, freshly grated

Bring the milk and water to a boil in a large saucepan. Add the rice and cook over medium heat, stirring frequently. Cook this rather less than an ordinary *risotto*: approximately 20 minutes and no longer. Add salt and pepper and then the cream. Mix until totally blended.

While the rice is cooking, clean the chicken livers and chop them coarsely. Melt the butter in a saucepan, add the chicken livers, sage, and nutmeg. Cook very briefly. The livers must not be allowed to harden.

Heat a large platter and spoon *risotto* onto it. Sprinkle with half the Parmesan. Then add the chicken livers with their juice and the sage leaves on top. Serve the remaining Parmesan in a bowl for guests to sprinkle over their individual dishes.

A Valpolicella would be a fine accompaniment to this unusual *risotto*.

NOTE

I call it Risotto Mantovano because it was in a restaurant in the city of Mantova that I first tasted it. I tried to find out about its origin but all the owner of the restaurant could tell me was that it was a specialty of his city. Nor would he give me the recipe but I have tried it many times since that first experience and the result has been exactly the same as the dish I tasted in Mantova.

Risotto alla Milanese

Risotto, Milan style

Serves 6

2 quarts good broth, beef or chicken
2 tablespoons butter
1 tablespoon bone marrow (optional)
2 tablespoons fat from a roast, either beef or veal
1 small onion
1 pound Italian rice
1 cup Parmesan cheese, freshly grated
Salt and freshly ground black pepper
  ¹/₄ teaspoon saffron powder
2 tablespoons heavy cream (if you are not
  including the marrow, then use 3 tablespoons
  cream)

Bring the broth to a boil and keep it simmering. Melt the butter in a saucepan, then add the marrow and the fat. Slice the onion very thin and add the slices to the butter mixture. When it begins to color, add the rice. Stir briskly with a wooden spoon until the rice is completely coated and glistening. At this point, start adding broth, one ladle at a time, and reduce the heat to a simmer. Keep stirring. The rice should not get dry but should also not be drowned in broth. The cooking time is about 25 minutes, depending upon the quality of the rice.

After 15 minutes, add the Parmesan, reserving 3 tablespoons for later use. Taste and add salt and pepper. Five minutes before removing the rice from the heat, add the saffron and mix well. (In old recipes, the saffron was added almost at the beginning but that was when saffron came in little pods and it took time to dissolve. Now saffron comes in powder form and should not be added too soon or it might lose some of its flavor.)

One minute before removing the rice from the heat, add the heavy cream and mix, cooking half a minute longer. Spoon the rice onto a hot platter or into a shallow bowl; cover with the remaining Parmesan and serve immediately.

A light red wine like a Bardolino or a Valpolicella goes best with this dish. In our opinion this is one of the greatest examples of Northern Italian cuisine.

NOTE

The creamy substance that surrounds the rice, made of butter, cream, and cheese, makes it a unique dish. It continues, however, to cook the rice even after it has been removed from the stove. Not only should risotto therefore be eaten immediately, it should also not be served in a deep bowl because the bottom would remain hotter than the surface and would continue cooking. It is a dish that needs loving care, but it is so worthwhile!

 # Risotto Padovano

Risotto, Padua style

Serves 6

2 quarts broth, chicken or beef
3 or 4 chicken livers
1 small onion
2 stalks of celery
½ cup oil
6 tablespoons butter
1 cup green peas, fresh and shelled
¼ pound ground veal
Salt and freshly ground black pepper
1 pound (2 cups) Italian rice
¾ cup Parmesan cheese, freshly grated

B ring the broth to a boil. Keep it simmering.
Clean the chicken livers and remove the membranes. Chop coarsely. Chop the onion and celery, but not too fine. Heat the oil in a saucepan, add the onion and celery, and sauté until wilted. Add half the butter and then the peas. Cook for 3 to 4 minutes, then add the veal and the chicken livers. Season with salt and pepper and cook, stirring, for a couple of minutes. Add the rice and mix well over low heat. When the rice is well coated with butter, start adding the broth a little at a time, allowing one ladle of broth to be absorbed before adding the next.

After about 20 minutes from the time you began adding the rice, try one grain (careful: nothing is as hot as rice!). It should be a little underdone. Add the remaining butter, another ladle of broth, and cook for 5 more minutes. Just before serving, add half the Parmesan, mix to blend, and spoon onto a

hot platter. Sprinkle the remaining cheese over it or serve separately, allowing each person to add as much Parmesan as desired.

The veal in this recipe would require a white wine; however, all that Parmesan, on the other hand, would call for red. I opt for the latter. There is a very special wine from the region, called Venegazù. It comes both red and white. When de Gaulle was the guest of the Italian government, the red Venegazù was served at the state dinner. It would be a splendid companion for this dish. It is, however, hard to find. A Merlot could replace it, or a really good Valpolicella. This dish, though rich, is not too heavy. It could be followed by a light veal *piccata* with a green vegetable (no peas, please!).

 # Risotto al Barolo, I

Risotto with Barolo wine

Serves 6

1 bottle Barolo wine
1 pound Italian rice
1 quart broth, chicken or beef
Salt and freshly ground black pepper
4 tablespoons butter
1 cup Parmesan cheese, freshly grated

Pour a bottle of fine Barolo into a large saucepan. Bring it to a boil and cook until reduced to half the quantity. Add the rice and stir. Continue cooking, uncovered, over low heat. When all the wine has been absorbed, add the broth, a little at a time, stirring and waiting for 1 ladleful to be absorbed before adding the next. Add the salt and pepper sparingly: the wine adds a distinct flavor that doesn't require much additional seasoning.

Exact cooking time can't be given since it varies according to quality of rice. It should be between 20 and 30 minutes, but it also depends on the desired effect. Bite 1 grain and when you feel that 5 minutes more or so of cooking time are required, add the butter and half the Parmesan. Mix well and serve with the rest of the Parmesan in a separate dish for each person to sprinkle over his or her own plate.

The wine to be served with this *risotto* is, of course, Barolo.

NOTE

The purplish color of this risotto might not appeal to some people. The taste more than makes up for it.

 # Risotto al Barolo, II

Risotto with Barolo wine

Serves 4 to 5

3 tablespoons butter
1 cup Italian rice
½ bottle Barolo wine and the equivalent amount
  of chicken or beef broth
Salt and freshly ground black pepper
1 cup Parmesan cheese, freshly grated

Melt the butter in a saucepan, add the rice, and mix until it is glistening and well coated.

Pour the wine and broth together. Heat. When the liquid starts to boil, reduce heat. Start adding this liquid to the rice, a little at a time. Wait until 1 ladleful has been absorbed before adding the next. Add the salt and pepper. Don't add too much because the flavor of the wine doesn't require much additional seasoning.

When the *risotto* is almost done (after about 20 minutes), add half the Parmesan. Mix well, continue cooking until done and serve immediately with the remaining Parmesan in a separate bowl. Each person will sprinkle a little of it over individual dishes.

Serve this with the same wine you use in cooking. Extravagant though it might seem, dishes prepared with a lot of wine should be prepared with the best wine available, lest the dish be destroyed by an inferior wine.

NOTE

This Risotto al Barolo is supposed to be a very old recipe, but I have been unable to find it in any old cookbook. I assume that it is the invention of a contemporary cook. I herewith express my gratitude to the unknown chef.

 # Risotto allo Champagne

Risotto with Champagne

Serves 4 to 5

1 pound Italian rice
2 quarts broth, chicken or beef or a mixture of
  broth

¼ *stick* + *1 tablespoon butter*
2 cups Champagne
1 cup + *3 tablespoons Parmesan cheese, freshly*
  grated
Salt and freshly ground black pepper

Follow the recipe for a plain *risotto* (see page 95), with the following exception: as soon as the rice is shiny and coated with the butter, add 1 cup of Champagne instead of broth. Then proceed as described until you are ready to add the last ladle of broth. Instead of broth, that last ladleful should be a cup of Champagne. Follow by adding the Parmesan cheese, salt, and pepper.

Serve your *risotto*, accompanied, of course, by the same Champagne you have used in your cooking.

 # Risotto alla Vodka

Risotto with Vodka

Serves 6

½ *teaspoon hot red pepper – peperoncino*
1 ounce Vodka
2 quarts broth, chicken or beef
4 tablespoons butter
1 pound Italian rice
Salt
½ *cup Parmesan cheese, freshly grated*
4 tablespoons heavy cream

Add the *peperoncino* to the Vodka and let stand.
Bring the broth to a boil and continue to simmer slightly. Melt the butter in a saucepan, add the rice, and stir rapidly to avoid sticking. Over medium heat sauté the rice lightly until it is glistening and coated well. Continue stirring and add the broth, 1 ladle at a time. Lower the heat and continue to add broth as soon as the previous ladleful has been absorbed. Add salt to taste. After about 15 minutes, add the Parmesan and keep stirring. After about 20 minutes (total cooking time is approximately 25 minutes, depending on quality of rice), add the cream and mix well. Try 1 grain

between your teeth: if it is still "bitable" but not raw, and it is held together by the creamy substance made of broth, butter, cream, and cheese, add the Vodka with the *peperoncino*. Mix well. Spoon onto a hot platter or into a shallow bowl and serve immediately without any additional Parmesan.

I hesitate to make any wine recommendation because of the Vodka in this dish.

NOTE

This is obviously not a classic Italian dish. Vodka has become fashionable in Italy in recent years, as it has in many other countries. Italians, however, have a marvelous talent for incorporating new things into their classic cuisine. This risotto is a typical example of a new ingredient added to an old recipe, with great results.

 # Risotto con le Mele

Risotto with apples

Serves 6 to 8

2 quarts broth, chicken or beef
3 tablespoons butter
3 tablespoons oil
1 pound Italian rice
5 apples, preferably golden delicious
Lemon peel
½ cup dry white wine
½ cup + 3 tablespoons Parmesan cheese, freshly
  grated
Salt and white pepper
Pinch of nutmeg, freshly grated

Bring the broth to a boil. Melt 2 tablespoons of butter in a saucepan, then add the oil. When it is very hot, add the rice and stir until the rice is coated and shiny. At this point, start adding broth to the rice, a ladle at a time. The rice should not get dry but should also not be submerged in liquid.

Peel and core the apples and cut them into cubes ½-inch in diameter. Melt the remaining spoonful of butter in a skillet and add the apple cubes and the lemon peel. Sauté the apples and set aside.

Tagliatelle with 4 Cheeses

When the rice is half done (about 12 minutes), add the wine and stir. Add the ½ cup of Parmesan, salt, pepper, and nutmeg. Add the apples and stir carefully: the apples should not disintegrate.

When the rice is done (approximately 25 minutes), spoon onto a hot platter or into a shallow bowl. Avoid deep bowls because the hot rice continues to cook and tends to become what we call in Italy *stracotto,* which is the worst that can happen to a *risotto.* Sprinkle the rest of the Parmesan over the top and serve immediately.

The combination of apples and cheese obviously requires a red wine: something like a Merlot, light and gentle on the palate. But if this unusual dish were to inspire you to new experiments, there is no reason why you shouldn't try a Prosecco: white, dry and slightly effervescent.

Risotto con Asparagi

Risotto with fresh asparagus

Serves 4 to 5

1 pound fresh asparagus
1 quart broth, chicken or beef
1 stick butter
1 small onion
1 cup rice
½ cup dry white wine
2 tablespoons heavy cream
½ cup Parmesan cheese, freshly grated
Salt and freshly ground black pepper

Clean the asparagus and discard the hard portions. Cut the tender parts of the stems into pieces of about 1 inch, keep the tips separate. Bring the broth to a boil. Heat half the butter in a saucepan. Slice the onion, add to the butter, and allow it to get transparent. Add the asparagus pieces, stir, and add the rice. Stir rapidly. When the rice is coated with butter, add the wine and allow to evaporate, then add broth 1 ladle at a time. The rice should never get too dry but should not be drowned — just barely covered with liquid.

After about 10 minutes, add the asparagus tips and continue to stir while adding broth. When the rice is almost done (about 25 minutes), add the

cream, Parmesan cheese, and, at the very end, the rest of the butter. Taste and add salt and pepper. Mix well and serve very hot. Eat immediately.

The wine you drink with this *risotto* is a question of personal choice. It also depends on what you want to eat afterwards. Either a dry red or a white would be acceptable, provided the red is not too heavy. A Merlot, from nearby Friuli to the east, or a Bardolino from nearby Lake Garda to the west, would go as well as a Tocai, a lovely white wine from Friuli, or a Soave, a lovely white from Lake Garda.

NOTE

This dish is a specialty of Venice, where it is called Risoto coi Sparasi; and this is what it would be called on most menus. Venice is one of the Italian cities where the dialect is still spoken by everyone, from the aristocracy to the "Gondolieri." This is done in moderation, however. When Venetians talk to foreigners (and anyone who comes from outside the city limits is a foreigner), they speak the official Italian.

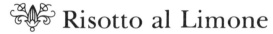 Risotto al Limone

Risotto with lemon

Serves 6

2 quarts broth, chicken or beef
1 stick butter
2 cups Italian rice
2 tablespoons oil
½ cup Parmesan cheese, freshly grated
1 egg yolk
Juice of ½ lemon
Rind of ½ lemon, grated

Bring the broth to a boil and keep it simmering. Melt half the butter in a fairly large saucepan, then add rice. Stir with a wooden spoon until rice is shiny and totally coated with butter. Add the oil and keep stirring. Start pouring the broth into the rice, 1 ladle at a time. As soon as it bubbles strongly, reduce the heat and keep adding broth. The rice should never be dry but should also never be totally submerged. Continue stirring to prevent sticking. After about 25 minutes, the rice should be almost done (exact cooking time depends upon quality of rice). Try 1 grain of rice; when it needs to be cooked for just about 2 more minutes, add the rest of the butter and the

cheese. Mix well. Beat the egg yolk with the lemon juice, then add the grated rind (when grating the rind, do not include the white part, which is very bitter). Remove the rice from the heat for a moment so that the yolk won't "cook" as you add it to the rice. Place back on heat and cook, stirring well, for a minute longer. Taste it again. If it still tastes not quite done, add another spoonful of broth and stir again; the whole cooking time should be about 30 minutes.

If desired, more cheese may be added individually as guests help themselves. But this is entirely up to every person's taste; no additional cheese is actually needed.

This is a very special and unusual *risotto*. Some people feel that it is particularly suited for a summer luncheon or a light dinner. A very dry white wine should be drunk with it. There is a wine from the region of Vicenza, which is not available in this country. It is called Durello, and it is perfect with this *risotto*. However, a California Pinot Chardonnay would go well also. well also.

 # Risotto con Piselli alla Veneziana, I

Risotto with peas, Venetian style

Serves 6

2 quarts broth, chicken or beef
1 stick butter
2 slices prosciutto, diced
1 small onion, thinly sliced
2 cups Italian rice
Salt and freshly ground black pepper
2 cups small peas, shelled
1 tablespoon parsley (optional)
1 cup Parmesan cheese, freshly grated

Bring the broth to a boil and keep it simmering. Melt half the butter in a saucepan, then add the *prosciutto*. When very hot, add the onion. When the onion is transparent, add the rice and stir until it is well coated with butter. When the rice glistens, start adding the broth, 1 ladle at a time. Allow the first ladle to be absorbed before adding the next, but don't allow the rice to get dry. Add salt and pepper to taste. When rice is half done (about 10 to 12 minutes), add the peas. Continue adding broth and continue stirring. When

the rice is almost done (about 25 minutes but, to be sure, bite 1 grain; it should be firm but not hard), add the parsley, Parmesan, and, just before removing pot from heat, the rest of the butter. Serve immediately because the rice gets mushy even after having been removed from stove.

A dry Tocai from the Friuli region, nicely chilled, would go well with this dish. Or, if you feel like drinking a red wine, try a ruby red Merlot, also from Friuli.

 # Risotto con Piselli alla Veneziana, II

Risotto with peas, Venetian style

Serves 6

2 pounds peas in their pods
2 quarts broth, chicken or beef
1 stick butter
2 slices prosciutto
2 cups Italian rice
Salt and freshly ground black pepper
½ cup Parmesan cheese, freshly grated

Shell peas, wash pods, and add the pods to the broth. Cook for about 30 minutes. When the pods are soft, purée them in a blender with a little of the broth. Add this mixture to the remaining broth; you will have a rather thick greenish soup. If the young fresh peas are unavailable, use small canned peas (1 16 oz. can) and add the liquid to the broth.

Melt ½ stick of butter in a saucepan; when it is hot, add the chopped *prosciutto*, rendering the fat from the meat. Add the rice and stir until it is well coated. Start adding the broth 1 ladle at a time. Add salt and pepper to taste and cook over medium heat until the rice is half done. Add the peas if you are using fresh ones. If you are using canned peas, wait until the rice is almost done and stir them in carefully so that they won't disintegrate.

Add the Parmesan and test some rice grains to determine if the dish is done. When the grains are firm but not hard, the rice is ready. Before removing the pot from the heat, add the rest of the butter. Stir and serve immediately.

Rice dishes will go well with either red or white wine, but with the peas and the *prosciutto* added, it would be preferable to serve a light red.

NOTE

This is another version of the most famous of all Venetian rice dishes. Risi e Bisi used to be a festive dish when Venice was an independent republic. The fame of her cuisine reached all countries on the Mediterranean sea and various ways of preparing Risi e Bisi developed.

If you are lucky enough to have your own vegetable garden, pick the peas when they are very young or try to find them at a farm market.

 # Risotto con Pepperoni

Risotto with peppers

Serves 6

2 quarts broth, chicken or beef
1 stick butter
1 pound Italian rice
3 fresh red peppers
2 tablespoons oil
Salt to taste
1 cup Parmesan cheese, freshly grated

Preheat the oven to 400°. Bring the broth to a boil and continue to simmer. Melt ¾ stick of butter in a saucepan and add the rice. Stir until the rice is completely coated with butter and shiny. Start adding the broth a little at a time, stirring to avoid any sticking to the bottom of the saucepan. The rice should be covered with broth but should be visible under the surface.

Place the peppers in a hot oven (400°) for about 5 minutes. Remove and peel. Cut into bite-sized pieces. Heat the oil in a skillet, add the peppers, and cook for about 10 minutes or until the peppers look wilted.

Try a grain of rice between your teeth: it should be bitable but not raw. Add salt to taste. The total cooking time is about 25 minutes, depending upon the quality of the rice. When the rice is almost done, stop adding broth. The grains should be held together by a creamy substance but not by a liquid. Add half the Parmesan and stir. At the last moment, add the rest of the butter.

Spoon the *risotto* onto a warm platter or into a shallow bowl. Avoid deep bowls because the bottom part of the *risotto* will continue to cook. Sprinkle the rest of the Parmesan over the *risotto* and cover with peppers.

The strong taste of peppers requires a wine with a strong personality. Any one of the reds of the Valtellina (north of Lake Garda) would go well. Their names are Grumello, Sassella, or Inferno. I like them in that order.

NOTE

This dish can be made more elegant by buttering a ring mold, filling it with the risotto, unmolding immediately on a warm round platter, and filling the center with the peppers.

 # Risotto con l'Uvetta
(Risotto con l'ueta, in Venetian dialect)

Risotto with raisins

Serves 4 to 5

2 tablespoons butter
2 tablespoons oil
1 small onion
½ cup dry white wine
2 slices prosciutto, chopped (if unavailable, use
   boiled ham)
1 cup Italian rice
4 cups broth, chicken or beef
2 tablespoons small raisins
1 tablespoon parsley, finely chopped (optional)

Melt the butter in a saucepan and add the oil. Chop the onion, or slice it very fine, and add it to the butter. Allow the onion to get blonde. Add the wine and let it evaporate over medium heat. Add the *prosciutto* and mix. Add the rice all at once. Stir until the rice is well coated and shiny. Lower the heat and add 1 cup of broth. Continue stirring. Add the raisins and continue to add broth when the previous cupful has been absorbed.

The cooking time depends on the quality of the rice, but should be approximately 25 to 30 minutes. Bite 1 grain of rice to see if it is done; it should be neither mushy nor raw. Just before removing rice from heat, add the chopped parsley, if desired.

The same wine as is used in cooking should be served with this dish. A Tocai from the Friuli would be ideal.

NOTE

The Oriental influence, often encountered in Venetian cuisine, is quite evident in this dish. Some people don't prepare it like a risotto, but add all the broth at once, cover tightly, and let the rice cook over low heat for about 15 minutes.

 # Risotto con Luganeghe

Risotto with pork sausage

Serves 6 to 7

2 quarts broth, chicken or beef
4 tablespoons butter
1 small onion (optional)
2 to 3 links 100% pork sausage, depending
    upon size
1½ cups Italian rice
½ cup dry white wine
Salt and freshly ground black pepper
1 cup Parmesan cheese, freshly grated

Bring the broth to a boil. Reduce heat and continue to simmer. Place half the butter in a large saucepan; when it is melted add the onion, finely chopped. Skin the sausage and cut into chunks. When the onion is translucent, add the sausage and stir. Turn the sausage pieces until their fat is rendered. Add the rice and stir constantly until the rice is well coated and glistening. Add the wine and, a little at a time, the broth. Continue stirring; allow the broth to be almost absorbed before adding the next ladleful. The rice should never be allowed to dry out but neither should it ever be totally submerged in the broth.

When the *risotto* is half done (after about 15 minutes cooking time), add the salt and pepper and the remaining butter. Continue stirring. Add half the Parmesan and finish cooking. The exact cooking time cannot be given as it depends upon the quality of the rice. Italian rice tends to remain firm longer and yet the grains are held together by a creamy substance, made of butter, broth, cheese, and, in this case, pork sausage. Sprinkle the remaining Parmesan over it before serving, or serve the cheese separately in a bowl for people to sprinkle over their individual dishes.

Serve with a Merlot, the ruby red wine of Friuli. The wine served with a dish should usually be the same as the one used in preparing it. But not for

this *risotto*. Tradition wants that a white wine be used in cooking, but it would be impossible to serve a light white wine with this very rich dish. It is a winter dish, ideally suited for a cold Sunday luncheon. Personally, I find it too filling to be treated as a first course, as other *risottos* are. It could be followed by a vegetable dish, or by cheese and fruit.

NOTE

It is extremely important that the sausage be of the finest quality. Surely there is a butcher somewhere in your neighborhood who makes his own sausage.

 Risotto con Scampi

Risotto with shrimp

Serves 6

1 pound fresh shrimps
1 stalk of celery
1 small onion
Salt
3 cups broth, chicken or beef
2 tablespoons olive oil
2 medium-sized tomatoes, very ripe (or the
   equivalent of canned tomatoes)
½ cup white wine
1 stick butter
2 cups Italian rice

Wash the shrimps carefully. Place the celery and onion in a saucepan with water (just enough water to cover the shrimps). Bring the water to a boil, add some salt, and then add the shrimps. When the water returns to a boil again, cook for only 1 minute. Let cool. Remove the shrimps with a slotted spoon, carefully remove their tails, and reserve. Discard the veins. Place the heads and tails in a mortar and break them up with the pestle. Add these to the water in which the shrimps have boiled, cover, and simmer for an hour. Strain. You should have about 2 cups of liquid. Add the broth and bring to a boil.

Heat the oil, then add the tomatoes, cut into chunks and with as much of the seeds removed as possible. Add the shrimps (if they are large, cut them in half). Add the wine and simmer until the liquid is gone.

Melt half the butter in a saucepan, add the rice and stir with a wooden spoon until the rice is glazed and shiny. Add the broth, 1 ladle at a time. Allow 1 ladle to be absorbed before adding the next. After 10 minutes, add the rest of the wine. Continue stirring and adding broth.

Just before rice is done (total cooking time should be about 25 minutes, according to the quality of the rice), add the shrimp-tomato mixture, stir gently; add the rest of the butter. Stir and serve immediately.

Risotto with fish or seafood does not require Parmesan cheese.

A Pinot Grigio, a slightly fruity white wine, would be the ideal companion for this dish.

NOTE

If you can't find shrimps in their shells, add the onion and celery to the water in which you boil the shrimp. After removing the shrimps, continue to boil the vegetables until the liquid is reduced to 2 cups. Add the vegetables to the broth.

 # Risotto con Scampi e Peoci

Risotto with shrimp and mussels

Serves 6

2 pounds mussels
1 pound fresh raw shrimps
4 tablespoons butter
4 tablespoons olive oil
½ small onion
1 clove garlic
1 pound Italian rice
1 quart broth, chicken or beef
Salt
Black pepper, freshly ground
2 tablespoons parsley, finely chopped

Clean the mussels by brushing them with a small wire brush until all visible encrusted sand is removed. The classic method of cleaning them is to rinse them in seawater, but since this is rarely practical, just wash them in heavily salted water. Pat dry with a paper towel. Place the mussels in a pan over high heat. After a few minutes, the shells will open. Remove the

mussels from their shells and strain the liquid through a cloth. Add the liquid to the broth.

Remove the shells from the shrimp. Discard the shells. Clean the shrimps, removing the vein if desired.

Melt 2 tablespoons of butter in a large saucepan and add the oil. Add the onion half; add the garlic. When the butter-oil mixture is very hot, add the rice. Stir rapidly with a wooden spoon. When the rice is well coated and glistening, reduce the heat and start adding broth a little at a time. Stir constantly. Add the broth whenever the rice seems to get dry. After approximately 20 minutes, chop the shrimps coarsely. Remove the onion and garlic from the pan and add the shrimps and mussels. Taste the rice and add salt and pepper to taste. When the rice is almost done, add the remaining butter and the chopped parsley. Serve immediately.

If you want to make the dish especially elegant, keep a few large mussels for decoration and place them on top of the *risotto* at the moment of serving. Do not add Parmesan to a seafood *risotto*.

A Tocai, from the region near Venice, or a Pinot Grigio would go well with this typically Venetian *risotto*.

NOTE

This is an elegant and expensive risotto, but it is worth the price and the effort.

 # Risotto con Zucchini

Risotto with zucchini

Serves 6

Sauté 2 or 3 medium-sized zucchini in oil. Keep warm. Prepare a basic *risotto* (see page 95), using the same ingredients as given in that recipe.

When the *risotto* is half done (after about 15 minutes cooking time), add half the zucchini and continue stirring the *risotto*, but not quite as vigorously as you normally would. The little zucchini rounds should not be totally mashed.

Add the Parmesan to the *risotto*, except for 2 or 3 tablespoons to be used later. Try a grain of rice to test whether it is done: it should be *al dente* or bitable, but should not taste raw.

Spoon the *risotto* onto a heated platter, cover with the rest of the zucchini, and sprinkle remaining Parmesan on top.

Serve with a ruby red Merlot from the Friuli. Or, if not available, try this dish with a young Chianti.

NOTE

This is a summer dish when zucchini are in season. I have such a weakness for them that I can't resist, at times, buying them out of season, and I am always sorry. Zucchini, kept in storage for a long time, are unfailingly bitter. When their color has turned a dull green and their tips are slightly soft, stay away from them.

 Risotto Verde

Green risotto

Serves 6

1 stick butter
2 cups Italian rice
2 quarts broth, chicken or beef
½ cup cooked spinach, well drained
Salt and freshly ground black pepper
½ cup Parmesan cheese, freshly grated

Melt half of the butter in a saucepan, add the rice, and stir until the rice is coated and shiny.

Bring the broth to a boil and continue to simmer. When the rice is coated, start adding broth 1 ladle at a time. Reduce the heat under the rice and keep adding broth, stirring to avoid any sticking to the bottom of the pan. The rice should never be allowed to dry, but should also never be drowned in broth.

Place the spinach in a blender and add just enough broth so that the spinach becomes puréed (about 30 seconds at high speed). When the rice is almost done (about 25 minutes cooking time), add the remaining butter and the puréed spinach. Mix well and taste; if the rice doesn't seem quite done, add another bit of broth and cook, stirring, for another couple of minutes. Add salt and pepper and mix very well. Serve very hot and eat immediately, sprinkling cheese over each individual portion, serving the grated cheese in a separate dish allowing guests to serve themselves.

Serve with a dry white wine or a very light red.

 # Risotto al Salto

Flipped risotto

Serves 4

2 cups leftover risotto
2 whole eggs
1 tablespoon butter
1 tablespoon oil
½ cup Parmesan cheese, freshly grated

Place the *risotto* in a bowl and break it up with a fork. Add the eggs and mix carefully, being sure not to mash the rice.

Melt the butter in a skillet, add the oil, and allow to heat but not to brown. Add the *risotto*-and-egg mixture and cook over high heat until bubbles appear all around rice. Lower the heat and run a spatula around the edges to prevent the rice from sticking. When the surface becomes glossy (about 3 minutes) place a plate over the rice, rapidly turn the pan over, and slide the rice mixture back into skillet and allow to brown on the other side. Sprinkle half of the Parmesan over the rice and briefly place a lid over the skillet. Remove the lid as soon as the cheese has melted. Slide the rice onto a warm platter and sprinkle with the remaining cheese or serve the cheese on the side.

Like most dishes that contain a lot of cheese, *Risotto al Salto* requires a red wine. A Bardolino or a Valpolicella from Lake Garda would be fine, as would a Merlot from the Friuli region.

NOTE

Risotto leftovers can also be baked in the oven. Timid cooks, who are afraid of the "al salto," meaning turning the rice, should place the rice-and-egg mixture in a baking dish, cover it with cheese, and bake it in a preheated 350° oven for about 15 minutes, or until the cheese is totally melted. This Frittata di Riso may also be eaten cold.

The classic version of Risotto al Salto is actually made without the addition of eggs. Heat an iron skillet until very hot, melt 2 tablespoons of butter, and place the leftover risotto in it and brown. Insert a thin spatula under the rice to make sure it doesn't stick to the pan. Lift an edge slightly to see if the bottom is golden and, if so, flip it over rapidly with a plate. I have added the eggs to this recipe to make the preparation easier.

 # Timballo di Riso

Baked risotto in a mold

Serves 6

1 cup breadcrumbs
3 cups risotto (see page 95)
4 oz. mozzarella cheese
2 whole eggs
½ cup breadcrumbs

For the filling:
2 tablespoons+1 teaspoon butter
1 small onion (optional)
1 cup fresh mushrooms, or ⅓ cup imported dried
1 cup small green peas
Salt and freshly ground black pepper
½ cup besciamella (see pages 22-23)
¾ cup Parmesan cheese, freshly grated

Coat an 8-inch mold well with oil (mold should have no hole in the center and the sides should not be fluted). Sprinkle the bottom and sides well with breadcrumbs so that the mold is well coated. Use your hands if needed to make them stick to the sides.

Prepare a *risotto*, keeping the rice rather more *al dente* than you would normally. Cut the *mozzarella* into small cubes and add them to the rice while it is still very hot. Beat the eggs well with a wire whisk and add them to the *risotto* when it is slightly cool. Mix well. Press about ¾ of the *risotto* into the mold, using your hands to press it against sides and bottom of mold. There should be a deep well in center of mold. Reserve the remaining *risotto*.

Preheat the oven to 375°. Melt 2 tablespoons of butter in a skillet, slice the onion (if desired) and add it to the butter, allowing it to wilt. Remove the sandy parts from the mushroom stems; if necessary, peel the caps. If the mushrooms are white and fresh, wipe them with a wet paper towel, then slice both stems and caps. Add these to the pan, cover, and cook over very high heat for about 4 minutes (if dried mushrooms are used, soak them in warm water for at least ¼ hour, squeeze out the water, chop coarsely, and add them to the skillet).

Add the peas to the pan, lower the heat, and cook until all the liquid is absorbed and the peas are done. Taste, and add salt and pepper. Mix the mushrooms and peas with the *besciamella* and add half the Parmesan. Mix well. Spoon the mixture into the center of the mold. The mixture should not

fill the mold to the rim. Cover with the remaining *risotto,* pressing lightly with your hands. Sprinkle breadcrumbs over the top, then sprinkle the remaining Parmesan over the crumbs and dot with the rest of the butter.

Place mold in the center of the oven and bake for about 1 hour. The top should be golden. Remove from oven and shake the mold slightly from side to side to loosen the edges. Let it stand for at least 15 minutes before placing a warm platter over the top and turning the mold rapidly upside down to unmold the *timballo.*

This *timballo* may be served either with a light red wine, like a Bardolino, or a fruity wine, like a Pinot Grigio. I consider it one of the great dishes of Italian cuisine. Either as a first course for a formal dinner, followed by a poached fish, served with mayonnaise, or as a complete luncheon, followed only by cheese and fruit. If it is served as a first course and you wish to serve only one wine, you will of course opt for a white wine.

NOTE

There are many variations for the filling of this timballo. For those who like variety meats, the mushrooms may be replaced with sweetbreads, cut into bite-sized pieces, or with chicken livers. Another version calls for filling the center with sweet Italian sausage, peeled, cut into chunks, and fried in its own fat. For this version, no besciamella is required, and the timballo will be accompanied by a red wine and a sturdy one at that (an Inferno, or a Grumello from the Valtellina region).

In any case, it is a rewarding dish because it is both delicious and beautiful. But it is not easy to make; and, no matter how often I prepare it, I never fail to pray when I unmold it.

 # Timballo di Riso alla Romana

Rice mold, Roman style

Serves 8

1 small onion
4 tablespoons butter
½ pound chicken livers
½ pound Italian (plum) tomatoes
1 cup dry white wine
1 quart broth, chicken or beef
1 pound Italian rice
½ cup Parmesan cheese, freshly grated
Pinch of nutmeg, freshly grated (optional)
Salt and freshly ground black pepper

Chop the onion very fine. Melt 3 tablespoons of butter in a saucepan, add the onion, and cook until transparent. Clean the chicken livers and discard all extraneous parts. Chop coarsely and add to the onion. Peel the tomatoes and chop coarsely, removing the seeds as much as possible. Add these to the livers and mix until the tomatoes are quite wilted. Add the wine and stir until liquid is absorbed.

Preheat the oven to 400° Bring the broth to a boil and keep it simmering. Add the rice to the liver-tomato-onion mixture and mix well until the rice is well coated. Start adding the broth a ladle at a time, stirring constantly to avoid sticking. When the rice is almost done (about 20 minutes cooking time), add the Parmesan and mix well. Taste, and add salt, pepper, and nutmeg. With the remaining butter, coat a ring mold carefully so that the whole inside is equally coated. Fill the mold with the rice mixture, pressing it down gently and so that the mold is totally filled. Place the mold in the oven and bake for 5 to 6 minutes. Remove it from the oven and let it stand for a couple of minutes. If necessary, loosen the edges with a sharp knife; place a platter (previously warmed) on top of the mold, and rapidly turn the mold over onto the platter. If desired, fill the center with additional chicken livers or with buttered peas. Serve immediately.

As the recipe calls for white wine, the same wine should be served with the *timballo*. The white wines from the region around Rome are fruity enough to compete with the chicken livers. I suggest a Frascati, chilled.

NOTE

In risotto recipes, the cooking time is given as approximately 25 minutes; here it is reduced to 20 because of the additional baking time. The quantity of butter used is somewhat less than in other rice recipes because the chicken livers are very rich.

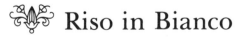 # Riso in Bianco

Steamed rice

Serves 6 to 8

2 quarts water
Salt
2 cups rice, either Italian or long grain
2 tablespoons butter (optional)

In a large saucepan, bring water to a strong boil, then add the salt. Pour the rice in all at once and stir with a wooden spoon. Stir several times during cooking. Cooking time depends somewhat upon quality of rice, but is approximately 20 minutes. The only way to test if the rice is done is to bite a grain. It should be neither mushy nor raw.

When done, remove from the heat. Over the sink hold the pot in which rice was cooked in one hand and, with the other hand, hold a colander. Pour the rice into the colander. Place the empty pot back on the hot burner without turning on the heat. There should be enough heat left in it (be it gas or electric). Place the colander with the rice in it over the pot. Fluff up the rice lightly with a fork.

If desired, place butter at room temperature in a warm bowl and pour the rice into the bowl. Mix. If what you want is dry rice, just remove it from the colander, spoon it onto a platter or bowl, and serve hot.

NOTE

I had not intended to write this recipe. After all, what could be simpler than boiling rice and making it come out dry, al dente, and fluffy? Apparently it isn't that simple. And, after another helping of soggy, overcooked rice, I decided to add this recipe to put an end to mushy rice.

Ris an Cagnon

Rice with fontina cheese

Serves 4 to 5

1 quart water
1 teaspoon salt
1 ½ cups Italian rice
¼ pound fontina cheese
3 tablespoons butter

In a large kettle bring water to a strong boil over high heat. Add salt. Add the rice and boil over high heat, stirring frequently for about 20 minutes, or until rice is still firm under your teeth. Drain but reserve ½ cup of the water. Place the rice in a bowl that has been well heated. Add just enough of the cooking water so that you can see it. The rice should be moist but not covered with liquid. The water should be visible among the rice kernels. If there is too much water, the cheese will be diluted.

Cut the *fontina* cheese into tiny pieces. Add these to the rice and stir constantly until the cheese has completely melted and blended with the liquid. Melt the butter in a skillet and allow it to brown. Pour the browned butter over the rice and mix well. Serve very hot.

This is a dish from the Piedmont and the Piedmont is one of the finest wine regions of Italy. One of its lighter wines would go well with this dish: a Dolcetto d'Alba or a Freisa.

NOTE

This is the simplest way to cook rice and one of the most delicious. The rice, however, should be Italian rice. The cheese too should be real fontina, a cheese from the Piedmont with a light brown rind and a distinct flavor and texture. Swiss cheese has been tried as a substitute and it doesn't work.

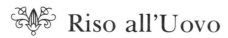 Riso all'Uovo

Rice with eggs

Serves 4 to 5

2 quarts water
Salt
1 ½ cups Italian rice
2 tablespoons butter
2 egg yolks
½ cup Parmesan cheese, freshly grated

In a large saucepan bring the water to a boil. Salt lightly. As soon as the water boils strongly, add the rice all at one time and keep boiling over medium high heat.

Have the butter at room temperature. Warm a bowl or a tureen and place the butter in the bowl. With your hands, or with a fork, break up the butter into small pieces.

After about 20 minutes cooking time, taste the rice: if it seems almost done, add the egg yolks and Parmesan to the butter, and beat lightly. Drain the rice and pour into the bowl. Mix well and serve immediately. This should be done as rapidly as possible, so that the eggs and cheese are mixed evenly.

This is an old recipe of the province of Milan. We don't call it *Rice Milanese* because that automatically brings to mind saffron. *Riso all'Uovo* is a

very delicate dish and may be served with either white or red wine. Personally, I would prefer a white: fruity, like a Terlano or a Pinot Grigio.

NOTE

It is necessary to use Italian rice for this recipe because you will find that the long grain rice doesn't have enough texture.

 Sformato di Riso all'Uovo

Rice and egg mold

Serves 4 to 6

1 quart water
2 cups Italian rice
Salt
4 whole eggs
3 tablespoons heavy cream
½ stick butter
½ cup Parmesan cheese, freshly grated

B ring the water to a boil in a large kettle. When it boils strongly add the rice. Stir to avoid sticking, but keep the water at a strong boil. Add salt and stir every now and then.

Generously butter a 9-inch ring mold. In a bowl, beat the eggs lightly, add the cream, and cook briefly in a skillet but don't allow to set completely: about 1 minute.

When the rice is done (about 20 to 25 minutes cooking time), add the butter and cheese; add pepper if desired and mix well. Fill the mold with the rice mixture and unmold immediately onto a hot platter. Pour the egg and cream mixture over the top of the rice, letting the sauce fill the cavity of the mold. Sprinkle additional cheese over top if desired. Serve immediately.

All rice dishes that don't contain meat should be served with white wine. This dish, however, has a strong egg flavor. Any light wine, white or light red, would go well with it.

NOTE

There is no real need to press the cooked rice into a mold and to go through the tribulations of unmolding it. Place a small bowl upside down in the center of a large

round platter and arrange the cooked rice around it, pressing it together with a spoon. Remove the bowl and pour the egg mixture into the center and round the top. This has to be done rapidly so that the rice doesn't get cold.

It is imperative that Italian rice be used in this recipe. Long grain rice doesn't have the necessary texture.

 # Riso e Prezzemolo, I

Rice with parsley

Serves 4

1 quart broth, chicken or beef
2 cups rice, preferably Italian
2 tablespoons butter
4 rounded tablespoons parsley, finely chopped
½ cup Parmesan cheese, freshly grated
Salt and freshly ground black pepper

Bring the broth to a strong boil and immediately add the rice. Stir well and lower the heat a little to medium. Cook, stirring frequently. Taste the rice after about 20 minutes; it should be done and the broth should be all absorbed. Melt the butter in a saucepan and add some of the parsley. Pour onto the rice. Add the Parmesan and taste again; add salt if needed (Parmesan is quite salty so you may not need much salt). Add additional parsley, stir and serve very hot.

This is not a real *risotto*. It is an easy dish that doesn't require constant supervision as does a *risotto*. Typical of Milan, it is served with a light red wine: Bardolino or Valpolicella. All that parsley might overpower a light white wine.

 # Riso al Prezzemolo, II

Rice with parsley

Serves 6

2 quarts water
Salt
1 pound Italian or long grain rice

2 tablespoons parsley, finely chopped
1 small clove of garlic, sliced
2 tablespoons butter
1 tablespoon olive oil
1 cup Parmesan cheese, freshly grated

Bring the water to a strong boil in a large saucepan (the more space rice has to cook in the better). Add salt and then the rice; stir immediately. From then on the rice needs stirring. Cook for about 20 minutes or until rice is *al dente;* the grains should be "bitable," neither mushy nor raw.

Chop the parsley along with the slice of garlic. Melt the butter in a saucepan, and add the oil. When the rice is almost done, add the parsley to the butter (parsley should never cook more than a couple of minutes or else it gets bitter). Drain the rice well. Spoon the rice onto a platter or into a shallow bowl, cover with Parmesan, and pour the steaming butter-parsley mixture over the top. Don't mix. As people help themselves, the ingredients will blend.

This is not a regular *risotto*, though some people call it that. Either a sturdy white or a light red wine may be served: anything from a Pinot Grigio to a Bardolino.

Pasta

The word *pasta* actually means dough, or paste. Toothpaste is *pasta dentifricia* in Italian. In gastronomic terms, *pasta* covers everything from spaghetti to *tagliatelle*, from macaroni to *ziti,* to *lasagne*, and to all the other shapes and forms pasta can be made into.

In some restaurants in Italy, where the owner's wife or the owner himself does the cooking, they waste no time on fancy menus. A member of the family will appear at your table and then, according to what part of Italy you find yourself in, the litany of first courses starts: "*Spaghetti al Pomodoro, Maccheroni al Forno, Lasagna Gratinata . . .*" and so it goes on from the simplest spaghetti dish to the elaborate *ravioli.* If none of these get a positive reaction from you, the litany will continue with *Minestre in Brodo,* or First Courses in Broth.

If you find yourself in the region of Milan, the emphasis will be on *risotto* dishes and a couple of pasta dishes will be mentioned at the end, just in case . . . . In and around Venice on the other hand, a series of *polenta* dishes will be mentioned first, then some rice dishes, and at the end a couple of pasta dishes.

It is really from Bologna southward that pasta is king.

There are many variations for making pasta. The best thing is to try out a few and decide which way suits you best. Then stick to the method that gives you the best results, whether the experts agree with you or not. Some people will shudder if you mention that your pasta is made with a spoonful of oil; others won't like the idea of a drop of water. Just use the method that works best for you.

There are people who feel that making your own pasta is too much trouble. They are of the opinion that the commercial product is perfectly adequate. This is certainly true of elbow macaroni and of the various types of *pastina* (tiny rings or stars usually cooked in broth). I doubt that anyone nowadays will take the trouble to make them in their own kitchen. But when it comes to *tagliatelle, taglierini,* or any of the other forms of thin noodles, people are bound to change their minds, once they have tasted the homemade product. This is especially true for *tortellini* or *ravioli,* which require paper-thin pasta in order not to be too heavy. If you are a pasta lover, invest in a pasta-making machine. It simplifies life enormously.

In the following recipes, I give directions for making pasta both with a rolling pin and with a pasta machine. If you choose the latter, your machine will come with instructions. Don't follow them to the letter. The instructions will tell you to set the machine to setting #1, put the dough into the top, turn the handle, and, as the dough emerges somewhat flattened, set the machine to setting #2 and continue rolling your dough. Not so. After the dough emerges from setting #1, fold it as you would a letter, roll it again through the first setting and repeat this performance at least three times. Then, and only then, set your machine to setting #2 and continue to turn the handle until your dough has rolled through the last setting. At that point it should be as thin as you want it. It is now up to you to cut it into the shape of your choice. Your machine has an attachment that will make wide noodles *(tagliatelle),* thin noodles *(taglierini),* or spaghetti.

Pasta machines are available in most department stores with well-equipped housewares departments, as well as in many hardware stores. It is a worthwhile investment.

 Pasta all'Uovo, I

Egg pasta

Serves 6

3 cups flour
4 whole eggs

Pinch of salt
Few drops oil

See Illustrated Techniques, pages 351-353

Make a mound of flour on a wooden board of ample dimensions. In fact, the bigger the board the better. If your kitchen table has a wooden surface, use the whole table. Personally, I prefer a marble-top table and find any kind of formica surface hard to work on, but that is a very personal thing and is due in part to habit.

Make a deep well in the center of the mound and break the eggs into it, one at a time. Add the salt and, working rapidly with a fork, start mixing the eggs with the flour. At each stroke of the fork, bring a little more of the flour to the eggs, while you shield the mound of flour with the other hand, lest the eggs run through it and down the table-top. When the eggs and flour are mixed, start kneading the mixture with your hands. The size of eggs varies and you might find that you need a little more flour or that you have a little flour left over. Don't let that throw you: add a little if needed or discard what you don't.

When you have a homogeneous dough, moisten your hands with a few drops of oil and moisten the surface on which you are working with another few drops. Get your longest possible rolling pin and rub it lightly with oil (this should be done every time you use it, no matter how old the pin is). Flatten the dough with your hands, fold it in thirds as you would a letter, then flatten it with a rolling pin. If the dough should stick to the pin, rub a little flour over it. Fold the dough again and repeat. Do this until the dough glistens and little bubbles form on the surface. It is now ready to be rolled thin.

Roll the dough away from you. Remember that you want a round sheet of pasta. As you start, you will form an oval at your end of the dough. Move the dough slightly clockwise and continue working with the pin. This might be difficult the first time, but you will learn quickly. The secret lies in turning the pasta slowly and always in the same direction. The pleasure you will get from the first round sheet of thin pasta is well worth the effort. The ideal thickness of pasta should be that of a quarter.

Remember that it is easier to work with a small amount of flour and eggs in the beginning. If you want to feed 6 to 8 people, you can make the pasta in 2 installments. Keep in mind that you have to work quickly. Keep the dough away from drafts because pasta dries out fast and any draft speeds the drying process. Once it is dry there is nothing you can do to thin it.

Let's assume that you have mastered the process of making the dough and have a beautiful, round sheet of pasta in front of you. Now comes the fun. Roll up the pasta as if it were a sheet of Christmas wrapping, then cut it into strips of whatever width you wish. You can make *tagliatelle* (about ¼-inch

wide) or *tagliarini* (about ⅛-inch wide) and you can invent your own size and shape. The important thing is that you spread your pasta (once it is cut into the desired shape). Don't let it stick together, but, rather, spread it out onto your working surface. Lightly flour your table top and let the pasta dry for about 5 to 10 minutes before cooking it. The room should be well aired.

If you own a pasta machine, proceed as indicated above until you have a homogeneous dough. Then, instead of flattening it with your hands and rolling it thin with a rolling pin, shape the dough into a long loaf and cut it into about 3 chunks. Fasten the pasta machine to the edge of the table, insert 1 chunk into the opening at the top, and crank the handle. When a leaf of dough emerges, fold it like a letter and insert it again into the machine, *without switching to the next setting*. Repeat this 3 or 4 times. Then go on to the next setting and thickness. Continue, always folding the dough between operations, until you reach the last setting. Once the desired thickness of dough is obtained, continue running the dough through the last setting 2 or 3 times without folding it between operations. The ideal thickness should be $^1/_{16}$ inch. If this seems difficult, at least for the first few times, $^1/_8$ inch is permissible, but barely.

NOTE

The recipe should really read "serves 6 according to nationality" because if you look at some portions served in Italy, the amount of pasta I mentioned will barely be enough for 4.

 ## Pasta all'Uovo, II

Egg pasta

Serves 4

2 cups flour
1 whole egg
1 egg white
Pinch of salt
1 teaspoon olive oil
½ eggshell full of water

Make a mound of flour on a wooden board or on a marble surface. Make a well in the top of the mound. Break the egg into the well, add the additional egg white, the salt, and the olive oil. Fill half an eggshell with water and add the water to the eggs. (This is an old recipe and

you may, of course, use the equivalent measure of the content of half an eggshell.)

With a fork, start mixing the ingredients, incorporating a bit of the flour with each movement of the fork. (The quantity of flour used has to be approximate because the size of eggs varies. I advise using large eggs, but even so you might find that you need to add an additional spoonful of flour or that you have a bit left over). When the eggs, oil, and water are absorbed, work the dough with your hands for several minutes. When the dough is ready, it usually forms little bubbles on the surface. Proceed as in the previous recipe, either using a rolling pin or a pasta machine. The thickness of the dough, when ready to be cut into noodles, should be between $^1/_8$ to $^1/_{16}$ inch. The thinner the better, of course.

 # Pasta all'Uovo, III

Pasta with eggs

Serves 4 to 6

4 cups of flour
3 whole eggs
1 teaspoon salt
¼ cup of water

Make a mound of the flour on a wooden board or on a marble top table. Make a well in the flour deep enough to hold the other ingredients. Break the eggs, one at a time, into the well. Add the salt. Start mixing lightly with a fork. As the eggs get absorbed by the flour, add water a little at a time. When the water too is absorbed, start kneading the dough with your hands. It takes a little practice to know when the dough is ready to be flattened and made into desired shapes; you can feel when the dough is homogeneous. It will be neither hard nor sticky in your hands and there will be small bubbles on the outside. At this point, start flattening the dough with a rolling pin. Dust both the surface on which you are working and the rolling pin with a little flour to prevent the dough from sticking.

If you have a pasta machine, shape the dough into a long loaf and cut it into 3 chunks. Fasten the machine to the edge of the table and place 1 chunk at a time into the opening of the machine. Follow the instructions that accompany the machine with an exception: instead of switching from first

setting to second after passing the dough through, continue on setting #1 for at least 3 times, folding the dough in between each time. If you are working the dough by hand, follow the instructions as given on pages 125-26.

When the dough is less than ⅛ inch thick, start cutting it into the desired width. Cut it with a knife, if you have used a rolling pin, or use the machine. Once you have your *tagliatelle* or *tagliarini*, spread them on a cloth and allow to dry for at least 5 minutes or a maximum of one hour.

It is important that the room where the pasta dries be well aired. If your kitchen is small, open the window. If your kitchen has no window, spread your cloth with the pasta on a table in another room. Pasta, properly dried, will last for several days stored in a cool dry place.

I used to be against freezing pasta, but then I tried it and much of my prejudice vanished. I won't say that it tastes exactly like freshly made, 5-minute-old pasta, but then, in my opinion, no frozen food does. I would say that pasta takes to freezing as well as any other food.

Cooking Pasta (General Instructions)

The following procedure is the same for all kinds of pasta.

First of all, you need a large pot and a lot of water. Even the best-made pasta will be ruined if it is crowded when it is cooked. The water should be well salted (you can't properly add salt once the pasta is cooked) and it should be boiling vigorously before you add the pasta. As soon as you drop the pasta into the water, stir it with a long wooden spoon. Then leave it alone. Once the water has started to boil strongly again, no stirring is necessary. There is no rule against stirring, though, if you enjoy it.

It is impossible to give the exact cooking time for pasta. The time depends on how dry the pasta was when you started out; it also depends on how many eggs were used, and finally it depends on your own taste. I hope that you like your pasta *al dente,* meaning not too mushy, but bitable. The only solution is the one it has always been: fish one *tagliatella* (or whatever pasta you are cooking) out of the water and taste it. The cooking time will vary between 3 and 5 minutes. But, make no mistake: one minute more or less makes a big difference. After all the trouble you have taken to make your pasta, don't ruin it by overcooking.

While the pasta is cooking, prepare a bowl in which to place it. Many Italians like to use a tureen. It is deep enough and ample enough, and it gives a kind of cozy look to the pasta. Whatever bowl you choose, I recommend that you butter the serving bowl, pour the drained pasta into it, stir, then add whatever sauce you choose — or even just more butter and grated Parmesan cheese.

Have the colander ready. If you wait until the pasta is done, during the time you spend getting it (and maybe even having to look for it) the pasta will continue to cook in the hot water even if the heat has been turned off. Be sure you have a large colander, possibly one that is wider than deep. Pour the water with the pasta into the colander and shake it vigorously. Or better still, place the colander over the pot in which the pasta has been cooking and place the pot back on the stove on the burner. Although it is turned off, the burner will be hot enough to give whatever water might be left clinging to the pasta a chance to evaporate.

To cook storebought spaghetti or macaroni, proceed the same way. The cooking time might be a few minutes longer because packaged pasta is harder than the fresh homemade kind. To find out when it is done, there still is no other system than the one we have mentioned before. Lift one piece out of the water and bite into it.

The choice of the spaghetti (or macaroni, or *ziti*, or *penne*) you buy is important. If your spaghetti have been behaving badly, meaning if they tend to get mushy on the outside while the inside is still raw, switch to another brand. The flour that is used in making commercial pasta is very important. And only by experimenting will you find out which brand suits you best.

I used to think that pasta, once it was cooked, could not be reheated. And for many types, this is true. Fine *tagliatelle* or *capelli d'Angelo* would stick together and become a mushy mess. But I shall never forget what a Neapolitan friend of mine said, who was a pasta expert:

"You mean you have never taken some leftover macaroni, sprinkled them with *Parmigiano*, dotted them with butter, and browned them in the oven until the tops were a golden crust? You haven't lived."

I tried it immediately. Now I have lived.

Tagliatelle ai 4 Formaggi, I

Tagliatelle with 4 cheeses

Serves 6

Water
Salt
1 pound tagliatelle or tagliarini, either
   homemade or dry

(continued)

¾ *cup light cream*
⅓ *cup Swiss cheese, grated*
⅓ *cup Gouda or Edam, grated*
½ *cup mozzarella, grated*
1 *cup Parmesan cheese, freshly grated*
Black pepper, freshly ground

In a large kettle, bring water to a boil and add salt. Add the *tagliatelle* or *tagliarini*. If they are fresh, the cooking time will be about 5 minutes or less, depending upon the thickness of the pasta. If dry pasta is used, the cooking time will be about twice that much. The only way to tell is to bite a small piece to see if it is cooked.

Meanwhile, pour the cream into a large saucepan and add the cheeses a little at a time, reserving half the Parmesan for later. Simmer over very low heat; the cheese has to melt completely. When the mixture is smooth, taste it and, if needed, add salt and pepper.

When the pasta is done, drain it very well, rinse it very briefly with cold water, and pour it all at once into the saucepan with the cheese. Mix rapidly until the pasta is well coated. Heat a serving bowl by running hot water over it or placing it briefly in a warm oven. Transfer the pasta to the bowl and sprinkle the remaining Parmesan over it (or serve in a separate bowl for each person to sprinkle a little over each individual portion).

This is a very rich dish and requires a rich red wine. A Brunello di Montalcino would not be wasted on it, but a good Chianti would go well too (Brunello is a Chianti, but it is the king of Chiantis).

NOTE

There are many versions of Pasta ai 4 Formaggi. The above version seems to be the best suited to the cheese we have in the United States. The mozzarella available in supermarkets is not ideal for this. If you can buy real mozzarella, kept in a basin of water, you will get better results. If you use this type, you will have to shred the cheese, rather than grate it. The mixing of the pasta with the cheeses by adding pasta to the cheese mixture instead of pouring cheese mixture over the pasta is my variation and makes a big difference. The pasta and cheese mix much better.

For the calorie conscious, I have tried a mixture of half milk, half cream instead of all cream, but it didn't work. The mixture didn't get creamy enough.

 # Pasta ai 4 Formaggi, II

Pasta with 4 cheeses

Serves 6

*1 pound pasta (tagliatelle, tagliarini, spaghetti
  or any kind of pasta to your liking)*
¾ cup light cream
½ cup Swiss cheese, grated
*⅓ cup pecorino, grated (If available, pecorino
  Toscano rather than Sardinian or pecorino
  from southern Italy. Pecorino Toscano is
  somewhat less sharp)*
¼ pound fontina, slivered
1 cup Parmesan cheese, freshly grated

Proceed as in the preceding recipe to prepare the pasta, melt the cheese, then mix it with the pasta.

Pasta ai 4 Formaggi is not an old recipe. It has materialized in the last few years and everyone — cook, hostess, or restaurateur — has his or her own version. Personally, I like the above selection of cheeses best. The important thing is that they all be of excellent quality.

As for the pasta itself, it is quite true that any kind may be prepared *ai 4 Formaggi*, but somehow *tagliatelle* seem to lend themselves best. My only explanation is that they have a broader surface for the cheese to cling to.

 # Tagliatelle al Burro e Ricotta

Tagliatelle with butter and ricotta

Serves 6

Water
Salt
1 pound tagliatelle, either homemade or dry
4 tablespoons butter
1 container (10 oz.) skim milk ricotta
Black pepper, freshly ground
½ cup Parmesan cheese, freshly grated

Bring a lot of water to a strong boil in a large kettle. (Remember: the more space and the more water pasta has to cook in, the better). Add salt. Add the pasta and stir every now and then with a long wooden spoon. The exact cooking time can't be given since it depends upon the thickness of the pasta. Approximate cooking time is 4 to 5 minutes for fresh homemade pasta and about twice that much for store bought.

Meanwhile, melt the butter in a large saucepan. Add the *ricotta*. *Ricotta* is a bland creamlike cheese, sold in most supermarkets in plastic containers (10 oz. is ¾ of a container). I prefer the skim milk variety. When opening the container, you will find a little liquid on top. Empty the container onto a paper towel and pat the *ricotta* dry before adding to the butter. Over low heat, mix the butter and *ricotta*. Add salt and pepper, using quite a bit of both because the *ricotta* is very bland.

When the pasta is cooked, drain and rinse briefly with cold water. Then add the pasta to the hot butter-*ricotta* mixture and mix very well until the pasta is well coated. Serve very hot with Parmesan cheese in a separate little bowl, for each person to sprinkle over the individual dishes.

It is a rule that cheese should be accompanied by red wine. The same goes for dishes that contain a lot of cheese. Personally, I would choose a light red wine, a Bardolino for instance, with this dish. But *ricotta* is a very bland cheese and, if your preference runs to white wines, I say why not? Drink a Bianco Toscano with it and enjoy it.

NOTE

Theoretically this butter-ricotta-Parmesan mixture could be a sauce for any kind of pasta. In reality, it is at its best with noodles of any width or with spaghetti. I have tried it on macaroni and it didn't work. My only explanation is that the insides of the macaroni contain a little moisture, no matter how well you drain them, and this thins the cheese mixture.

 # Pasta con Tonno e Piselli

Pasta with tuna and peas

Serves 6

Water
Salt
1 pound tagliatelle, either homemade or dry
1 can (6½ oz.) tuna, packed in oil
½ cup olive oil

3 tablespoons butter
1 can (7 oz.) tiny peas
3 tablespoons parsley, finely chopped
Black pepper, freshly ground

Bring the water to a boil in a large pot. The more space and the more water pasta has to cook in, the better. Add salt. Add the pasta. If homemade *tagliatelle* are used, the cooking time will vary between 3 and 5 minutes, according to the thickness of the pasta. If dry pasta is used, it will take about 10 minutes. The only way to tell is to bite into a small piece.

While the pasta cooks, drain the tuna and chop finely but don't purée. Place the tuna in a saucepan, add the oil, and simmer. Heat a deep bowl by running hot water over it and then place the butter in the bottom of the bowl. Keep warm.

Add the peas to the tuna and simmer a few minutes longer. Add the parsley to the tuna and peas 1 minute before removing from heat. (Parsley should never be allowed to cook longer than 1 minute because it gets bitter).

Drain the pasta and place it in the bowl with the butter. Mix well so that all *tagliatelle* are well coated. Pour tuna-pea mixture over the pasta and serve immediately.

A Verdicchio, white and fruity, or a Frascati would be the best wines to serve with this Springlike dish.

NOTE

I used canned peas in this recipe because it is almost impossible to get fresh small peas. If you are lucky enough to grow your own, by all means use them.

Some people will automatically sprinkle Parmesan over this dish. They are wrong. Fish and cheese don't mix.

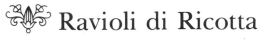 Ravioli di Ricotta

Ricotta ravioli

Serves 8

Prepare the filling following the instructions given below and using the ingredients indicated.

Prepare the pasta dough (see pages 124-128) and, either using a pasta machine or a rolling pin, make a long strip, rolling the dough as thin as

possible. The strip should be about 6 inches wide. Place the strip on a long table (if your kitchen table is not long enough, use your dining room table with a white cloth over it).

Using a teaspoon, place a small mound of filling near the edge (not too close) of one side of the strip of pasta. Leaving a one-inch space between them, make a row of mounds along the strip of dough. Fold the other half of the strip over the mounds of filling and press the edges together firmly. Using a *ravioli* cutter, cut off the excess dough from the edges. Then, using the *ravioli* cutter, cut between the mounds pressing the edges together firmly with your hands. All this has to be done rapidly because the dough dries quickly and the edges won't stick together once it dries. If the dough should seem too dry, moisten it slightly with water. Make sure the edges of the little squares are well closed, or they will open when you cook them.

The Filling:

2 pounds fresh spinach
1 container (15 oz.) skim milk ricotta
1 cup Parmesan cheese, freshly grated
Salt
Pinch of nutmeg, freshly grated (a little more if
  desired)

Cook the spinach after having washed it several times in a basin full of water (a little sand in the spinach can ruin the best *ravioli*). Squeeze out all the water, taking a small amount of spinach between your hands and squeezing hard. Repeat until all the spinach is dry. Chop very fine. If you have a food processor, place the cooked spinach in it 2 or 3 handfuls at a time and run the motor for about 6-7 seconds each handful.

In a bowl, mix the chopped spinach with the *ricotta*, ½ of the Parmesan, the salt, and the nutmeg. Mix well.

Cooking the Pasta:

Be sure the room where you make the pasta is not drafty; the pasta will dry too fast and will become hard by the time you have it ready to cook.

Spread the *ravioli* out so that they won't stick together. If necessary, sprinkle with a little flour.

Bring the water to a vigorous boil in a large pot. Add a few *ravioli* at a time. When the *ravioli* rise to the surface, remove them from the water with a slotted spoon and place them on a warmed platter. Continue until all the *ravioli* are done.

Melt a stick of butter in a saucepan and let it brown. Pour the browned butter over the *ravioli*, sprinkle with the remaining Parmesan, and serve.

Gnocchi, Roman Style

Either a white or a red wine would go with these *ravioli* since *ricotta* is a bland cheese and would not overpower a dry white. If you use a red, it should be a gentle red: a Valpolicella or a Bardolino.

 # Maccheroni al Forno

Baked macaroni

Serves 6

3 large ripe tomatoes
Salt and freshly ground black pepper
Water
1 pound elbow macaroni or other short
   macaroni
3 tablespoons butter
8 ounces mozzarella
½ cup Parmesan cheese, freshly grated

Preheat the oven to 375°. The tomatoes should be ripe and of the meaty kind, like beefsteak tomatoes. Slice the tomatoes to ⅛-inch thickness. Place them in a sieve, salt liberally, and let them stand for at least ½ hour; they should shed most of their water. Butter an 8-inch baking dish or soufflé dish. Make a layer of tomato slices on bottom of dish. Cook the macaroni in salted water, leaving them slightly more *al dente* than you normally would. Drain and mix with 2 tablespoons of butter.

Cut the *mozzarella* into thin slices. Make a layer of *mozzarella* on top of the tomatoes. Cover with a layer of buttered macaroni. Sprinkle Parmesan on top of the macaroni. Cover with a layer of tomatoes. Continue until all ingredients have been used. The top layer should be of macaroni, sprinkled with Parmesan. Sprinkle with black pepper, dot with the remaining butter, and place in preheated oven. Bake for about 35 minutes, or until the top is lightly browned.

Serve with a friendly Bardolino, slightly cooler than room temperature.

NOTE

This is a very easy, inexpensive dish. If you have leftover ham or even a piece of pot roast, grind it in a meat grinder or a food processor and make a layer of meat halfway between the other layers.

Timballo di Maccheroni

Macaroni mold

Serves 6

½ cup breadcrumbs
1 whole egg
½ pound chicken livers
2 tablespoons butter
½ cup dried mushrooms or 1 cup fresh
  mushrooms, sliced
1 pound ripe tomatoes, peeled, seeded, and
  chopped
Pinch of nutmeg, freshly grated
1 pound short macaroni or rigatoni
Water
Salt

Preheat the oven to 350°. Butter a 9-inch mold with butter. The mold may be metal or glass but should have straight, not fluted, sides. Coat with ¼ cup breadcrumbs. Beat the egg well and pour it into the mold. Move the mold from side to side and slightly up and down until the egg coats the layer of crumbs. Coat the egg with the rest of the crumbs.

If dried mushrooms are to be used, soak them in lukewarm water for about 10 minutes, then squeeze out water and chop coarsely. If fresh mushrooms are used, remove all sandy parts before slicing.

Wash the chicken livers, remove membrane or fat, and dry them on a paper towel. Heat the butter in a skillet, add the mushrooms, and then the chicken livers. Cook over low heat. Add the tomatoes to chicken liver-mushroom mixture. Add nutmeg and simmer for about 6-7 minutes, stirring a couple of times.

In a large kettle, bring water to a boil and add salt. When the water is boiling hard, add the macaroni and cook for about 6-8 minutes, or until half done. Remove pot from fire, drain well. In a bowl, mix the cooked macaroni with the juice from the chicken liver-mushroom-tomato mixture. Mix well and pour half of the macaroni into the mold. With a spatula, distribute the macaroni so that the mold is evenly half filled. Add the liver-mushroom-tomato mixture and cover with the rest of macaroni. The mold should be filled but not heaping full.

Cover the mold with aluminum foil and place it in hot oven. After 30 minutes, remove the foil and examine the surface. If it seems brown enough,

cover again and allow to bake 30 minutes longer. If it seems too pale, remove the foil and bake uncovered for the additional 30 minutes. Before the days of foil, a *timballo* used to be covered with buttered parchment.

After the second 30 minutes of baking, remove the dish from the oven and allow it to stand for 5 minutes before unmolding the *timballo* onto a platter; before unmolding, loosen the edges slightly with a small sharp knife.

This is a spectacular and hearty dish, served either as a first course for dinner or a main course for lunch. In either case, a light dry wine, a young Chianti or a Gragnano, would go well with it. There is no problem with Chianti. Either the rooster or the "putto" on the label assures you of its authenticity. Be careful with Gragnano. It might just be an indifferent wine from around Naples that has been labeled Gragnano.

 # Sformato di Tagliatelle e Prosciutto

Noodle and prosciutto mold

Serves 6

6 tablespoons butter
8 slices prosciutto
½ cup fresh mushrooms, sliced and tightly
  packed
½ cup tiny peas, fresh or canned
Water
Salt
1 package (8 oz.) noodles, or the equivalent
  amount of homemade

Preheat oven to 350°. Butter a 7-inch soufflé dish with 1 tablespoon of butter, making sure that sides and bottom of dish are evenly coated.

Prosciutto slices should all be the same size. Place the narrower ends of the slices in the center of the dish, press them against the bottom, then against the sides, and let the remainder of the slices hang over edges of the dish. When all 8 slices are in their places they should form a sort of star and almost cover the bottom of the dish.

Melt 2 tablespoons of butter in a skillet, add the mushrooms and cook, covered, over high heat for about 3 minutes. The mushrooms will be done and will also have kept their white color. Add the peas if tiny canned peas are used. (If fresh peas are used, reverse the process. Boil the peas for 5 minutes

or until tender, melt the butter in a skillet, add the peas, then add the mushrooms and cook as above). Reserve for later use.

Bring the water to a boil in a large saucepan. Add the salt and, when the water is boiling strongly, add the noodles. For this particular recipe, keep the pasta even more *al dente* than usual. If you use packaged noodles, cook them for about ½ the time given on the package. The only way to tell when the pasta is done is to bite into a little piece. You must be able to bite into it, not just to feel it slither down your tongue. Drain the pasta and immediately add 3 tablespoons of butter and toss lightly. Add the Parmesan and mix. Add the peas and mushrooms mixture and mix gently.

Pour the noodles into the soufflé dish, not pressing down too hard but filling it lightly. (If you have a little pasta left over, eat it as is, while nobody is looking.) Fold the ends of *prosciutto* over the top of the noodles and place the dish in preheated oven (350°) for 5 to 6 minutes — not longer because noodles might overcook.

Remove the dish from the oven. Let stand for a couple of minutes. Place a round serving platter on top of the soufflé dish, then rapidly turn upside down. Wait a minute to allow the mold to settle, then remove the soufflé dish. You should have a most intriguing looking mold, with the *prosciutto* hiding the noodles, to be discovered only when the dish is served.

Serve as first course, followed by a roast or fowl, or as a luncheon dish, followed by a salad, cheese, and fruit. It is marvelous and unusual for a buffet. The choice of wine will, of course, depend on the meat that follows, but I would recommend a light red wine. A northern Italian wine would be a logical choice, as the ingredients for this dish come from the North. A Valpolicella would be a good bet but, if you can find a Gragnano from the Bay of Naples, it might add a very pleasant sunny touch. Both wines are brilliant reds.

Gnocchi

Gnocchi are dumplings, for lack of a better word. But the infinite variety of Italian dumplings make them a very distant relative of American and German dumplings. They are a *minestra,* meaning a first course. On occasion they may be served with the main course.

Gnocchi may be made of potatoes, of cornmeal, of spinach, or of spinach and cheese. No matter what the ingredients used, they are usually lighter than their cousins of other nationalities. In some cases, as in the case of spinach dumplings, they have absolutely nothing in common with them. The only thing that makes them "dumplings" is their shape.

The classic *Gnocchi alla Romana* are made with *semolino* in Italy. I don't find the American semolina to be the same thing. I find white cornmeal gives much better results.

 Gnocchi di Patate

Small potato dumplings

Serves 6

6 medium-sized potatoes, preferably
  Russet potatoes
Water
½ teaspoon salt
2 cups flour
4 egg yolks

See Illustrated Techniques, page 354.

Peel the potatoes and boil in salted water until well cooked. Purée through a sieve or use a potato masher.

Place the puréed potatoes on a wooden board or a marble-top table. Mix, adding a little flour; as the mixture gets dry, add 1 egg yolk at a time. With your fingertips, mix the flour and potatoes, working rapidly and not kneading too much. When the mixture is dry enough to handle but not hard, you will have about half a cup of flour left over. Reserve for later use.

Roll the dough with your hands to form several sausagelike rolls about the thickness of your thumb. With a small knife, cut them into pieces about 1-inch long. You can use them as they are or, if you wish to complicate your life and be more traditional, take a dinner fork, prong side up, and roll each little dumpling rapidly over the prongs. The result will be slightly curved dumplings, decorated with small grooves. Roll lightly in remaining flour.

In a large kettle, bring the water to a boil. Drop the dumplings in when the water boils strongly. Cook the *gnocchi* 10 or 12 at a time; when they come to the surface, remove them with a slotted spoon. Place the *gnocchi* in an ovenproof dish, then cover with either butter and cheese or your favorite sauce. Place the dish briefly under the broiler, if desired, to melt the cheese on top.

Your choice of wine depends upon the sauce you add. The most sensational would be *Salsa di Gorgonzola* (see page 18) and good red wine with a lot of personality should be served with it. I would go so far as to suggest a fine Barolo.

Gnocchi Verdi

Spinach dumplings

Serves 6

2 packages frozen chopped spinach, or the
    equivalent fresh
1 pound skim milk ricotta
2 whole eggs
Salt and pepper, freshly ground
Pinch nutmeg, freshly grated
¾ cup Parmesan cheese, freshly grated
6 tablespoons flour, sifted
Water
1 stick butter

Preheat the oven to 400°. Cook the spinach in salted water. Allow it to cool. Taking a small amount of spinach at a time between your hands, squeeze out all the water.

Open the container of *ricotta* and place the contents in cheesecloth. Tie a knot at one end and let the bag hang over the sink until all the liquid has dripped out.

In a small bowl, beat the eggs lightly. In a large bowl, mix the spinach with the drained *ricotta* and add the eggs. Taste the mixture and add salt, pepper, and nutmeg to taste. Mix well, then add ½ cup Parmesan. Add approximately 3 tablespoons of flour or as much as the mixture will absorb, depending on how much liquid was left in the spinach. Mix ingredients very well and place the bowl in the refrigerator to chill for ½ hour.

In a large saucepan bring water to a boil and add salt. Spread the remaining flour on a board. With the help of a tablespoon, make round dumplings of the spinach mixture the size of a large walnut. Roll them lightly in the remaining flour without pressing down on the dumplings; they should remain as light as possible. Add the *gnocchi* to the vigorously boiling water, dropping dumplings gently into it, 1 or 2 at a time. In a heatproof flat baking dish (Pyrex or earthenware) large enough to hold all dumplings in 1 layer, melt half a stick of butter. As the *gnocchi* rise to the surface of the pot (about 1 minute cooking time), remove them using a slotted spoon and place them in the dish with the melted butter. When all the dumplings have been placed in the dish, melt the remaining butter and pour over the dumplings. Sprinkle with the remaining cheese and place the dish under the broiler for about 5 minutes or in a preheated oven for 10 minutes. Serve very hot.

A red wine, a Merlot or a Valpolicella, should be served with this delicious dish, which should really not be called "dumplings" at all. They are as light as the proverbial feather and very tasty. If you fear neither calories nor cholesterol, you may want to add 4 tablespoons of heavy cream to the butter you pour over them.

Gnocchi alla Romana, I

Gnocchi, Roman style, traditional version

Serves 6

6 cups milk
Pinch of salt
6 tablespoons butter
1 cup semolino or cornmeal (coarsely ground, if
  possible, but regular Quaker cornmeal may be
  used)
½ cup Parmesan cheese, freshly grated

Using a heavy, sturdy saucepan, bring the milk to a boil over medium heat. Add a pinch of salt and 1 tablespoon of butter. Hold the cup of cornmeal in 1 hand and pour very slowly into the pot, while stirring the milk rapidly with a long wooden spoon. Stir constantly until all the cornmeal has been absorbed, otherwise lumps will form. Continue stirring for about 10 minutes. The mixture should be very smooth and quite thick.

Wet a cookie sheet with cold water and pour the cornmeal mixture over it. Smooth the surface of the cooked cornmeal with a wet knife. Let it cool completely; the mixture should be quite firm.

Preheat the oven to 375°. With 1 tablespoon of butter, coat an oblong ovenproof dish, about 14″ by 9″. With a cookie cutter or a small liquor glass (about 2″ in diameter), cut cornmeal rounds. They should be about ¼-inch thick. Make a row of *gnocchi*, slightly overlapping the edges horizontally. Make a second row overlapping slightly over the first and so on until all of the cornmeal mixture has been used.

Melt 4 tablespoons butter in a small saucepan. With a small spoon, distribute the melted butter evenly over the *gnocchi*. Sprinkle the Parmesan cheese evenly over the whole surface, and place the dish in the preheated oven for about 15 minutes, or until tops of *gnocchi* are golden and the butter

bubbles all around them. Remove them from the oven and let stand at least 5 minutes before serving. If the *gnocchi* are still bubbling, they are too mushy; they have to calm down before being brought to the table.

This dish is universally known as *Gnocchi alla Romana* but scholars of Italian cuisine say that it originated in the Piedmont. This is a rich dish that requires a solid wine. An Inferno or a Chianti would be perfect with it.

NOTE

When I talk about semolina I don't mean the breakfast cereal but rather durum wheat, coarsely ground. In Italy it is called semolino. You might find it in some Italian groceries but if you don't, try cornmeal. We find that the white cornmeal is most satisfactory.

 Gnocchi alla Romana, II

Gnocchi alla Romana, modern version

Serves 6

3 cups water
3 cups milk
5 tablespoons butter
Pinch of salt
1 pound cornmeal, white or yellow
2 egg yolks
⅓ cup Parmesan cheese
2 tablespoons grated Swiss cheese

Pour the water and milk into a sturdy saucepan. Add 1 tablespoon of butter and a pinch of salt. Bring to a boil over medium heat.

Constantly stirring with a long wooden spoon, start pouring the cornmeal into the hot liquid (in Italian we say *a pioggia,* like a gentle rain). If you add too much cornmeal at a time, or if you stop stirring for a second, lumps will form and then the mixture has to be thrown out. Continue stirring for about 10 minutes after all the cornmeal has been absorbed. It might be wise to wear an oven mitt on the hand that does the mixing because this hot mixture occasionally "spits."

When the mixture is smooth and very thick, remove it from the heat. Quickly add 2 egg yolks and mix very well. Wet a cookie sheet with cold water,

then pour the hot mixture onto it as evenly as possible. Smooth the surface with the blade of a wet knife, and let it cool completely. The mixture should be quite firm.

Preheat the oven to 375°. Butter an oblong ovenproof dish (about 14″ by 9″) so that dish is very well coated all over. With a cookie cutter or a small liqueur glass (about 2″ round) cut small cornmeal rounds (*gnocchi*) and place them in a row, overlapping slightly, in the buttered dish. If the glass gets sticky, dip the edge in flour. Continue with a second row, slightly overlapping the first, and so on until all of the cornmeal mixture has been used. Melt the remaining butter in a small saucepan and, with the help of a spoon, cover the *gnocchi* evenly. Sprinkle Parmesan cheese over the whole surface, then pour the remaining melted butter over it. Sprinkle grated Swiss cheese over it.

Place the dish in the preheated oven for about 15 minutes, or until the tops of the *gnocchi* are golden and butter bubbles all around them. Remove the dish from the oven and let it stand for at least 5 minutes, or until the butter has stopped bubbling, before serving.

Serve with a good, fruity red wine. A Grignolino would go well with them, or even a Gattinara, one of Italy's noblest wines, from the region of Piedmont.

NOTE

Gnocchi alla Romana are made with semolino in Italy. The cereal of that name, sold in this country, is not the same thing. I find that Quaker cornmeal is the best substitute and (may the purists forgive me), even hominy grits gets good results. Before you discard the idea, read the following recipe.

 # Gnocchi alla Romana, III

Gnocchi made with hominy grits

Serves 6 to 8

2 cups medium coarse hominy grits
Salt to taste
1 stick butter
1 cup Parmesan cheese, freshly grated
Water

Cook the hominy grits as indicated on the package, stirring for about 30 minutes. Add salt to taste. Just before removing the pot from the stove, add a tablespoon of butter. Pour the hot grits onto a flat wet surface — a large platter or a marble-top table. Flatten the grits with the back of a wet

spoon to a ¼-inch thickness or less. Let cool completely; the grits should be quite firm.

Butter a rectangular ovenproof dish, coating evenly. Those brown glazed earthenware dishes that are available in most stores are the classic dishes used in Italy.

With a small glass (about 2″ to 2½″) or a cookie cutter of the same size, cut rounds of grits and place in the dish in neat rows, overlapping slightly. Sprinkle ⅓ cup Parmesan over the rounds. Melt the remaining butter and pour over the *gnocchi*. Place the dish in the broiler, not too close to the heat (about 7-inch distance). The edges of the *gnocchi* should be golden and the butter should bubble all around them (about 10 minutes in the broiler). Remove the dish from the broiler and let stand until the butter has calmed down. Serve with the remaining Parmesan in a separate bowl.

I am fully aware that hominy grits and *Gnocchi alla Romana* sound like a strange combination, but the result, though somewhat different from the one you get with imported *semolino* is more than acceptable. You should still serve a fruity red wine with this dish: a Gattinara from the Piedmont or, if your taste buds prefer, the wines of Valtellina, an Inferno, or a Grumello.

Egg Dishes

Eggs are used a great deal in northern Italy. They are plentiful and they lend themselves so well to dishes that are strictly Italian. This chapter includes recipes for *crespelle* (thin pancakes), omelettes, soufflés, and two characteristically Italian dishes: *frittate* and *tortini*. The difference between the *frittate* and *tortini* is that *frittate* are turned and cooked on both sides. *Tortini* are thicker and are cooked only on 1 side with the top left very soft.

Frittate are popular throughout Italy, with the exception of Sicily and Sardinia, where they are practically unknown. However, in the region of Friuli, the *frittate* are at their best. They are made with fresh cheese (another specialty of Friuli) with salami, herbs, and even potatoes. They can be eaten cold or hot, and they are always delicious.

The Friulani, the people of Friuli, are hard-working people. A Friulano farmer will rarely take time out to go home for lunch. He can take a *frittata* with him and eat it with a piece of bread when he gets hungry. If he works late and his family eats before he gets home, a *frittata* will be left for him on the kitchen table.

 ## Crespelle

Thin pancakes

10 to 12 *crespelle*

1 cup milk
¾ cup all-purpose flour
1 teaspoon salt
½ cup water
3 eggs
Pinch nutmeg, freshly grated (optional)
1 tablespoon butter

Pour the milk into a large bowl and add the flour, sifting it through a sieve. Add the salt and beat the mixture with a wire whisk until the ingredients are well mixed. Add the water and the eggs, 1 at a time, adding the second egg only after the first has been absorbed. Add the nutmeg, if desired, and let the mix stand for at least 30 minutes, but longer if possible.

When the time comes to fry your *crespelle,* take a paper towel and pick up a pat of butter with the edge of the towel. Rub an 8-inch omelette pan until it is well coated all over on the inside. Make sure the pan is perfectly clean and is never used for anything but eggs.

Place the buttered pan over fairly high heat and pour about ⅓ of an average kitchen ladle of the batter into the pan. Tilt the pan immediately in all directions so that the batter covers as much surface as possible, leaving only a bare edge all around. When the batter starts bubbling in the center and the edge starts getting golden, loosen the edge with a thin spatula. Shake the pan to loosen the whole *crespella*. Place a large platter or a wooden board near the stove and, when the *crespella* is done on 1 side, turn the pan upside down rapidly, letting the *crespella* fall onto the board or onto the platter. Repeat the operation with the next *crespella*. In the meantime, the first will have cooled off enough to be picked up and placed back in the pan, golden side up, to be fried on the other side.

Between pancakes, rub the pan with the buttered paper towel, picking up another bit of butter when the towel seems dry. The *crespelle* should be about 6½" in diameter.

NOTE

Every cook has his or her own method of making crespelle. I find this to be the easiest. You can flip them over if you want to show off (and if you are very skillful), or you can slide them onto a plate, place the pan upside down over the plate, and put them back in the pan that way. But I find the system I describe the simplest and fastest.

Crespelle lend themselves to an almost endless variety of uses, although the sweet version, with the crespelle filled with jam, sprinkled with sugar (called Palatschinken *in Germany), is not much used in Italy.*

 # Crespelle con Ricotta e Spinaci

Crespelle with ricotta and spinach

Serves 6

*1 cup (tightly packed) cooked spinach, finely
chopped*

(continued)

½ container (7½ oz.) skim milk ricotta
½ cup Parmesan cheese, freshly grated
1½ teaspoons salt
Black pepper, freshly ground
Pinch of nutmeg, freshly grated
12 6-inch crespelle (see pages 146-47)
2 tablespoons butter

The spinach should be dry. Squeeze it well between your hands before you measure it: the spinach should have no water in it.

Place the chopped spinach in a bowl. Add the *ricotta* (room temperature) and mix well with a wooden spoon. Add the Parmesan, salt, pepper, and nutmeg. Stir until totally mixed.

Lay 1 *crespella* on a flat surface and place a tablespoon of the mixture in the center. Roll the *crespella*, starting with the right edge folded over the center. Flatten the top of the roll lightly with the palm of your hand. Repeat for the remaining *crespelle*.

Preheat the oven to 350°. With 1 tablespoon of butter, coat a rectangular baking dish (or a brown earthenware dish) and place the filled and rolled *crespelle* in a neat row. There should be a little space between each of them. Dot them with the remaining butter and place in the preheated oven for about 15 minutes. Serve hot as a first course.

Serve with a light red wine: a Bardolino from Lake Garda or, if you plan a beef dish as main course, an Amarone, also from the Garda region.

NOTE

I use skim milk ricotta, sold in 15 oz. containers in almost all markets, because it comes closer to the Italian ricotta than the whole milk variety. If you find that the container, when you open it, has liquid on top, empty the container onto a paper towel and pat the ricotta dry with a second towel.

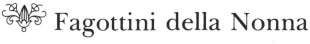 # Fagottini della Nonna

Grandmother's little bundles

Serves 4

1 pound fresh spinach
8 crespelle (see pages 146-47)
½ cup skim milk ricotta

Salt and freshly ground black pepper
1 ½ cups besciamella (see pages 22-23)
½ teaspoon tomato paste, preferably homemade
2 tablespoons butter
3 sage leaves or ½ teaspoon dried
⅓ cup Parmesan cheese, freshly grated
    (optional)

Wash the spinach carefully, then cook for 10 minutes or until done. Let cool. While the spinach is cooling, prepare the *crespelle*. They should be quite thin. Reserve.
Lightly butter an oblong baking dish.

Taking a small amount of spinach at a time, squeeze it between your hands until all the water has been eliminated. Purée in a foodmill or, if you have a food processor, use the sharp blade and run the motor for about 30 seconds. The spinach should be finely puréed. If necessary, run the motor for another 10 seconds.

Mix the spinach purée with the *ricotta* until well blended. Add salt and pepper. Place some of the mixture in the center of each *crespella* and then fold the sides of the *crespelle* over the mixture to form a square bundle rather than rolling them, as you would for other recipes. Arrange the bundles in the baking dish.

Prepare a fairly liquid *besciamella*, blended with the tomato paste. Spread this sauce over the bundles. Place the dish under the broiler, being careful to keep it far from the heat (at least 6 inches). Allow the *crespelle* to brown lightly; it will take about 10 minutes or less. The time varies according to the heat of the broiler.

Melt the butter in a saucepan and add the sage leaves or dried sage. Let the butter bubble for a few minutes so that it will absorb the taste of the sage. If you have used fresh leaves, remove them. Pour the sage-flavored butter over the *crespelle* and serve as a first course.

Serve the Parmesan cheese in a separate bowl for people to add if desired. This is a rich dish and many people will prefer it without the additional cheese.

NOTE

This is a specialty of that incomparable eating place called Locanda Cipriani in Asolo, slightly north of Venice. The recipe sounds perfectly logical and uncomplicated but the secret "Cipriani touches" such as the tomato paste and the sage leaves make this version stand out.

Timballo di Crespelle e Zucchini

Zucchini and crespelle mold

Serves 6 to 8

6 medium-sized zucchini
⅓ cup oil
1 clove garlic
Salt and freshly ground black pepper
Pinch of nutmeg, freshly grated
8 6-inch crespelle (see pages 146–47)
¾ cup Parmesan cheese

Wash the zucchini and scrape off the sandy parts or uneven spots. Don't peel. Cut them in half lengthwise and then into slices ⅓-inch thick. (If you have a food processor, place the zucchini, cut in half, in the tube and cut with the slicer. They will be sliced before you have time to look at them.)

Heat the oil in a large skillet where the zucchini won't be heaped on top of one another. Place the clove of garlic in the oil and sauté. When it begins to turn golden, remove and discard. Add the zucchini slices to the oil, then add the salt, keeping in mind that the zucchini are quite bland. Add pepper and cook over medium high heat, stirring now and then so they won't stick. Don't cover. Cook for about 20 minutes. The zucchini should be *al dente* and not mushy. Add a pinch of nutmeg and ½ cup Parmesan.

Preheat oven to 350°. Butter an 8-inch soufflé mold. Place 1 *crespella* on the bottom of the mold and line the sides with 4 of the remaining *crespelle*, making sure they cling to the sides of the mold. Fill the center of the mold with the zucchini-Parmesan mixture. Fold the edges of the *crespelle* over the center and cover with the remaining *crespella*. Sprinkle the remaining Parmesan cheese on the top and place in oven for 10 to 15 minutes or until Parmesan has melted.

Let the mold stand for 3 to 4 minutes. Place a round platter on top and turn the mold upside down.

If you wish you can sprinkle the Parmesan on top at this point instead of sprinkling it on top of the mold before placing it in the oven.

Serve this as first course, followed by a meat dish. It also looks beautiful on a buffet. The wine to serve with it depends upon the main course that follows. If you were to serve the *timballo* by itself for a light luncheon, a Soave di Verona would go with it. Soave is a gentle white wine from Lake Garda and won't interfere with the subtle taste of the zucchini.

NOTE

Keep in mind that you can make the crespelle ahead of time, as much as a few days, before making your timballo. We have been told that they may even be frozen, with a sheet of wax paper between each crespella, but have never tried this. The zucchini, however, have to be made just before you use them but your timballo can be ready before your guests arrive and you only have to put it in the oven while you are having drinks.

 # Frittata al Basilico

Frittata with basil

Serves 4 to 5

Small bunch (about 6 healthy stalks) basil
6 whole eggs at room temperature
4 tablespoons heavy cream
Salt and freshly ground black pepper
4 tablespoons butter
4 tablespoons olive oil
Parmesan cheese (optional)

Wash the basil, dry it with a paper towel, and chop the leaves well, discarding the stems. Break the eggs into a bowl and beat them well with a fork but don't allow them to get foamy. Add cream, salt, and pepper and stir.

In a heavy skillet (iron or heavy stainless steel), melt the butter over high heat; add the oil and allow to get very hot. Add the basil to the egg mixture and pour into skillet. Spread evenly with a spatula. Reduce the heat and allow the egg mixture to brown. Every now and then slide your spatula under the egg mixture to make sure that it doesn't stick to the bottom of the skillet. Allow the eggs to cook uncovered for about 5 or 6 minutes or until the edges are lightly golden. Slide the *frittata* onto a hot platter, cover with the overturned skillet, and, with a rapid movement, turn upside down so that uncooked side of the *frittata* is down. Cook over low heat for about 5 minutes, then slide onto a hot platter and serve. The inside of a perfect *frittata* should be soft. If desired, sprinkle top with Parmesan cheese.

Frittata is *the* Italian egg dish, which doesn't mean that we don't also have an *omeletta* — but it is a little less typical, a little less Italian. *Frittate* come in almost infinite varieties. Once you have learned how to make a basic *frittata*, you can invent your own versions.

Wine and eggs don't do very much for one another, but I like a dry white wine with any egg dish. Don't choose an important wine, however, because as I have said, eggs won't bring out the best in it. A Soave would be all right, and there is no reason why a young California Chablis shouldn't go with a *frittata*. Just make sure the wine has no more than 12% alcohol. A heavy wine has a way of overpowering eggs.

NOTE

If basil is not in season, forget about this recipe; dried basil won't do.

 # Frittata al Prezzemolo

Frittata with parsley

Serves 4 to 5

6 *whole eggs*
3 *tablespoons flour*
6 *tablespoons water*
6 *tablespoons Parmesan cheese, freshly grated*
⅓ *cup parsley, chopped*
Salt and freshly ground black pepper
4 *tablespoons butter*
Parmesan cheese (optional)

Separate the eggs: the yolks in one bowl, the whites in another. The eggs should be at room temperature. Beat the yolks lightly with a fork, adding the flour a little at a time, and alternating it with the water. Allow every bit of flour and every spoonful of water to be absorbed by the yolks so that no lumps form. When the egg yolks, flour, and water are well mixed, add the Parmesan, parsley, salt, and pepper.

Beat the egg whites with a wire whisk (or with an electric hand mixer), until moderately stiff. Fold the whites gently into the yolk mixture, using a rubber spatula. Over high heat, melt the butter in a skillet until very hot, but not brown. Pour the egg mixture into the skillet and flatten it with a spatula. Reduce the heat and brown well on 1 side (about 6 minutes), slide onto a plate, then cover plate with overturned skillet. Rapidly turn over so that the *frittata* is back in the skillet, but with the uncooked side down. Brown the other side for about 5 to 6 minutes, still over medium heat. Slide the spatula along the edges

Frittata with Basil

to make sure the *frittata* doesn't stick. When it is done, slide it onto a serving platter and sprinkle with a little Parmesan (optional).

All *frittatas* should be served with a light dry white wine, chilled, of course, but not so cold that it freezes your taste buds.

 # Frittata al Piri-Piri

Frittata with red hot pepper

Serves 4

1 large white onion
1 tablespoon oil
½ cup broth (chicken or beef)
Pinch of salt
6 whole eggs, beaten lightly
Pinch of Piri-Piri (or very hot red pepper)
2 tablespoons butter
2 tablespoons oil

Slice the onion; the slices should be very thin. Place the oil in a skillet, heat and add the onion. Stir, cooking over high heat until golden. Add the broth and the pinch of salt. Cook, covered, over very low heat. Stir now and then. Add more broth if necessary. Cook the onion until it is almost dissolved; the cooking time depends on thinness of onion, but it takes more or less an hour to get the onion to this point. When ready, pour off the juice and reserve it for a sauce.

Put the eggs in a bowl (glass, porcelain, or stainless steel that is used only for eggs), then add the onion and a dash of *Piri-Piri*. In a skillet, heat the butter and oil, but don't allow it to brown. Pour the egg-onion mixture into the pan and cook, uncovered, over high heat until the edges are golden. Using a plate or a lid, turn the *frittata* over. Slide it back into skillet and cook on other side. While the *frittata* is cooking, slide the spatula under the edges every now and then to prevent sticking. The cooking time should be no more than 5 minutes on each side. The inside of a perfect *frittata* should be slightly soft.

No wine is suggested with this dish. Your palate will have to calm down before you can taste any.

NOTE

This is a recipe from a famous restaurant in Milan: Pino alla Parete. The owner is a great cook and a supporter of visual arts. He also likes to be "different." Piri-Piri is a kind of pepper friends bring him from Africa. It is the hottest we have ever tasted, but the hot pepper used in Mexican food will do.

 # Frittata Friulana

Frittata, Friuli style

Serves 6

8 whole eggs
2 tablespoons shortening, such as Crisco
Salt and freshly ground black pepper

B eat the eggs very well with a fork or a wire whisk. Both the yolks and the whites should be totally mixed and foamy.

Use a frying pan made of iron, not too large (about 6 inches), and with a rather high rim. Place the fat in the pan over high heat and tilt it so that the bottom and sides are evenly coated. Beat the eggs again just before pouring them into the hot fat. Reduce heat and cook until the edges are golden. The center should remain quite moist. It may be turned and cooked on the other side if it is to be eaten cold.

Serve with a cold Tocai from Friuli (no relation to the Hungarian Tokay, which is sweet).

NOTE

This Frittata Friulana is different from all other frittatas. It should be at least 2 inches high and can never be stuffed and folded; it is frequently not turned.

 # Frittata con le Patate

Frittata, Friuli style with potatoes

Serves 6

8 whole eggs
2 large potatoes, peeled

(continued)

2 tablespoons oil
1 small young onion, chopped
Salt and freshly ground black pepper
2 tablespoons shortening, such as Crisco

Place the eggs in a bowl and beat well until foamy.
Grate the potatoes (if you have a food processor, place the raw peeled potatoes, halved or quartered according to size of potatoes, in the feeding tube, and run the grater for 1 second).

Heat the oil in a skillet over high heat, and add the onion but don't allow it to brown. Add the grated raw potatoes and fry for 3 to 4 minutes. Add this to the bowl with the beaten eggs. Add salt and pepper. Beat again briefly. Place fat in deep, heavy frying pan and turn to coat sides. Place egg mixture in pan and reduce heat, cook until edges are golden.

There is no rule against frying the *frittata* on both sides. If you prefer to have a golden crust on both sides, place a plate on top of the skillet and turn the skillet upside down. Make sure the skillet is still coated enough to fry the eggs on the other side: if not, add ½ teaspoon fat, slide the *frittata* back into skillet with the uncooked side down, and cook for 4 to 5 minutes. Don't allow the inside to harden. The advantage of cooking it on both sides, in my opinion, is that it is equally good served hot or cold.

Serve this *frittata* with that pale golden Tocai, one of Friuli's best white wines.

NOTE

The difference between a Frittata Friulana and one from any other region of Italy is that the former is twice as thick and the inside is quite soft. It has a totally different texture.

Frittata Friulana con Salame

Frittata, Friuli style with salami

Serves 6

8 whole eggs, beaten well
3 slices Italian salami (each ¼-inch thick)
2 tablespoons shortening, such as Crisco
Salt and freshly ground black pepper

Beat the eggs as in preceding recipes. Peel the salami and dice (cubes should be ¼-inch by ¼).

Over high heat melt the shortening in an iron skillet and tip the pan to coat sides. Add half of the eggs and salt and pepper. Sauté over high heat. When the edges begin to turn golden, add the salami, sprinkled over the whole surface, and allow to set in the eggs. Pour the remainder of the eggs over the salami, lower the heat to medium, and cook until the edges are brown. Place a plate over the skillet, turn upside down. Make sure there is enough fat left in the skillet; if not, add a bit of shortening. Slide the *frittata* back into the pan, brown side up, and cook for another 5 minutes or so. Don't allow the center to harden. This particular *frittata*, however, has to be turned because the salami is uncooked and would have a hard texture otherwise.

I have suggested a Tocai, a dry white wine from Friuli, with all *frittatas*. With the salami, however, I would switch to a Merlot. It, too, is a wine from Friuli, the most beautiful ruby red, and can stand up to the bite of any salami.

NOTE

Make sure you taste your salami before adding it; if it is very spicy you might go lighter on the salt and pepper.

 ## Frittata Friulana con Spinaci e Menta

Frittata, Friuli style with spinach and mint

Serves 6

½ cup cooked spinach, tightly packed
1 small leek
2 tablespoons oil
4 leaves wild mint
8 whole eggs
2 tablespoons shortening, such as Crisco
Salt and freshly ground black pepper

Chop the spinach and leek (only the white part). Heat the oil in a skillet, and add the spinach and leek, sautéing for a couple of minutes. Chop the mint coarsely and add. When all the ingredients are well coated with oil and when all the water that might have remained in the spinach has evaporated, beat the eggs very well with a fork or a wire whisk until foamy. Add the spinach mixture, beating a little longer.

Melt the shortening in an iron skillet with rather high sides. Pour the egg-spinach mixture in and cook, starting over high heat, then reducing the heat until the edges start getting golden. If you wish to turn the *frittata*, this is the time to do it. If you don't want to turn it, allow the edges to get quite brown. Remove from heat, loosen with a spatula, and allow to stand for a few minutes before placing it on a platter.

Serve with a Tocai, chilled only slightly.

NOTE

Mint grows wild all over Friuli, but then all herbs seem to flourish there. My friends have bushes, 4 feet high, of the most beautiful rosemary, whereas I struggle with a tiny plant on my windowsill. It gets very cold in Friuli; I've no explanation!

 # Tortino con Ricotta

Tortino with ricotta cheese

Serves 4

3 heaping tablespoons skim milk ricotta
4 tablespoons butter
5 whole eggs
2 teaspoons salt
Black pepper, freshly ground

Have the *ricotta* at room temperature. Place the cheese on a paper towel to absorb excess liquid.

Beat the eggs lightly with a fork. Don't beat them too hard. Add 1 teaspoon salt.

Melt the butter over high heat in an 8-inch skillet. When the butter is melted, pour the eggs into the skillet. As soon as the edges begin to bubble, lower the heat to medium. With a small spatula, push the eggs toward the center of the skillet, allowing the liquid eggs and butter to run under the eggs. This will produce a rather thick *tortino*. It should be about 1-inch thick in the center.

When the eggs are almost cooked and only the center of the *tortino* is still soft, spread the *ricotta* over the center. Sprinkle with the remaining salt and with the pepper. Cover the skillet as tightly as possible. Turn off the heat. Let the *tortino* stand for a few minutes to give the *ricotta* a chance to warm.

This is a different and delicious dish for people who like eggs for breakfast. If that is when this *tortino* will be served, no wine is served with it. If it is served for lunch, it requires a light dry wine: a Soave di Verona or a Tocai from Friuli.

NOTE

This tortino may also be eaten cold, but not refrigerated. I have at times cut it in half and placed 1 side on top of the other, with the ricotta side in. That way it can be wrapped in aluminum foil and taken on a picnic.

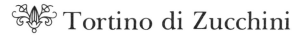

Tortino di Zucchini

Tortino with zucchini

Serves 4 to 5

2 medium-sized zucchini
6 tablespoons butter
6 whole eggs
1 tablespoon cream or 2 tablespoons milk
Salt and freshly ground black pepper
3 tablespoons olive oil
2 tablespoons grated Parmesan cheese

Choose the zucchini carefully. They should be bright green and glossy. Squeeze the tips lightly when the grocer isn't looking. If they are very firm, the zucchini are fresh. Avoid soft zucchini; they are bitter.

Wash zucchini carefully and rub with a rough towel to remove any sand. Don't peel. Remove the stems and dark spot on top where the blossoms had been. Cut into slices the thickness of a quarter.

Melt 2 tablespoons of butter in a skillet and sauté the zucchini until transparent. Meanwhile, in a bowl beat the eggs lightly with the cream or milk; add salt and pepper to taste.

Melt the remaining butter over high heat in another skillet and add the olive oil. Pour the egg mixture into the skillet and immediately add the fried zucchini, spreading them evenly over the eggs with a spatula but being careful not to break them. When the edges of the eggs are golden (about 5 to 6 minutes), slide the *tortino* onto a plate.

When the *tortino* is on serving platter, sprinkle with Parmesan cheese.

This *tortino* may be served hot or cold. If you wish to serve it cold, allow it to cook 2 or 3 minutes longer or until the center is well done.

If a wine is to be served with this dish it should be a very dry white wine: a Soave or a Durello. The latter is still hard to find in this country but it is worth looking for.

Omeletta con Mozzarella e Ricotta

Mozzarella and ricotta omelette

Serves 4

6 whole eggs
4 tablespoons cream
Salt
½ stick butter
2 tablespoons shredded mozzarella
2 tablespoons ricotta

Beat the eggs with a fork and add cream and a little salt.

Melt the butter in an omelette pan, then add the eggs over low heat and watch carefully for the moment when the edges get solid. Tilt the pan slightly and, using a spatula, fold the edges toward the center. Shake the pan slightly to make it slide to the lower edge of the pan.

Have the *mozzarella* and *ricotta* ready (both must be at room temperature) and place both in the center of omelette when it is still quite runny. Add a pinch of salt since both cheeses are bland. At this point, fold in half, as you would with any other omelette and let it cook for a few seconds to make sure the cheeses are melted and hot. Slide onto an oval platter and serve immediately.

Serve with a dry white wine: a Durello or a Pinot Grigio, in spite of the presence of cheese, which usually requires a red. The mixture of eggs and bland cheese seems to be overpowered by a red.

NOTE

This is not the easiest dish to make and might require a little practice but it is one of the great egg-cheese mixtures I know.

Omeletta con Funghi

Omelette with mushrooms

Serves 4

½ pound fresh mushrooms
⅓ cup fresh parsley
1 stick butter
Salt and freshly ground black pepper
3 tablespoons dry Marsala wine
½ teaspoon flour
6 whole eggs
3 tablespoons olive oil

Clean the mushrooms by cutting off the brown or sandy parts of the stems and rubbing the caps with a wet towel. Peel the caps only if they have dark spots. Slice the mushrooms.

Wash the parsley and dry it well on a paper towel before chopping. This is important because wet parsley will cling to the sides of your knife and will be hard to chop.

Heat half of the butter until very hot but don't allow it to brown. Add the mushrooms, a pinch of salt, and the Marsala and turn heat very low. Sprinkle the flour over the mushrooms and stir it into the Marsala with the help of a wooden spoon so that no lumps form. Add the chopped parsley when mushrooms are almost done, about 4-5 minutes. Remove from heat.

In a bowl break the eggs; add pepper and very little salt. Beat lightly with a fork until the whites and yolks are well mixed. Heat the remainder of the butter in a heavy skillet, add the olive oil. When the mixture foams, pour in the egg mixture and distribute it evenly with a spatula. Then don't touch the eggs until edges are golden but not brown. If you want a rather firm omelette, cover the skillet with a lid for 1 minute.

Place the mushroom mixture in the center of the eggs, distributing it evenly but leaving an edge all around. When the center of the omelette is done, loosen the edges with a spatula, fold half over the other half and, always with the help of a spatula, slide onto a hot platter. If a little of the butter-Marsala mixture should be left in the skillet, pour it over the omelette and serve immediately.

With the Marsala it is difficult to suggest a wine. Some people might even forego it. Personally, I would drink a Soave di Verona with this dish, Marsala or no Marsala.

 Soffiato di Prosciutto

Ham soufflé

Serves 6

6 eggs, separated
½ pound lean ham
2 tablespoons butter
2 tablespoons flour
1 cup cold milk
Salt and freshly ground black pepper
3 tablespoons Parmesan, freshly grated
1 tablespoon breadcrumbs
Pinch of nutmeg, freshly grated (optional)

There are 2 ways of making this *soffiato:* one with a food processor and one without it. If you have a processor, cut the ham into chunks, place the chunks in the processor, and run the motor for about 10 seconds. Melt the butter in a skillet and add the flour, stirring rapidly with a wire whisk. When the mixture starts foaming, add the cold milk, continue mixing and allow to cook for 6 to 7 minutes. The mixture should not be too thick. Add the ham to the mixture and let it cool.

Preheat the oven to 400°. Beat the egg yolks lightly with wire whisk and add to the cooled ham mixture. Add salt and pepper and nutmeg, if desired. Add the Parmesan and mix well. Beat the egg whites until stiff and fold them into the mixture, using a rubber spatula.

Coat a 7-inch soufflé dish with butter and then with breadcrumbs. Make a 3-inch to 4-inch collar of aluminum foil and tie it around the edge of the soufflé dish. Pour the mixture into the dish, and bake for about 35 minutes or until the top of the *soffiato* is golden. Serve immediately either by itself or with a mustard sauce.

If you do not have a food processor, chop the ham and place it in a blender. Add the milk and run the blender for about 30 seconds at low speed and then 30 seconds at high speed. Melt the butter in a skillet. Add the flour and when the mixture foams, stir in the milk and ham and allow it to cook for 6 to 7 minutes. Continue the recipe as given earlier.

If you don't own a blender, chop the ham with a *mezzaluna,* a moon-shaped chopping knife, and proceed as you would for the remainder of the recipe.

A Merlot from the Friuli region would be an ideal companion for this dish. If a Merlot is not available, a young Chianti will be happy with it.

NOTE

Don't expect this soffiato to grow as tall as a cheese soufflé would. The ham is a heavier ingredient. On the other hand it doesn't fall as easy as other soufflés.

 ## Soffiato di Ricotta

Ricotta soufflé

Serves 4 to 5

1 container (15 oz.) skim milk ricotta, drained
1 teaspoon salt
1 cup Parmesan cheese, freshly grated
6 eggs, separated
1 tablespoon butter

Place the *ricotta* in a bowl, add salt and Parmesan cheese (reserving 1 tablespoon for later use), and stir until well blended.

Preheat oven to 400°. Add the egg yolks to the *ricotta* mixture, 1 at a time, adding the next only when the previous one has been blended in.

Beat the whites until quite stiff and fold into the *ricotta* mixture, using a rubber spatula and working carefully.

Butter an 8-inch soufflé dish, making sure sides and bottom are well coated. Using a spatula, transfer the *ricotta* mixture to the soufflé dish. Sprinkle the remaining Parmesan on top, dot with the butter, and place in oven for about 30 minutes or until top is golden.

This dish makes an ideal luncheon course, followed by a salad and a light dessert. It is also less rich than a regular cheese soufflé, made with white sauce and a fat cheese. Both *ricotta* and Parmesan are lean cheeses. Serve with a Valpolicella from Lake Garda. Make sure the wine is slightly chilled before serving.

NOTE

This soffiato will not rise as high as a soufflé made with besciamella, but it will also not collapse into nothingness within minutes. In fact, it may be eaten cold the next day when it will taste like a sort of quiche without the crust. The important thing in this recipe is that the Parmesan be very flavorful. It should be the best Italian Reggiano, aged at least 2 years, yellow, and not chalky white.

 # Uova in Cereghin con i Crostini

Eggs, the clergy way, with croutons

Serves 1

1 slice stale white bread
2 tablespoons butter
1 whole egg
Salt and freshly ground black pepper

Cut the bread slice into cubes and fry in butter until golden, using a small frying pan. Push these croutons to the edge of pan so that they form a circle. Carefully break 1 egg in the center of the pan so that the yolk remains intact in the middle and the white mixes with the croutons.

It is hard to pin down exactly where this dish originated, but *Cereghin* is a clergyman in Milanese dialect. The fried egg, obviously, looks like his tonsure.

The eggs for this recipe may be fried, 2 or 3 at a time in a large frying pan, but this makes it harder to form the crouton circles. They are a delicious breakfast or brunch dish. If you have a house guest, you will create a sensation if you serve this fried egg in *Cereghin*.

Fish
Pesce

Italians are passionate fish eaters. It is no wonder, with that long and narrow peninsula they live on surrounded by all that water. Italians boil, broil, and fry their fish, as well as make fish soup. Fish soup is particularly a dish of great pride and competition among various regions. Venice has its *broeto* and looks with some contempt upon Livorno (Leghorn) where they add sharp spices in order to give their fish soup some taste. Venice cooks its lesser fish (cheaper qualities, that is) in water with a little lemon juice and a couple of tomatoes. After an hour or so this mixture is puréed through a sieve. Pieces of the finest fish, cooked separately and with all bones removed, are added to the *broeto*. Nothing is added that might alter the taste of fish. The preparation of a perfect *broeto* takes about 3 to 4 hours. Once upon a time this was perfectly acceptable. Now it is hard to find someone who will devote that time to a fish soup.

There is no longer the infinite variety of fish in the Italian market that used to exist. Cheap but exquisite fish, called simply *pesce misto*, seem to have disappeared. There still are, however, the majestic *orate*, which are similar to the North American bass and the *triglie*, which are red like our red snappers. There are also *merluzzi* (whiting) and fresh anchovies and sardines to be stuffed, fried, or baked. What has disappeared completely are the little *frittolini*, small fish stores where little anonymous fish were constantly being deep-fried in enormous pots of hot oil. They were sprinkled with salt and sold in cornucopias of brown paper. We used to buy them after school on our way home the way American kids buy candy. We came home smelling of fish and fried oil and were severely punished because *fritture* (deep-fried foods) were bad for our health. These days the *frittolini* are gone; we are told that there are a couple left in small towns on the coast of the Adriatic but haven't found any.

It is quite true that some fish are scarce and very expensive because the Adriatic, like all seas, yields less fish than it used to. Pollution has taken its toll and we are only slowly repairing the damage.

One of the extraordinary sights of Venice is the fishmarket at Rialto (the famous bridge that looks like an inverted V) early in the morning when the barges have just arrived. It is a fascinating moment, both for the variety of fish

and the variety of people who have come to buy them. Restaurant owners, private cooks, gourmets, housewives, and workmen go to market early in the morning. Although fish has become expensive and fewer people can afford it, the scene is still a lively one. The dialogue between sellers and buyers is lusty and earthy, reminiscent of the *Commedia dell'Arte*.

A fish, if that is what it is, that should be mentioned here is the Venetian *bisato*, the eel of the Adriatic. According to experts, it is superior to the freshwater variety. The reason why I can't give a recipe for its preparation is that I can't bring myself to cook it or eat it. There are plenty of recipes for eel available elsewhere, if you want to cook that slithery creature.

The following recipes are for Italian uses of fish available in this country. These include bass, red snapper, salmon, swordfish, sea trout, scrod, sole, and others, in addition to shellfish.

 # Broeto

Venetian fish soup

Serves 6

1 quart water
2 pounds small mixed fish
2 fresh tomatoes
½ lemon
1 pound striped bass
1 pound red snapper or similar fish
2 tablespoons butter
3 tablespoons oil
1 clove garlic
Salt
1 tablespoon parsley, finely chopped (optional)

Bring the water to a boil in a large saucepan. Remove the heads from the small fish, and rinse them under running water. Place the fish into the boiling water, along with the tomatoes and the lemon half. Simmer for 30 minutes. Remove the fish from the water with a slotted spoon. Remove all visible fish bones, then purée the fish by pushing it through a sieve. Strain the water in which the fish was cooked. Put both the fish broth and the puréed fish back into the saucepan.

Separately poach the bass and the red snapper for about 20 minutes.

Remove the bass and snapper from the pot and remove the bones. Cut into pieces somewhat larger than bite size.

Heat the butter and oil in a skillet. Add the garlic. When the garlic is blonde, remove and place the fish pieces into the oil-butter mixture. Sauté on both sides. When the fish is slightly colored, add it, along with the oil and the butter, to the puréed fish. Simmer for 5 minutes. Taste and add salt if needed.

Serve in deep dishes, over slices of fried white bread, if desired, or by itself with a little parsley. This is nicely accompanied by a dry white wine: a Venegazù or a Tocai.

NOTE

This is an elegant fish soup albeit an expensive one. Also, it might get you in trouble with your fish market. The request for 2 pounds of mixed small fish and for 1 pound of bass and 1 pound of snapper can produce some nasty looks from the man who sells you the fish, unless he happens to have small slices handy. What I do is market with a friend who wants to try her hand at broeto. If a bass weighs 2 pounds, we have it cut in half (take the part with the tail if you can; it is better). Broeto is so delicious that it's worth the effort. In addition to all its virtues, this soup is even better if prepared several hours in advance. If you use fried bread, that has to be prepared at the moment of serving, however.

 # Zuppa di Pesce alla Livornese

Fish soup, Leghorn style

Serves 6

2 pounds assorted fish and shellfish (striped
  bass, swordfish, red snapper, halibut, shrimp,
  clams)
1 small onion
1 clove garlic
1 stalk of celery
½ teaspoon rosemary leaves
1 cup olive oil
1 tablespoon tomato paste
6 cups + 2 tablespoons water
1 teaspoon flour
½ cup white wine
Salt and freshly ground black pepper
6 slices stale Italian bread

Choose fish with a strong backbone. Avoid filets of any kind because they fall apart too easily and because the bones add flavor. Wash the fish carefully and reserve.

Chop the onion, garlic clove, celery stalk, and rosemary leaves. Heat the oil in a deep pot, then add the chopped vegetables. In a small bowl, dissolve the tomato paste in 2 tablespoons of water. Add the flour and mix until the flour is dissolved. Add this to the oil and stir. Pour in the wine and allow it to evaporate. Add the water and bring to a strong boil.

Add the fish to the boiling broth, starting with the toughest variety first. If swordfish is used, add it first, then the striped bass and the red snapper. Add halibut, shrimp, and clams about 10 minutes later. When all the seafood has been added, cook for about 10 minutes over medium heat. Add salt and pepper to taste.

When the fish soup has finished cooking, spoon out the pieces of fish and remove the large bones. Place the fish back into the broth.

Toast the bread slices in the oven. When they are golden, place a slice in each individual dish. Spoon the fish soup and fish pieces over the bread.

Serve this soup with the same white wine that you used in preparing the soup.

NOTE

If some soup is left over, use it as a sauce for pasta, adding 2 tablespoons of chopped parsley when you reheat it. Keep in mind, however, that no cheese should ever be added to the fish sauce.

 # Thick Fish Soup

Serves 6

½ cup olive oil

1 clove garlic

1 tablespoon fresh basil, finely chopped, or ½ teaspoon dried

1 can (16 oz.) whole tomatoes, seeded, but with their liquid

1 pound assorted fish (striped or sea bass, red snapper, fresh salmon)

½ pound sea scallops

5 cups water
Black pepper, freshly ground
Salt
2 tablespoons parsley, finely chopped
1 ounce Aquavit

Heat the oil in a deep saucepan. Add the garlic and the chopped fresh basil. When the basil is wilted, remove the garlic. Add the tomatoes (and dried basil if you are using that instead) and mix well with a wooden spoon.

Wash the fish carefully but don't remove the bones. Add the fish to the oil, starting with the thickest fish first. Start adding the water 1 cup at a time over medium heat, mixing constantly. The soup should boil gently. Add the scallops before adding the last cup of water. (If there is a great deal of water in the tomatoes, you might want to reduce the quantity of water to 4 cups.) Add the pepper and taste the soup before adding salt.

Add the parsley a couple of minutes before the soup is done. Add the Aquavit, let stand for a couple of minutes, and then serve. The total cooking time is about 30 minutes.

This soup is a combination of many fish soups from the past and it has been adapted to the types of fish we know in this country. It may be served either by itself or with side dishes of steamed rice. The steamed rice may also be added to the soup. The soup should be served in deep dishes or bowls.

It may sound incredible but the fish in this soup may be so rich that a red wine would go as well as a white.

Pesce in Cartoccio

Baked fish in aluminum foil

Serves 6

1 fish of about 3 pounds (striped bass, red
  snapper, or sea trout)
6 shrimps with their shells
6 mussels
1 tablespoon flour
½ teaspoon oregano
2 sprigs of fresh rosemary
Salt and freshly ground black pepper

(continued)

⅓ cup olive oil
½ cup dry white wine

Preheat oven to 475°. Rinse the fish and shrimps under running water and pat dry. Clean the mussels well. Place a sheet of aluminum foil (or parchment paper) on a flat surface. The paper should be about twice the size of the fish. Sprinkle the center of paper with half a tablespoon of flour. Place the fish on the flour. With a sharp knife, cut the spine of the fish where the head is attached but don't remove the head. Sprinkle the remaining flour over the fish. Sprinkle the oregano, rosemary, salt, and pepper into the cavity. Pour the oil and white wine over the fish, lifting the edges of the aluminum foil slightly so that no liquid will run off. Place the shrimps and mussels around the fish. Fold the foil over the fish and close tightly, folding and refolding the edges of the foil.

Place the wrapped fish in a large baking dish and bake for about 30 minutes (allow 10 minutes per pound of fish).

Move the fish, unopened, to a serving platter. Unwrap and fold the foil back. Serve as is. Removing the fish from the foil to a serving platter would cause you to lose some of the juice. Served in the foil, the fish remains surrounded by juice. Cutting the spine serves two purposes: the fish won't shrink or curl, and it is much easier to serve. Once one side of the fish has been eaten, simply lift the spine off and discard. No need to turn the fish before serving the other side.

Serve this fish with a dry white wine, the same wine that was used in cooking the fish. A light wine from northern Italy would be the best choice: a Lugana or a Pinot Grigio.

NOTE

To clean mussels, sprinkle them with a little flour, mix them with your hands so that all the mussels are coated, then rinse them under running water. All the sand will stick to the flour and wash off.

 Pesce al Vino Bianco

Fish in white wine

Serves 4 to 6

2 to 3 pounds fish (striped bass, sea bass, or any
fish of firm flesh. If you can find a large trout
or other fresh water fish, it would do well.)

(continued)

Fish Soup, Leghorn Style

2 scallions
2 small white onions
3 fresh mushrooms, as large as possible
Salt
2 tablespoons butter
1 carrot
1 stalk of celery
½ teaspoon peppercorns
3 cups dry white wine (approximately)
3 tablespoons parsley, finely chopped

Wash the fish under cold running water. Pat dry with paper towel. Place it on the tray of a fish poacher. Open the fish and cut the spine carefully where the head is attached with a pair of sharp kitchen scissors. *Don't remove head* and make sure you don't cut through the flesh in back of the neck. The fish will cook much better if the spine is cut and will be much easier to serve.

Chop the scallions, 1 small onion, and the mushrooms. If you have a food processor, use the sharp blade and run the motor for 1 second. Add salt and 2 tablespoons of butter to the mixture. Using a spoon, fill the inside of the fish with the mixture.

Place the tray with fish on it in the poacher. Place carrot, celery, the second onion, peppercorns, and some salt on and around the fish. Slowly pour the white wine over the fish, barely covering it. Place the lid on the fish poacher and simmer over low heat until the fish flakes easily — about 30 minutes, according to the size of the fish.

To make sure the fish is done, lift one side carefully and check if the spine is white. If there is the slightest trace of blood visible, cook 10 minutes longer. Nothing is worse than underdone fish.

Remove the tray from the pan and slide the fish onto a warm platter. Keep warm. Pour the poaching liquid through a sieve and add the chopped parsley. If the liquid seems too thin, mix a little butter with a small amount of flour and add. Otherwise, leave out the butter-flour. Reduce the liquid to about 1½ cups. Pour over the fish and serve at once.

The only accompaniment to this flavorful dish is boiled potatoes. The same wine as used in cooking should be served with it. I would recommend a white dry Tocai.

Pesce Lesso con Salsa

Poached fish, served with sauce

Serves 6 to 8

1 small onion
1 carrot
2 stalks of celery
2 bay leaves
½ lemon
Water
1 striped bass, approximately 4 pounds
1 teaspoon peppercorns
½ teaspoon cloves
Salt

Place all the vegetables and spices, as well as the lemon half, on the bottom of a fish poacher. Wash the fish carefully under cold running water. Place the fish on the tray and pour lukewarm water into the poacher until the fish is barely covered. Turn on the heat very low and bring the water to a boil as slowly as possible. When it starts boiling, the fish should be almost done. Test with a fork: if it flakes easily, turn off the heat. If it is not ready, continue to simmer for a few additional minutes.

If the fish is not served immediately, lift the tray out of the poacher and place it diagonally over the pan. Cover with aluminum foil or wax paper. The fish will be out of the water but will be kept warm by the steaming water underneath.

Serve with mayonnaise or *Salsa di Capperi* (see page 27), or *Salsa al Dragoncello* (see page 25).

Serve only boiled potatoes with it. Sprinkle the potatoes with a little chopped parsley for looks. A gentle Soave di Verona should be drunk with this dish.

 ## Sardelle in Saor

Fish, sweet and sour

Serves 4

1 pound sardelle, or smelts or whitebait
Oil for deep frying

(continued)

2 tablespoons flour
½ cup olive oil
2 cups white wine vinegar
2 medium-sized onions, sliced
2 tablespoons pine nuts
2 tablespoons small raisins
Salt

Clean the smelts, heads removed, and dry well on a paper towel. Heat the oil in a saucepan until a drop of water dropped on the surface will make a sizzling sound. Spread the flour on a wooden board and roll the fish in the flour. They should be lightly coated. Deep-fry to a crisp. Remove the fish from the oil with a slotted spatula and place the fish on paper towels to absorb excess oil (thrifty Venetians will pour leftover oil in a bottle and use it the next time they fry fish).

In a saucepan heat the olive oil and add the sliced onions. Sauté until pale blonde. Add the vinegar, reduce heat, and simmer for about 5 minutes.

In an earthenware or porcelain dish make a layer of fried fish in neat rows, overlapping slightly. Sprinkle a few raisins and pine nuts over the fish; pour a little of the oil-onion-vinegar mixture over it. Make another layer of fish, add nuts and raisins and some of the liquid mixture. Place a lid on the dish and let it stand in a cool place, but not in the refrigerator, for about 24 hours. Serve as a first course.

No wine would be served with this dish because the vinegar would kill it.

NOTE

This is the classic recipe and definitely of Oriental origin. Nowadays some people prepare it without the raisins or the pine nuts.

For a special Venetian holiday in mid-July this dish is prepared with delicate filets of sole instead of sardelle, a far more expensive version. Sardelle in Saor, especially if served in one of those shiny brown earthenware casseroles, look marvelous and intriguing on a buffet.

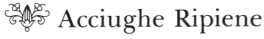 Acciughe Ripiene

Stuffed fresh anchovies

Serves 6

2 pounds fresh anchovies
½ cup very fine breadcrumbs from stale white bread

½ cup parsley, chopped very fine
3 tablespoons capers
Very little salt
¾ cup olive oil
Juice of 1 lemon
2-3 tablespoons water

Preheat oven to 375°. Wash anchovies under cold running water. Remove the heads but leave the spines. If you have a food processor, place enough stale bread in the container to make ½ cup breadcrumbs. Run the motor for 30 seconds; the crumbs will be very fine. If you don't own a processor, place the bread between 2 sheets of wax paper and roll with a rolling pin.

Wash the parsley and dry it well. Place it in the food processor and run the motor for another 30 seconds. If, instead, you use a *mezzaluna*, make sure the parsley is very dry. Otherwise it will stick to the sides of the blade and will make chopping more difficult.

Chop the capers (preferably large ones, preserved in vinegar; if capers preserved in salt are used, wash before using). Mix the parsley, capers, and almost all the breadcrumbs together. Reserve 1 tablespoon of breadcrumbs for later. Moisten the mixture with a few drops of oil. Open the anchovies and, with your hands, stuff a little of the mixture into each one. Lightly press each closed with your fingers.

Coat an 8″ by 12″ baking dish with a little oil. Place the fish in a row, then make a second row. The tops of the fish should overlap the fish in the preceding row. Continue until all the fish are placed in neat rows. Salt lightly (capers are salty).

Mix the oil and lemon juice with a wire whisk and add the water. Pour this gently over the fish, being careful not to disturb them. Sprinkle the rest of the breadcrumbs over them. Place in preheated oven and bake for 10 minutes. Place under broiler for an additional 5 minutes or until the tops are crisp.

Serve with additional lemon juice, if desired.

I learned this recipe in Portofino. It was served with a dry white wine called Portofino. There is not enough of that wine for export but you might be able to find a Coronata, equally fresh dry and delicious.

NOTE

You might think that stuffing anchovies is too much trouble. It isn't. Once you have seen how much stuffing the first little fish can take, it only takes seconds for each one.

You might not be able to find fresh anchovies. Whitebait will do, or even small smelts. Be careful with the latter, however. Their flesh is not as firm as that of anchovies and they might fall apart when you serve them. Use a long spatula to serve them.

Trancio de Pesce Spada o Tonno alla Griglia

Boston scrod (or swordfish), baked or broiled

Serves 4 to 6

1 thick slice Boston scrod or swordfish, about 2
   pounds
1 teaspoon salt
½ stick butter
2 scallions, chopped
6 anchovy filets
1 teaspoon capers
1 teaspoon parsley, finely chopped

Preheat oven to 450°. Coat a baking dish with oil. The dish should be large enough to hold the fish comfortably.

Wash the fish and pat it dry with a paper towel. Place in the oiled dish and salt lightly. Place the dish in the center of preheated oven and bake for about 12 minutes or until the fish flakes easily (exact cooking time depends on thickness of fish).

If you prefer to use the broiler, place the fish in broiler for about 6 to 8 minutes. Whether oven or broiler are used, the fish should not be turned because it breaks easily.

To prepare the sauce, melt the butter in a small saucepan, then add the scallions but don't allow them to brown. Chop the anchovy filets, capers (if capers packed in salt are used, rinse before adding), and parsley. Remove the fish from the oven or broiler and pour the sauce over it.

Serve immediately accompanied by boiled potatoes. Prepared with the caper-anchovy sauce, it makes a perfect main course after a *risotto* or a pasta dish. It also lends itself well as first course for an elegant dinner, followed by a veal or chicken dish. The wine should be a good Soave di Verona or a Verdicchio.

NOTE

We don't have any scrod in Italy but this is one way of cooking fresh tuna or swordfish. Scrod has a lighter flesh and takes less time to cook. I consider it one of America's finest fish. If none of these are available you might want to try shark; you will find it delicious.

Sogliole Fredde al Vino Bianco

Cold filets of sole in white wine

Serves 4

1 pound of sole or flounder filets
8 large fresh shrimps
1 cup dry white wine, a little more if needed
Juice of ½ lemon
¼ cup olive oil
2 tablespoons capers, chopped fine
Dash of black pepper, if desired

Preheat oven to 400°. Wash the fish filets and pat dry. With the tips of your fingers, go over them very lightly, lengthwise; first in one direction then in the opposite. You will feel if there are any tiny bones on the sides. Remove them, of course.

Place the fish filets in a shallow baking dish. Clean and devein the shrimp and place alongside. Pour the wine over the filets and shrimps. They should be almost covered. (The shrimps are thicker than the filets and will stick out a little; that's all right.)

Place the baking dish in the center of the preheated oven. Remove when the shrimps are pink and the filets flake easily (about 10 minutes). Let stand in their juices until cool.

Remove the fish and shrimp from the liquid. Cut the fish into bite-sized pieces and cut the shrimps in half lengthwise. Divide the filets and shrimps into 4 portions and place in individual little bowls.

Pour the wine in which fish has cooked into a bowl. Add the lemon juice and oil and beat with a wire whisk or an electric mixer until the mixture is smooth and slightly thick. Divide the sauce as evenly as possible into 4 portions and pour over the individual dishes. Let each marinate for an hour or so.

Chop the capers as finely as possible and sprinkle a little over the center of each dish shortly before serving. Grate a little pepper on top if desired. No salt is needed; the capers are salty enough.

Serve as a first course with lemon wedges. Elegant!

Serve the same wine with the dish as was used in cooking; a Verdicchio or a Durello. If both are hard to find where you live, a Soave would do very well.

Spigola in Forno

Baked striped bass or red snapper

Serves 6

1 striped bass or red snapper, approximately 3
    pounds
2 tablespoons butter
2 tablespoons fine breadcrumbs
1 cup dry white wine
Juice of 1 lemon
1 clove garlic, chopped fine
2 tablespoons capers, chopped if they are large
Salt
¾ cup olive oil
2 tablespoons parsley, chopped, and several
    sprigs for decoration

Preheat oven to 375°. Wash the fish under cold running water. Pat dry with a paper towel. With a sharp knife or with kitchen scissors, cut the spine where it is attached to the head, being careful not to detach the head. Cutting the spine will prevent the fish from losing its shape while baking. Also, when half of the fish has been served, the bone is easily discarded with no need to turn the fish before serving the second half.

Coat an oval or rectangular ovenproof dish with oil. Place the fish in the center of the dish. With a sharp knife, make a couple of diagonal incisions into the skin, being careful not to cut deeply into the flesh. This will prevent skin from breaking while the fish bakes.

Melt the butter in a small skillet and add the breadcrumbs. Cook until golden, then pour over the fish. Mix the wine with the lemon juice and pour over the fish. Mix the garlic with the capers, and sprinkle over fish; salt very lightly (capers are salty).

Pour the oil over the fish and bake in preheated oven for about 1 hour. Remove from the oven, and test with a fork: there must not be the slightest trace of pink near the spine. If there is, bake the fish 10 minutes longer. The exact cooking time is hard to give, since ovens vary and also because a few ounces of fish might make a difference. Sprinkle with parsley.

Serve with boiled potatoes but don't serve a salad with this dish. Baked oil and raw oil simply don't go together.

A Pinot Grigio or a Soave, both dry northern Italian wines, will go well with this.

NOTE

Fish from the Mediterranean are different from fish from U.S. waters. But I find a striped bass or a red snapper to be as good as any fish anywhere. Both of them lend themselves eminently to this preparation.

 Pesce Spada con Verdure

Swordfish on a bed of vegetables

Serves 8

½ cup oil
2 medium-sized onions, chopped
2 medium-sized heads Boston lettuce
1 cup fresh spinach
1 carrot, washed and scraped
Salt and freshly ground black pepper
1 can (8 oz.) peeled Italian tomatoes
1 swordfish steak 1" thick, about 3 pounds
1 cup dry Vermouth (white Italian)
1 teaspoon dried oregano
10 black olives, Italian or domestic
6 anchovy filets (optional)

Preheat oven to 375°. Heat the oil in a large skillet then add the onions. Remove the tips of the lettuce leaves and chop the rest; add to the onions. Chop the spinach and add to the onion-lettuce mixture. Cut the carrot into thin strips and add. Add salt and pepper to taste. Cover the skillet and cook over medium heat for 2 to 3 minutes. Add the tomatoes and cook uncovered for about 5 minutes or until the liquid is almost all absorbed.

Spread the vegetable mixture over the bottom of an ovenproof dish. Cut the swordfish into strips about 3 inches wide, and place on top of the vegetables. Pour the Vermouth over it. Sprinkle oregano over the fish. If Italian olives are available, chop the olives and sprinkle over fish. If you are using large glossy California olives, halve them and arrange in a pattern: they will only be decoration as they have very little taste. Place the dish in oven and bake for about 20 minutes. If desired, garnish with strips of anchovies before serving.

Swordfish is a rich and tasty fish. It would overpower a delicate wine like a Soave or a Lugana. The whites from Capri and Ischia are now available in many parts of the United States and would hold their own. If they are not available, a white wine from Tuscany or a Frascati (both quite fruity) will do very well.

 # Pesce Spada al Pomodoro

Swordfish with tomatoes

Serves 4 to 5

2 large slices of swordfish, each ¾-inch thick;
   each slice should weigh about 1 ½ pounds
½ cup oil
1 tablespoon flour
2 tablespoons butter
4 large ripe tomatoes, or the equivalent canned
   tomatoes peeled, seeded and chopped
Salt and freshly ground black pepper
½ teaspoon oregano (optional)
2 filets of anchovies
1 teaspoon capers

Wash the swordfish steaks and pat them dry with a paper towel. Remove the gray skin all around them. Heat the oil in a skillet large enough to hold the fish steaks without crowding. Coat the fish lightly with flour and place them in the hot oil. Brown the fish on one side then, very carefully with a long spatula, turn and brown on other side. Reduce heat to medium.

Melt the butter in a saucepan and add tomatoes, salt, and pepper, and oregano if desired. Simmer over low heat.

Chop the anchovies and add them to the fish.

When the liquid from the tomatoes is absorbed, add the tomatoes to the fish. Continue cooking over medium heat, moving the fish every now and then to prevent sticking. Turn once, very carefully, so as not to break the fish. The total cooking time should be about 30 to 35 minutes, depending on the thickness of the fish steaks. When the fish flakes easily and is almost done, sprinkle the capers over the fish.

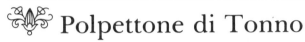

Transfer the steaks to a warm platter, pour the cooking liquid over the fish, and serve with boiled potatoes.

A Pinot Grigio should be drunk with it.

NOTE

Go easy on the salt in this dish. Anchovies and capers are salty. If the dish should be too rich for your taste, pour off some oil before adding the tomatoes to the fish.

Polpettone di Tonno

Tuna loaf

Serves 4 to 6

1 can (6½ oz.) tuna
½ cup Parmesan cheese, freshly grated
1 egg
Pinch of nutmeg, freshly grated)
½ teaspoon dry mustard (optional)
Water
Capers

Drain the tuna and place in a bowl. Break up with a fork then purée with a pestle until smooth. Add the Parmesan and mix well, either with the back of a tablespoon or with a pestle. Add the egg and the nutmeg, add the mustard if desired, and continue working the mixture, first in the bowl with the spoon or pestle, then with your hands. Shape the mixture into a long, narrow loaf and wrap in cheesecloth or a linen napkin as tightly as possible. Tie knots at both ends.

Bring the water to a boil in a long, narrow saucepan. Place the fish loaf gently into the boiling water and simmer over medium heat for about 30 minutes, covered; don't allow the water to evaporate.

Let the pan cool for a while, then lift the loaf out of the water and place it, still wrapped, on your wooden board. Allow it to cool completely. Unwrap carefully and, when the loaf is cold, slice it with a very sharp knife. Place the slices on a platter and garnish the loaf with slices of lemon and wedges of hard-boiled eggs. Add a few capers, if desired, and serve with mayonnaise as either a first course or a main course.

This dish requires a rather sturdy white wine, such as a white Tuscan wine or a white Corvo from Sicily.

NOTE

> This dish can easily be changed into a much larger course by simply doubling the ingredients.
>
> If you want to present the Polpettone di Tonno on an elegant buffet, hollow out a dozen cherry tomatoes carefully, salt them, turn them upside down on a platter to let all water drain out, then fill them with a rather thick mayonnaise and place them around the tuna loaf. In Italy, where cherry tomatoes are unknown, we use plum tomatoes (also known as Italian tomatoes) halved.
>
> We have always said that fish and cheese don't mix. We still do. This recipe is the one exception. It comes from Friuli and Friulani are exceptional people.

 ## Scampi all'Olio e Limone

Shrimps with oil and lemon

Serves 4

40 medium-sized raw shrimp
2 quarts of water
Pinch of salt
⅓ cup olive oil (it ought to be the finest you can
  get)
Juice of ½ lemon
Black pepper, freshly ground

Wash the shrimps under cold running water but don't peel. Fill a fairly large pot with water and add the salt, then the shrimp. There should be plenty of water on top of the shrimp and plenty of space between the level of the water and the rim of the pot. Place over high heat and bring to a strong boil. Turn off the heat almost immediately; the shrimp should be a lovely pink. Let them stand until they are cool enough to touch. Peel and, if necessary, devein.

In a small bowl, beat the oil and lemon juice with a fork. Place the shrimp in a bowl (glass or porcelain; avoid metal and particularly wood). Pour the oil and lemon mixture over the shrimp, add the freshly ground pepper and serve lukewarm.

Scampi, in Venice where they come from, are always served lukewarm because they are freshly cooked. They are served in what we would consider soup dishes rather than in fancy bowls on a bed of lettuce. The pepper is added at the last moment.

Venetians are known as *ciaccoloni*, or as being very talkative. They are, but I have noticed recently that, when they eat *scampi*, they are quiet and give their tastebuds a silent chance.

Scampi have become as expensive as gold. They are served with a delicate white wine — something like a Tocai.

NOTE

The trouble with this recipe is only that scampi are not shrimp, nor are they prawns. They are scampi, tender soft little curly pink creatures of the Adriatic. Their flavor is so delicate that they require nothing more than the seasoning given above, nor do they usually need to be deveined. Shrimp, no matter how fresh, are tough by comparison. They are also larger. Ten shrimp per person might be a little much; you might want to make it eight, particularly if you want to serve this as a first course. Whether they are scampi or shrimp, however, refrigerating them kills the flavor.

Poultry
Pollame

Of all the foods I have enjoyed since my childhood, poultry has changed the most it seems to me. When I was a little girl my family was sure that I would some day become a surgeon, only because of the skill with which I was able at a tender age to eat chicken with a knife and fork leaving the bones completely clean. Medicine had nothing to do with it. I just loved chicken and was not going to forego the tiniest morsel (fingers were, of course, taboo; at least on the rare occasions when I was permitted to eat with my parents). Now that no one prevents me from using my fingers I don't enjoy the chicken so much anymore — not as much as those scrawny flavorful chickens of my childhood anyway. I still eat them, of course, and I prepare them in all sorts of ways, but I take precautions when I buy them.

First of all, I try to buy smaller birds. It might be just an impression, but I believe that the fatter and bigger the chickens are, the less taste they have. Then I cut off all those bits of yellow fat at the tail end and around the thighs. And I do that whether I intend to fry, broil, stew, or boil the bird. Even so, the amount of fat in chickens is incredible.

I love boiled chicken with lots of vegetables, but I now cook it a day ahead of time. When it's done, I refrigerate it until I can skim off all the fat that comes to the surface. Otherwise the soup is pretty nearly inedible, at least for my taste.

A few years ago I spent some time in Puerto Rico, in the house of friends who spend their winters there. I feel I don't know a country until I know its markets, so I went marketing. I bought a couple of local chickens. Most unprepossessing they were. Compared to ours, they were underdeveloped and from a cosmetic viewpoint they had nothing to recommend them. I boiled them in very little water with a lot of local vegetables, grown by my hosts (what you buy in the markets comes from the U.S. and is chosen for its durability rather than for its flavor). When they were done, the chickens themselves tasted like real country chickens and so reminded me of my childhood that I didn't dare touch them with my fingers! But the real joy was the broth: I

refrigerated it and there was almost no fat but there was enough gelatin for six eggs in jelly!

Of course there is no need to go to Puerto Rico for tasty chickens: fresh herbs can do a lot for a chicken born to be bland. A sprig of fresh rosemary placed inside of a roasting chicken or rosemary leaves sprinkled over the pieces of a broiler can make a lot of difference. Freshly ground pepper, added at the moment of serving the bird, will help. But what has to be avoided is camouflaging the chicken instead of seasoning it. Don't overseason (especially with oregano)! Even in its present oversophisticated version, a chicken is a marvelous invention. Let it give you all the taste it has.

 # Pollo Arrosto al Rosmarino

Roast chicken with rosemary

Serves 6

1 2½- to 3-pound roasting chicken
2 tablespoons butter
3 sprigs rosemary, each about 2 inches long
Salt and freshly ground black pepper

Preheat the oven to 325°. Wash the chicken both inside and outside and dry with a paper towel. Place it on a flat surface, breast side up and, with a rapid strong movement of the palm of your hand, break the breastbone. You will hear a slight crack and the breast will be slightly flattened. Remove the fat from the tail end of the chicken and discard; it usually has a slight odor. With your fingers, loosen the skin over the breast and place a bit of butter (about ½ tablespoon) under the skin.

Place a sprig of rosemary inside the chicken and rub a little coarse salt into the cavity. Hold the chicken upside down and grate a little fresh pepper into it. Tuck a sprig of rosemary under each wing (between the wing and the breast). Tie the chicken if you find it necessary.

Place chicken *on its side* in a roasting pan. Place the pan in the center of the preheated oven. Restrain from opening the oven for about 20 minutes. After 20 minutes, the skin should have begun to get crisp. Rub it with a little butter and sprinkle a little coarse salt on the skin (the butter will prevent the salt from sliding off). Continue roasting for another 20 minutes, then turn the chicken on its other side; rub it with remaining butter, sprinkle another bit of coarse salt over it, and roast it for about 25 additional minutes. Increase the

heat to 400° and roast it for another 20 minutes (10 minutes on each side). The chicken should be light brown. The total cooking time is about 1 hour, 35 minutes, depending on the weight of the chicken. Test the thigh bone with a fork: juice should be clear without any trace of blood.

Remove the chicken from the pan and place it on a warmed platter, turning the chicken breast side down for a couple of minutes. This will allow the juices to flow into the breast which is the driest part of the bird. Serve the chicken with roasted potatoes or *Patate alla Veneziana* (see pages 289-90) and a vegetable that takes kindly to the taste of rosemary, such as *Asparagi Fritti* (see pages 276-77) or *Carciofi alla Milanese* (see page 273).

A fine white wine is required: a Durello or a Lugana.

NOTE

Anyone knows how to roast a chicken but there are 2 things about this recipe that are important: to break the breast bone and to cook the chicken on its side. The first makes the breast juicier and makes the chicken easier to carve. The latter makes for a much more even color. If you roast it lying on its back it will get much browner on top than on the back. If you want to turn it upside down to brown the back, you will have a hard time keeping it in that position.

 Pollo al Sale

Chicken in salt

Serves 4 to 6

1 2½-pound broiling chicken
1 sprig fresh rosemary (3 inches long) or 2
   teaspoons dried
Black pepper, freshly ground
10 slices unsmoked bacon or fresh pork fat
   (called "fatback" in some parts of the country)
2 to 3 cups coarse salt

Preheat the oven to 350°. Wash the chicken and dry it with a paper towel. Remove the giblets from inside and reserve for another purpose. Place the rosemary inside the chicken and add a little pepper.

Tuck the wing tips under the wings and tie the legs together. Cover the chicken all over with the bacon or pork fat. Be sure the chicken is totally covered. There is no need to tie the bacon or pork fat around the chicken; it will cling to the skin, provided the slices are not too thick.

Place the chicken in a pot not much larger than the bird itself. Pour coarse salt over it until the chicken is totally covered. In this country, kosher salt is the best for this purpose. The salt has to be really coarse. Don't be afraid to use too much; it won't harm the chicken.

Cover the pot tightly and place it in the center of the preheated oven. Refrain from opening the oven, and don't remove the cover for 1½ to 2 hours, depending upon the weight of the chicken.

When finished, remove the pot from the oven and uncover. There will be a brownish crust on the salt. Break the crust with a strong spoon. Try to do it all at one time, so that the salt will break into a few pieces but won't be pulverized. Lift out the chicken. Remove the bacon or pork fat and discard. Place the chicken on a warmed platter, untie the legs, carve, and serve with *Patate alla Veneziana* (see pages 289-90).

Serve this chicken with a white Tuscan wine.

NOTE

This recipe is somewhat disconcerting for people who have never tried it. I believe that it is one of the most delightful ways of cooking a chicken. All the flavor is sealed in by the salt and you don't have to move a finger while it is cooking.

I don't add any salt to the chicken because a few grains might cling to it when you remove it from the salt. And it is better to add a bit of salt when you eat it rather than to oversalt it.

In some restaurants in the Italian countryside, especially in the outskirts of Milan, this same way of preparing chicken is done with clay. You order your chicken and watch the cook wrap it in wet clay. An hour or so later it is served. The waiters are very adept at hitting the clay once with a small mallet and lifting the chicken out of its wrapping.

 # Pollo al Latte

Chicken in milk

Serves 6

1 3-pound roasting chicken, cut up into serving
   pieces
2 tablespoons butter
1 generous teaspoon dried rosemary
Salt and freshly ground black pepper
2 cups milk

Wash the chicken pieces and pat dry. Cut off the fat from the rear, as well as the very fatty skin around the second joint.

Over high heat, melt the butter in a large skillet. The skillet should be wide enough to hold all the chicken pieces without crowding. Add the chicken pieces, followed by the rosemary. Cook uncovered, turning the pieces frequently to brown all sides. This should take approximately 20 minutes; during these 20 minutes add the salt and pepper, using rather more salt than you normally would (about 1½ teaspoons).

When the chicken is golden, add the milk. Bring the milk to a boil and reduce the heat. Cover and simmer over very low heat for about 20 minutes. The exact cooking time is hard to give because it depends upon the thickness of the chicken pieces; total cooking time is between 40 and 45 minutes. Remove the pieces and place on warmed platter. Turn the heat to high and, with a spoon, scrape all the bits of chicken off the bottom to blend with the milk. Pour the sauce in which chicken was cooked over the chicken pieces and serve.

A vegetable, any vegetable, may be served after the chicken. The chicken, with its sauce of butter, milk, and rosemary, should be eaten by itself. Any other flavor added to it would detract from it rather than enhance it.

A good white wine, like a Durello, should accompany the chicken dish.

NOTE

This is an adaptation of a recipe found in Milanese cookbooks of the early nineteenth century. The original calls for cream instead of milk and that seems a little rich for our cholesterol-conscious generation. One of these cookbooks is called The Cuisine for Frail Stomachs. Hardly.

 Pollo al Vino Bianco con Funghi

Chicken in white wine with mushrooms

Serves 6

½ cup imported dried mushrooms
1 cup water
1 3-pound roasting chicken, cut up into serving pieces
1 tablespoon flour
½ stick butter
1 cup dry white wine
Salt and freshly ground black pepper

Place the mushrooms in a bowl with 1 cup of water and let soak for about 15 minutes. Wash the chicken pieces and pat them dry with a paper towel.

Melt the butter in a skillet large enough to hold all the chicken pieces without crowding. Spread the flour on a flat surface and coat the chicken pieces lightly. When the butter is hot, add the floured chicken pieces and brown over high heat on all sides, turning them frequently to avoid sticking. When golden, add the wine and reduce the heat. Add the salt and pepper and cook slowly for about 20 minutes. Add the mushrooms with their water (a lot of the taste is in the water). Cover the skillet and cook over low heat for about 20 minutes longer. The total cooking time is approximately 45 minutes, depending on the size of the chicken pieces.

When the chicken is cooked, remove the pieces from the skillet and place on a warmed platter. Turn the heat to high and, with a spoon scrape all the bits of chicken from the bottom of the pan. Blend with the sauce and serve with the chicken.

The wine used in cooking should, of course, be served with the chicken: a Durello or a Pinot Grigio would go well.

NOTE

If you can't find imported dry mushrooms you may want to use fresh white mushrooms instead. Fresh mushrooms need no soaking, of course, but they should be cleaned carefully and the sandy parts of the stems should be cut off. Because fresh mushrooms have much less taste than the dried variety (which are wild mushrooms), use a full cup instead of ½.

 **Pollo Lesso con Besciamella**

Boiled chicken with white sauce

Serves 6

1 3-pound stewing chicken
Water
1 carrot
1 stalk of celery
1 small onion
2 bay leaves
Salt
Rice for risotto (see page 95)
1 cup besciamella (see pages 22-23)
¾ cup Parmesan cheese, freshly grated

Wash the chicken and pat it dry with a paper towel. In a saucepan not much larger than the chicken, bring the water to a boil and add the carrot, celery, onion, bay leaves, and salt (about 1 teaspoon). Place the chicken in the saucepan. It should be held in shape by the sides of the saucepan. The water should cover it but not drown it. Reduce the heat to medium and cook, well covered, for about 1 hour. Check every now and then to see that the liquid hasn't evaporated. If necessary, add a little water. When the chicken is done, drain the broth into another pot but leave a little with the chicken. Keep the chicken warm over very low heat.

Using the broth of the chicken, plus a little additional water, prepare a basic *risotto*. Meanwhile, make a *besciamella*, keeping it rather liquid. Add the Parmesan cheese to the *besciamella*.

Heat a large oval platter by running hot water over it. Make a bed of *risotto* in the center of the platter. Lift the chicken out of its pot. Clip the wing tips and remove the bones of the drumsticks. If desired, remove the skin. Place the chicken on top of the *risotto* and cover it with the *besciamella*. Serve immediately.

This dish is a complete meal and requires nothing but fruit as dessert. A dry white wine, a Soave di Verona or a Pinot Grigio, should be served with it.

NOTE

Except for the risotto and the besciamella, this dish may be prepared ahead of time. (The besciamella may be prepared a short time in advance. Place a couple pats of butter on top to avoid formation of skin.)

Discard the bay leaves, but the broth that remained in the pot with the chicken as well as the vegetables may be used to start a minestrone. Remember, in Italy food never is thrown out.

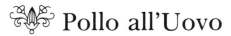

Pollo all'Uovo

Chicken with eggs

Serves 6

1 2 ½ to 3-pound roasting chicken
4 tablespoons + 1 teaspoon butter
4 tablespoons olive oil
3 cups water
3 cups chicken broth (homemade if possible)
Salt and freshly ground black pepper
2 egg yolks
Juice of 1 large lemon

Wash the chicken and pat it dry with a paper towel. Remove the wing tips but don't truss it or tie it. Put the liver aside; reserve the gizzards for another use.

Place the 4 tablespoons of butter and the oil in a saucepan not much larger than the chicken. Heat the butter-oil mixture but don't allow it to brown. Add the chicken. The sides of the saucepan should help retain the shape of the chicken. Reduce the heat to medium-low then add the water and broth. The chicken should not be totally submerged in liquid.

Place a sheet of wax paper over the saucepan and place the lid on top. Put a weight on top of the lid. Gently cook the chicken over low heat for about 1 hour. Toward the end of the cooking time, uncover the pot and taste the cooking broth. Add salt and pepper to taste. When the chicken is done, the liquid should be almost totally evaporated. Poke the thigh bone with a fork; the juice that comes out should be colorless. If there is the slightest trace of blood, add a little broth and cook, covered as before, for a few minutes longer.

Heat a large oval platter by running hot water over it. Remove the chicken from the pot and place it on the platter. Keep warm.

Melt the 1 teaspoon of butter in a small skillet. Chop the chicken liver coarsely and sauté for a couple of minutes. Don't overcook it or it will get tough.

Mix the egg yolks in a bowl with the lemon juice until well blended. Add the sautéed chicken liver and mix well. Add the egg mixture to the liquid left in the saucepan. Saucepan should still be hot but flame should be turned off. Egg mixture should be warm but should not cook.

Pour mixture over chicken and serve immediately. Serve with steamed rice or boiled potatoes and with a green vegetable.

I would serve a Soave di Verona with this dish. The other day I met someone who stated that it takes 3 wines to go with a chicken: one to accompany the wings (white and sturdy), one with the breast (very delicate and white), and finally a light red to go with the dark meat. I bow to him but I shan't complicate my life to that extent. It's an amusing thought, though.

NOTE

There are 2 ways of serving this chicken. It may be cut into pieces as soon as it is done, then covered with the sauce, or it may be left whole, covered with the egg sauce and carved at the table. Somehow I find the latter method more elegant.

 Pollo Ripieno Disossato

Stuffed boneless chicken

Serves 6

1 3-pound roasting or frying chicken
2 cups water
5 slices of white bread
1 cup Parmesan cheese, freshly grated
2 egg yolks
Pinch of nutmeg, freshly grated
Salt and freshly ground black pepper
½ teaspoon rosemary
¼ cup dry white wine

Preheat the oven to 375°. Wash the chicken both inside and out. Pat dry with a paper towel. Holding the chicken by the wings, sear the leg joints over a high flame for a few seconds. Turn the chicken around and, holding it by the legs, sear the wing tips. The yellowish skin will peel off easily.

Place the gizzards in a saucepan along with the water and simmer.

Place the chicken on a table, holding it neckside up. Pull back the skin from the neck and feel for the wishbone; break it and remove it. With a short, very sharp knife, cut the flesh from the bone, being careful not to cut the skin of the chicken. Stay as close to the bone as possible. Continue to pull down skin until you reach the second joint. Cut through the joint, pull down the skin, and remove the bone from the second joint. The wings and drumsticks should not be removed. Add the carcass of the chicken to the gizzards. The "Pope's nose" should stay attached to the chicken.

Remove the rind from the bread, and break the slices into a mixing bowl. Add the Parmesan cheese, egg yolks, nutmeg, salt, and pepper; mix well. Moisten with 2 tablespoons of cooking liquid from the gizzards. Mix again. The mixture should be firm but not hard; if it seems too stiff, add a few more drops of broth.

Hold the boned chicken neckside up and salt it inside and out. Sprinkle half the rosemary into the chicken cavity. Stuff the chicken with the bread and cheese mixture. Sew both openings, then lay the chicken on its back and pat it lightly to give it shape.

Fold the wing tips under the wings, cross the legs, tie a string around the "Pope's nose," then around the crossed legs. Pull the string up and under wings. Tie in front.

Place the chicken in a baking dish. Pour ½ cup of the gizzard broth and ⅓ cup wine into the dish. Cover the chicken with aluminum foil and bake in preheated oven for 20 minutes. Baste occasionally. Remove the foil, reduce the heat to 350°, and continue baking for 50 minutes longer, basting every 10 or 15 minutes. The total cooking time is 70 minutes.

Remove the chicken from the baking dish and place on warmed platter. Pour the sauce from the dish over the chicken.

A dry white wine is required — one with a bit of personality because of the large amount of Parmesan in the stuffing. A Corvo Bianco would be perfect. Corvo is a fine wine that has recently become available in this country.

Petti di Pollo alla Crema

Chicken breasts with cream

Serves 6

6 *whole or boned chicken breasts*
2 *tablespoons flour*
4 *tablespoons grated Parmesan cheese*
1 *teaspoon thyme*
1 *tablespoon fresh chopped rosemary or ½*
   teaspoon dried
½ *teaspoon dried sage*
1 *cup light cream*
Salt and freshly ground black pepper (optional)

Preheat the oven to 350°. If you are using whole chicken breasts, bone them. Cut the meat into halves. Beat the cutlets lightly with a wooden mallet without breaking apart the meat; just flatten the breasts slightly.

Mix half the Parmesan cheese with the flour. Spread the mixture on a wooden board, and coat the chicken breasts on both sides. Arrange the breasts in a shallow ovenproof baking dish. Sprinkle the chicken evenly with a mixture of the thyme, rosemary, and sage. Cover with the cream.

Place the dish in the preheated oven, but don't cover it. After about 5 minutes, pierce each chicken breast lightly with a fork and move them slightly so that they won't stick to the bottom. Sprinkle with the remaining Parmesan cheese. If salt or pepper is desired, this is the moment to add it, but remember that the Parmesan is slightly salty and that this is enough for most palates.

Bake for about 10 more minutes. The exact cooking time can't be given because the thickness of the chicken breasts varies. When done, they should be pale blonde and golden at the edges and not dry but soft.

Serve the chicken either in the baking dish or move to a decorative platter. If the chicken breasts have to be transferred, warm the platter and remove the breasts from the baking dish very carefully. Place the breasts in the center of the platter and surround them with *Riso in Bianco* (pages 118-19).

A rather robust white wine would go well with the chicken-and-cheese dish: something like a Verdicchio, a Bianco di Toscana, or a Frascati.

 # Petti di Pollo al Vermouth

Chicken breasts with Vermouth

Serves 4

2 chicken breasts, boned and cut in half
1 tablespoon flour
Salt and freshly ground black pepper
3 tablespoons butter
1 tablespoon oil
1 cup dry white Vermouth

Place a sheet of wax paper over the chicken breasts and flatten lightly with a rolling pin or the flat side of a wooden mallet.

Spread the flour on a working surface, place the breasts on the flour, and turn them to coat them lightly. Salt and pepper lightly.

In a large skillet, melt the butter over medium heat and add the oil. Sauté the chicken breasts for about 2 to 3 minutes on each side, depending on the thickness of the meat. If your skillet is not large enough to hold the breasts all at one time without touching each other, sauté only 2 halves at a time.

When the breasts are golden and done (test with fork), remove them from the skillet, place on warmed platter, and keep warm.

Add the Vermouth to the skillet. With a spatula, deglaze by scraping the particles loose from the bottom of the pan. Reduce the liquid to about 2 tablespoons, then pour this over the chicken breasts and serve with *Riso in Bianco* (pages 118-19), or *Carciofi all Milanese* (page 273).

A Sauvignon (the grapes came from France but are doing splendidly in Northern Italy) would add an ideal touch.

NOTE

Personally, I prefer to serve accompanying dishes separately, particularly if the main dish has a sauce. I hate to see it run into the vegetables or into the rice. It makes serving a little more complicated but it is worth it. By suggesting rice as accompaniment I am thinking of an American household. In Italy, rice dishes are usually a first course and are rarely served with the main course.

Some people don't particularly like the taste of Vermouth. In this recipe it might be replaced with a dry white wine. Use 1½ cups of wine instead of 1 cup of Vermouth.

Spezzatino di Pollo al Pomodoro e Vino Bianco

Chicken sautéed with tomato and white wine

Serves 4 to 6

1 2½-pound roasting chicken, cut up into 8
    pieces
2 tablespoons butter
⅓ cup oil
1 teaspoon dried rosemary
2 tablespoons salsa di pomodoro (see page 20)
1½ cups dry white wine
½ cup small peas, fresh or canned
½ teaspoon salt
Black pepper, freshly ground

Remove the wing tips from the chicken. Melt the butter in a large skillet and add the oil. While the butter and oil heat, wash the chicken pieces under cold running water. Pat dry with a paper towel. When the butter-oil mixture is hot, place the chicken in the skillet. Be sure the skillet is large enough so that there is a little room between pieces; if they are crowded in the pan they won't cook properly.

Cook over high heat, uncovered, for 5 to 6 minutes, turning pieces frequently to make sure they brown evenly and don't stick to the bottom of the skillet. If fresh peas are used, boil them briefly in slightly salted water. (If canned peas are used, don't discard the liquid they come in; it contains the best part of their taste).

When the chicken is golden, add the rosemary. Reduce the heat and add

the water from the canned peas (if fresh peas are used, skip this step). Dissolve the tomato sauce in the wine and pour it over the chicken. Cover and simmer over low heat for about 20 minutes. Check every now and then to see that the liquid hasn't evaporated. If needed, add a little water.

After 20 minutes, add the peas, taste the liquid, and add salt to taste. Turn the chicken and continue simmering for another 20 minutes. The total cooking time should be about 45 to 50 minutes, depending on the size of the chicken pieces.

Before removing the chicken from the skillet, sprinkle a little freshly ground pepper over the chicken. Place the pieces on a warmed platter, pour the sauce over the chicken, and serve at once.

Serve this chicken with the same wine you have used in cooking. It should be a Soave di Verona or a Lugana from Lake Garda.

NOTE

This preparation of Spezzattino di Pollo uses very little oil or butter and no flour to coat the chicken. The sauce will never be greasy and, even if it stands for a while on a buffet, the sauce won't have that "glazed" look, due to too much fat and flour.

No vegetable is necessary to accompany this dish; the peas and tomato sauce are sufficient. It should, however, be served with a good crusty bread. With a sauce like this it seems perfectly proper to clean your plate with a piece of bread.

Gallina al Vino Rosso

Hen in red wine

Serves 6

⅓ cup imported dried mushrooms
1 hen (or a 3- to 4-pound large roasting
  chicken), cut up
2 tablespoons flour
4 tablespoons butter
4 tablespoons salt pork, cubed
3 shallots, sliced
3 cups of dry red wine
1 oz. Grappa or another unflavored Eau de vie
  (or Vodka)
Pinch of nutmeg, freshly grated
Salt and freshly ground black pepper

Soak the mushrooms in a bowl of water.

Wash the hen pieces and pat them dry with paper towels. Spread the flour on a flat surface and coat all the pieces of fowl evenly. In a large skillet melt half the butter and add the salt pork and shallots. When the shallots are blonde, start adding the pieces of fowl, a few at a time, turning them with a wooden spoon as you add them, to brown them evenly on all sides. When all the pieces have a nice light brown color add the wine, moving and turning the pieces to avoid sticking. Add the Grappa. Reduce the heat and simmer until the fowl is done. The total cooking time depends on the tenderness of the meat — approximately 40 minutes. Test with a fork and, if the fowl seems done, remove the pieces from the skillet. Place on a warmed platter.

Strain the cooking liquid through a sieve into a small saucepan. Squeeze the water out of the mushrooms and add them to the gravy. Add the remaining butter and simmer the sauce for a couple of minutes. Taste and add salt and pepper. Pour over the pieces of fowl and serve with mashed potatoes.

The red wine for this meal should be a good wine: a Valpolicella would be perfect.

NOTE

In Italy, this dish is prepared with a faraona, or "prairie hen." I find that a hen, the kind they use in the south for smothered chicken will do.

As for mashed potatoes, they are not an Italian specialty. But Italians, knowing a good thing when they see one, make very good mashed potatoes and eat them with dishes like this. Use your favorite way of making them.

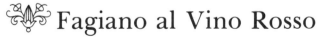 # Fagiano al Vino Rosso

Pheasant in red wine

Serves 5 to 6

1 3-pound pheasant
Salt and freshly ground black pepper
4 slices pancetta
2 tablespoons butter
1 cup small mushroom caps
1 cup dry red wine

R ub the pheasant with a mixture of salt and pepper. Place a small amount of the salt and pepper mixture in cavity of bird. Cover with slices of *pancetta* and tie the bird securely.

Melt the butter over high heat in a large skillet. As soon as it bubbles (and before it turns brown), add the pheasant. Turn on all sides so that the *pancetta* cooks evenly. As soon as the *pancetta* looks wilted, cover the skillet and reduce the heat. Simmer for about 15 minutes.

Add the mushrooms (peeled but not washed), then add the wine. Cover and simmer over low heat for about 1 hour turning occasionally.

The same dry red wine used in cooking should be served with the pheasant. If you are lucky and have a wild pheasant with strong gamy flavor, a "big" wine should be used — a Barolo or a Gattinara. If it is a bird brought up in captivity, any good dry wine will do — a young Chianti or a Merlot would be excellent choices.

NOTE

Pancetta is available in all Italian groceries and meat markets. If unavailable, unsmoked bacon or even fat unsmoked ham may be used.

 Petti di Tacchino Cardinale

Turkey breasts cardinale

Serves 6

1 cup milk
6 slices uncooked turkey breast, about ¾-inch
   thick
6 tablespoons butter
Salt and freshly ground black pepper
12 thin slices mozzarella cheese
6 slices prosciutto
3 teaspoons tomato paste

P our the milk into a deep dish, and place the slices of turkey breast in it. Let soak for 30 minutes. Pat dry, place between 2 sheets of wax paper, and lightly flatten with a wooden mallet (flat side).

Melt the butter in a skillet large enough to hold the turkey slices without touching one another. If you don't have a skillet large enough, cook the breasts a couple of slices at a time.

Brown the slices on both sides until golden. Add salt and pepper. Place a slice of *mozzarella* on top of each slice of turkey (the *mozzarella* should be smaller than the meat). Wrap a slice of *prosciutto* around both as if it were a little package. Then place another small slice of *mozzarella* on top.

Arrange the slices in a large ovenproof dish and place under the broiler until the *mozzarella* melts (about 3 minutes). Remove, place a dot of tomato paste in center of each slice, and place under the broiler for another minute. Don't place too close to the heat because the tomato paste should not burn. It should remain dark red like a Cardinal's hat. Remove from heat and serve.

Serve this turkey with fried artichoke hearts or with spinach or string beans. Avoid serving brussels sprouts or broccoli; they are too flavorful.

Serve a dry white wine: a Verdicchio or a Frascati, but make sure the wine is young. Neither of them has a long life. And, if you prefer red wine to white, here is your chance. In view of the *mozzarella* and the *prosciutto* in this recipe, a light red wine would be most acceptable; try a Bardolino from Lake Garda.

Veal
Vitello

Veal is undoubtedly the most popular meat in northern Italy, and the ways to prepare it are almost infinite. One of the best-known veal dishes is *La Cotoletta alla Milanese* (Veal Cutlet Milanese). It is the pride and joy of the cuisine of the province of Lombardy, one of the oldest and least known of all Italian cuisines.

History books mention breaded meat as far back as 1134 but they neglect to give us recipes. The *cotoletta*, as we know it today, first appeared in cookbooks that were printed around the middle of the nineteenth century. It was in the late nineteenth century that Milan was occupied by the Austrians. There exists a letter, written by Field Marshal Radetzky, then stationed in Milan and addressed to the Austrian chief of staff in Vienna, in which he carefully describes a veal dish he had eaten and greatly enjoyed. The dish became the *Wiener Schnitzel,* by no means the same thing as the *cotoletta*, whether it is because Radetzky's description was not correct, or because the Austrians preferred it that way. The *schnitzel* is a thin slice of meat covered by a thin crust. So much for those who say the *cotoletta is but an Italian version of the schnitzel.* The recipe traveled indeed, but in the other direction.

No matter what its origins, it is a deceptively simple dish that requires real skill. Once you have mastered it, the *cotoletta* will be a friend for life. It is equally good cold or hot. In fact the *Cotoletta Fredda* is a standard summertime dish in all good Milanese restaurants.

In Italy we prefer what is called *vitello da latte,* meaning animals that are less than 3 months old and are still milk fed. The meat is a very pale pink and very tender, yet flavorful. It is important that the meat be a very light pink, particularly for *scaloppine.* Animals are butchered differently in this country. The best meat, for both *scaloppine* and a veal roast, comes from the thigh of the hind leg of the animal. A lesson in anatomy is unnecessary, but some basic advice is needed for cooking veal.

The quantities of butter, or oil, given in the recipes are always approximate. Slightly more heat or a somewhat tougher cut of meat might require a little more butter or oil than indicated in the recipe. It could also

require a touch less than indicated. The difference will be infinitesimal.

For *scaloppine,* the main rule is that the skillet be piping hot and the butter almost smoking before you put the meat in. The meat will brown fast; as soon as the edges are golden, reduce the heat. The salt should be added toward the end of the cooking time.

Roasts may be placed in the saucepan with the butter and the oil. Once they are cooking, however, they should not be poked with a fork. Every tiny hole in the surface of the meat allows juices to escape, and it's the juices that retain the flavor in the meat. Roasts should be browned in a Dutch oven or saucepan deep enough so that the sides are higher than the meat. When the meat is browned, cover the casserole and cook the meat slowly over low heat. Remove the lid every now and then to check the liquid. If the liquid has evaporated, add a little broth. Turn the meat now and then but avoid piercing it with a fork. Use a spatula and a spoon.

Veal is seldom boiled, except when a piece of veal is added to a *Bollito Misto* (see pages 232-33). For that recipe, the same rule applies that applies to all other meats: bring the water to a very strong boil before lowering the meat into it. The strong boil seals the surface of the meat and prevents the juices from escaping.

•

 ## Vitello Arrosto a Modo Mio

My own roast of veal

Serves 6

10 tablespoons butter
1 sprig rosemary
4 or 5 leaves fresh sage (or ½ teaspoon dried)
2 bay leaves
½ teaspoon peppercorns
1 teaspoon salt
1 2-pound filet of veal

Place the butter and spices in a pot not much larger than the piece of meat. Place the meat on top without melting the butter first. As the butter melts, it begins to permeate the meat. Cover and cook over very low heat for 2 hours. Uncover every now and then and turn the roast but only as briefly as possible. The humidity that forms inside the pot helps to cook the

meat. After 2 hours, pierce the meat with a fork; the liquid that comes out should be totally colorless, and the meat should be light brown. If it seems too pale, increase the heat, uncover, and, turning frequently, cook for about another 10 minutes until the roast has a golden color.

Place the meat on a hot platter and allow it to rest a couple of minutes. Slice, strain the juices through a sieve, and pour them over the meat. The roast needs the juice to avoid drying out.

A white wine from the region of Lake Garda — a Soave or a Lugana — are a natural with this dish.

NOTE

Leftover roast of veal is delicious. All the fat from the gravy clinging to the outside of the roast should be scraped off. The cold veal can be served with mustard, or cut into slivers and added to a chef's salad.

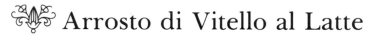 Arrosto di Vitello al Latte

Roast of veal in milk

Serves 6 to 8

3 tablespoons butter
1 3-pound roast of veal, rolled
Salt
1 heaping teaspoon rosemary (dried) or 2 sprigs
  fresh
2 cups milk
1 teaspoon flour (optional)

Preheat the oven to 325°. Melt the butter in a pot with a tight-fitting lid. When the butter is hot, add the meat. Follow with salt and rosemary. Turn the meat so that all sides are equally coated with butter. Remove the pot from the heat before the veal browns (about 10 to 15 minutes).

Pour 1 cup of milk over the veal, cover the pot, and place it in the center of the preheated oven. Check the liquid once or twice during the next hour and baste the meat or turn it in the liquid. After 1 hour add the second cup of milk and increase the oven temperature to 375°. Turn the veal during the second hour and baste. At the end of the second hour, the meat should be done and the liquid should be reduced to about 1½ cups. It should also be

quite thick (the quality of the gravy depends upon the amount of cartilage in the meat). If there is too much liquid and if it doesn't seem thick enough, place the meat on a warmed platter, and pour a little liquid over it to keep it from drying out. Place the pot back on the stove and boil the sauce, uncovered, over medium heat until it is reduced somewhat. If you wish to thicken the sauce, pour a ladleful into a small bowl, wait a couple of minutes for the liquid to cool, then add 1 teaspoon of flour. Mix until the flour is dissolved completely. Add this paste to the gravy and cook the sauce a few minutes longer, stirring.

Some people like to strain the gravy before pouring it over the meat or putting it into a gravy boat. Personally, I like the tiny fragments of meat and the rosemary. (If sprigs of fresh rosemary are used, they must, of course, be removed.)

The veal should rest for a few minutes before being carved. If it is a rolled roast, the string should be removed. The slices should be fairly thick because the meat will be very tender and would crumble if you try to cut it too thin.

This roast deserves a fine white wine: a white Pinot Grigio.

NOTE

Leftovers, if there are any, should be placed in the refrigerator. The next day, all the fat can be removed easily from the gravy. Underneath the top layer of fat there will be a delicious mixture of and juices and milk. Served cold, the meat can be sliced easily, and goes well with Insalata Mista Cotta, (see pages 307-8).

Dried rosemary should be washed before adding it to the meat. Place the rosemary leaves in a cup of cold water and let stand for about ½ hour. You will find a little dust and even bits of wood or bark at the bottom of the cup; the rosemary will float on top. The rosemary "needles" get soft when cooked and need not be removed from the gravy.

 Vitello Arrosto alla Crema

Roast of veal with cream

Serves 6

1 stick butter
2 bay leaves or 1 sprig fresh rosemary
*1 2-pound filet of veal (if not available, a rolled
    roast)*
½ cup light cream
⅓ cup milk or broth, if needed
Salt and freshly ground black pepper to taste

Heat the butter in a heatproof roasting pan. If rosemary is used, tie it to the meat with a piece of string. If bay leaves are used, add them to the melted butter. Place the veal in the pan and brown on all sides. Pour the cream over the meat, reduce the heat, and continue cooking, basting frequently. The sauce should have the consistency of cream. Should it get too thick, add the milk. If a less rich sauce is desired, use a little broth instead of the milk.

The cooking time is 1 hour to 1½ hours, depending upon the quality of the meat. Try not to pierce the meat with a fork while it is cooking; pierce only at the end to determine if it is done. The liquid should be white without a trace of blood. Remember that veal is better overcooked (provided it doesn't dry out) than undercooked.

Remove the bay leaves or rosemary. Add salt and pepper to the veal, turning while seasoning it. Place the veal on a hot platter and let it stand for a few minutes, then slice it. Coat the slices with the cream sauce.
sauce.

This is a rich dish, although veal is leaner than beef. The addition of the cream and the butter makes up for that difference. A good white wine (not too light) should be served with it: Pinot Grigio, for instance.

NOTE

This is not a difficult dish to prepare but it requires patience. The veal roast has to be basted frequently. If you have to leave it for a while, cover it lightly with aluminum foil, although it still might dry out somewhat.

 # Arrosto di Vitello con Tartufo

Roast of veal with truffle

Serves 6

1 2-pound lean veal for roasting
2 slices prosciutto, cut into strips
1 small truffle, fresh or canned, thinly sliced
Salt and freshly ground black pepper to taste
2 tablespoons butter
2 tablespoons oil

Stuffed Roast of Veal

The cut of veal should be a rolled roast before it gets rolled; in other words, a rather thick slice of veal, rectangular in shape.

Preheat the oven to 375°. Place the veal on a board and place the strips of *prosciutto* on top, being careful not to place them too close to the edges. Follow by placing the truffle on top of the *prosciutto*, again being careful not to lay slices close to the edges of the veal. Salt and pepper lightly; the *prosciutto* is rather salty, so very little salt will be needed. Then roll the veal into the shape of a loaf and tie it with a string as you would tie a sausage — as tightly as possible.

Melt half the butter and add half the oil in a roasting pan that is not much larger than the veal roll. (The best are the old fashioned earthenware pans or a Dutch oven.) When both are hot but not burning, place the veal in the center of the pan. Place the pan in the preheated oven, covered. After 10 minutes, baste the veal with the juices that have collected on the bottom of the pan. Continue roasting in the oven, basting frequently and adding the rest of the butter and oil when the meat seems dry. After 45 minutes, uncover the veal and allow the top to brown, basting frequently. The total cooking time should be about 1 hour, 30 minutes. The veal is done when you prick it with a fork and the juice comes out clear without a trace of blood. The veal should be well done but not dry; that is why basting is imperative.

Place the roll on a board, untie it, and allow it to cool for a couple of minutes. Slice the meat, but not too thin. Place slices on a platter, overlapping slightly. Add a spoonful of water or broth to the liquid in the pan and scrape up all the particles of meat clinging to the bottom and sides. Pour this sauce over the meat and serve.

This is a dish that requires patience because of the frequent basting. A slightly fruity white wine, such as a Pinot Grigio would do it justice.

 # Vitello Tonnato all'Antica

Classic veal with tuna sauce

Serves 6

1 2-pound veal roast
2 anchovy filets
Water
1 medium-sized onion, stuck with 2 cloves
2 stalks celery

For the sauce:
1 can (6 ½ oz.) tuna, drained
2 anchovies, chopped
⅓ cup capers, packed in vinegar
1 cup olive oil
Juice of 1 lemon
1 tablespoon vinegar from the capers

The veal should not be a rolled roast; it should be the filet cut from the hind leg of the calf and the meat should be a pale pink.

Lard the meat with the 2 anchovy filets by cutting little slits into the meat. Place anchovy pieces about ¾-inch long into the slits. Wrap the meat tightly in cheesecloth and tie it at both ends.

Bring the water to a boil in a saucepan that is not much larger than the veal roll. Add the onion to the water. Place the veal into the boiling water and add the celery stalks. Cover and cook over medium heat for about 1 hour.

Let the pot with the meat cool. Lift the roll out of the water and place on a platter. (Don't discard the liquid; it makes a great *risotto*.)

Place the tuna in a bowl and mash it with a pestle, then add the anchovies. Continue working with the pestle. Drain the capers, chop 1 tablespoon as fine as possible, and add it to the tuna. The mixture should have the consistency of a paste. Start adding the oil a few drops at a time, working it into the tuna either with a small whisk or with a wooden spoon. When all the oil has been added, the sauce should be quite thick. Add the lemon juice and 1 tablespoon of liquid from the capers. Mix well.

When the veal is cold, unwrap it and slice thin. Pour some of the sauce over the meat and cover the platter tightly with wax paper. Place the rest of the sauce in a jar, and seal as tightly as possible. Before serving, pour the remaining sauce over the meat and sprinkle the rest of the capers on top.

A sturdy white wine should be drunk with this very rich dish: a white Tuscan wine or a Sicilian Corvo.

NOTE

This is the classic recipe. Today the sauce could be made in a blender, which would simplify it greatly. The amount of oil, however, would still be the same and the dish might be a little too rich for today's taste.

Vitello Tonnato Moderno

Today's veal with tuna sauce

Serves 6

1 2-pound leg of veal
Water
1 small onion, stuck with 3 cloves
1 carrot
1 stalk of celery
½ teaspoon salt
½ cup dry white wine
½ cup mayonnaise
1 can (8 oz.) tuna packed in olive oil
8 anchovy filets
3 tablespoons capers
1 tablespoon lemon juice (optional)
1 lemon, thinly sliced (optional)

The veal should not be a rolled roast but rather cut from the hind leg of the calf. It should be a pale pink.

Wrap the meat in a double layer of cheesecloth and make a knot at each end. Bring the water to a boil in a saucepan that will hold the meat and the vegetables rather snugly. Add the onion with the cloves, the carrot, celery stalk, and salt. Place the meat into the boiling water, with the cheesecloth ends hanging over the edges of the pot so the meat can be removed easily when it is cooked. Cover and cook over medium heat for about 1 hour. Add the wine and cook until tender, or for about another 20 minutes. The cooking time depends on the quality of the meat. When done, let the veal cool in its broth.

Prepare a mayonnaise with 2 eggs and keep it rather thick. Place the tuna, anchovies, and 1 tablespoon of capers in a blender. Run the blender at high speed for about 30 seconds. Add the mayonnaise and a tablespoon of the broth from the pot. Taste and add the lemon juice if desired. Place the sauce in a bowl and cover with plastic wrap; the sauce will get dark if exposed to air. Keep refrigerated until ready to serve.

Lift the veal out of the broth and remove the cheesecloth. Place the roll on a platter and, just before serving, slice as thin as possible. Cover the slices with the sauce and sprinkle the remaining capers on top. If desired, garnish with lemon slices.

A rather sturdy white wine will go well with this dish: either a Frascati or a white Tuscan wine.

NOTE

The success of this dish is dependent upon the quality of the meat. If the veal is stringy, no sauce will save it.

 Arrosto di Vitello Ripieno

Stuffed roast of veal

Serves 6

1 2-pound veal for roasting
½ pound boiled ham, sliced
1 cup chopped spinach, tightly packed
Water
6 tablespoons butter
½ cup Parmesan cheese or ½ cup ricotta
3 hard-boiled eggs
3 bay leaves
3 tablespoons oil
2 cups beef or chicken broth (if needed)
Salt and pepper to taste

Ask your butcher for the veal he uses to make a rolled roast of veal but don't ask him to roll it.

Place the veal on a flat surface, cover it with a sheet of wax paper moistened with cold water, and beat with a rolling pin, wooden mallet or the flat side of a skillet. Place the ham slices on top but don't place any too near the edges.

Wash the spinach in a lot of water, then boil for 8 to 10 minutes. Let cool, squeeze all the water out with your hands, and chop the spinach fine. If you have a food processor, place the spinach in the container and run the motor for about 10 seconds; it will be chopped just right and not puréed.

Sauté the spinach in 1 tablespoon of butter for a minute or so. Add the Parmesan or the *ricotta* to the spinach and mix. Spread this mixture evenly over the ham slices, again being careful not to spread too close to the edges. Place the hard-boiled eggs in the center of the spinach layer, one below the other. Roll the meat over itself, shaping it into a long sausage. Tie it as you would a sausage.

Melt the remaining butter in a heatproof roasting pan not much larger than the roast itself. Add the bay leaves and the oil. When the mixture is hot, place the meat in the pan and brown it, turning it on to all sides. Keep the pan uncovered and sauté over high heat. When the meat has a nice color, reduce heat to medium, cover, and simmer for 1½ hours. Check frequently to see if the juices have evaporated. If the roast looks dry, add a little broth. Turn the meat frequently and baste it with its own juices.

Remember that the veal has to be cooked through but it shouldn't dry out. To prevent it from drying out, baste frequently. To make sure it is totally cooked, test the meat with a fork. If the juice that comes out is not totally colorless, simmer for another 10 to 15 minutes.

When done, remove the meat and place on a warmed platter. Let it stand for a few minutes before attempting to slice and, when you do, don't try to slice it too thin.

Serve with added buttered spinach and roasted potatoes. Serve the veal with a very light red wine, like a Chiaretto del Garda or a Valpolicella.

 Petto di Vitello Ripieno

Stuffed veal breast

Serves 8 to 10

1 4- to 5-pound breast of veal with bones
3 slices white bread
2 cups cold water
2 tablespoons butter
2 tablespoons oil
1 large onion, coarsely chopped
*1 pound chopped meat (veal, pork, and beef
  mixed)*
½ cup Parmesan cheese, freshly grated
Pinch of thyme
½ cup chopped spinach, cooked and dried
½ cup pistachio nuts, shelled
Salt and freshly ground black pepper
1 whole egg
5 hard-boiled eggs
*1 ½-inch thick slice of boiled ham, cut into 5 or
  6 strips*

Water
2 carrots
2 leeks

Wash the veal breast repeatedly in cold water to keep it white. Pat it dry. Lay the meat flat, bone side up. With a small, very sharp knife remove the bones, cutting the meat as close as possible to the bone. It is not a difficult operation. If you poke a hole through the meat, don't worry. It can be mended. Don't discard the bones. If you have made holes in the meat, snip off small pieces from the edge of the breast and place them over the holes.

Soak the bread in the cold water. Melt the butter in a skillet and add the oil. Add the onion and sauté until transparent. In a mixing bowl, mix the chopped meat with the cooked onion, then add the Parmesan, thyme, spinach, and pistachio nuts. Squeeze the bread to remove the water and add this to the mixture. Season with salt and pepper, keeping in mind that the veal is bland and needs quite a bit of both. Finally, add the egg and mix well, kneading lightly with your hands.

With the veal breast flat in front of you, place the stuffing in the center of the meat. Flatten it slightly with your hands. Place the hard-boiled eggs in the center, one below the other. Lay the ham strips over and beside the eggs. Now roll the meat over the mixture like a jelly roll. Tuck in the stray ends. Tie the veal with a string, once lengthwise, then in 4 or 5 places horizontally. Don't worry if a bit of the filling shows at either end.

Wrap the meat (tied like a sausage) with two layers of cheesecloth. Make a knot at both ends. In a heatproof pan that is close to the shape of the meat (a long narrow pan), bring the water to a boil. As soon as it boils, place the meat roll into it. The cheesecloth ends should hang over the edges of both sides of the pan. Place the carrots and leeks around the meat. Add the bones from the veal breast and cover the pan. Simmer over low heat for 1½ hours. When the meat is done, let it cool in its cooking liquid.

Lift the meat roll out of the pan, using the ends of the cheesecloth as handles. Place on a platter. Reduce the cooking liquid to about half the quantity. Let cool, and strain it into a jar. Place the jar in the refrigerator. Discard the bones, carrots, and leeks. Weight the roll with a wooden board on top of the meat and a weight on top of the board. Let the meat sit overnight or for at least several hours. When ready to serve, unwrap carefully, and slice. Arrange the slices on a platter, with the stuffing displayed to the best advantage. The liquid will have jellied. Fit a pastry bag with a wide nozzle and fill with the gelatin. Squeeze the gelatin over the top and around the edges of the meat.

A dry white wine should be served with this dish, especially because the veal breast has a delicate flavor. This is when Soave, one of Italy's most popular wines, comes into its own.

NOTE

This dish has the great advantage of being at its best when prepared a day ahead. It can also be frozen. The gelatin should, of course, be added at the last moment.

Stuffed Veal Breast is ideal for a buffet or as a main course for a summer luncheon, accompanied by a salad. If it is served as first course at a formal dinner, it should be followed by a vegetable mold or a cheese soufflé.

Petto di Vitello Ripieno alla Friulana

Stuffed veal breast, Friuli style

Serves 8

1 3 ½-pound veal breast
2 slices (about 1 cup) bread
½ cup milk
4 chicken livers
3 tablespoons butter
½ teaspoon rosemary
½ teaspoon sage
1 tablespoon parsley, finely chopped
⅓ cup breadcrumbs
1 whole egg, beaten
Pinch of nutmeg, freshly grated
2 tablespoons oil
1 cup broth (optional)

Have the butcher bone the veal breast to be sure that there are no holes in the meat. Soak the bread in the milk.

Sauté the chicken livers in 1 teaspoon of butter for 3 or 4 minutes. The livers should remain quite rare. Chop the livers, and add the herbs. Squeeze the bread and discard the milk in which it was soaked. Add the bread to the livers, then add the breadcrumbs. Add the egg and mix well. Add the nutmeg and mix again. Stuff the veal breast with the mixture and sew the pocket closed so that none of the stuffing can leak out. Roll the stuffed veal breast and tie it with cord as you would a sausage.

In a saucepan not much larger than the veal breast, melt the remaining butter and add the oil. When the butter and oil are hot, add the rolled veal breast. Turn every 5 or 6 minutes, browning the meat lightly on all sides. After 30 minutes, cover the saucepan and simmer over low heat for an hour. Check frequently. If the meat seems dry add a little broth.

When it is done, let the veal cool for 10 minutes in a warm place, before slicing it. Serve with mashed potatoes and sautéed spinach.

The Friuli region produces a white wine that is an ideal companion to this dish. It is called Tocai and it is a very fragrant dry white wine. If it is not available, a California Pinot Chardonnay may be substituted.

 Ossibuchi

Serves 6

2 tablespoons flour
6 ossibuchi (veal shanks cut into 3 pieces)
1 stick butter
Peel of 1 lemon, grated, and 6 small strips of
     lemon peel
3 tablespoons tomato sauce (homemade, if
     possible, but a good commercial one may be
     used)
1 cup dry white wine
3 cups broth, beef or chicken
Salt

Spread all but ½ teaspoon of flour on a flat surface. Coat the *ossibuchi* lightly with the flour. In a heatproof casserole large enough to hold the *ossibuchi* upright, melt almost all the butter. Reserve 1 teaspoon of butter for later. Place the *ossibuchi* in the butter and brown on all sides. Add the grated lemon peel. When they are nicely brown add the tomato sauce and the wine. Bring to a boil over high heat, uncovered, and cook so as to evaporate the alcohol. Reduce the heat to low, add the broth, then cover and simmer. Check the sauce every now and then and add a little broth if needed; there should be quite a lot of liquid. The total cooking time is about 1 hour. When the *ossibuchi* are almost done, taste the sauce and add salt as desired. The juice

will probably be too liquid for a good sauce. Roll that reserved teaspoon of butter in the remaining flour and add it to the sauce, stirring when you do so.

Remove the *ossibuchi* from the casserole, and place on a warmed platter. Pour the liquid over them. Bend the 6 slivers of lemon peel into little curls and stick one into the center of each *ossobucho*. Serve with *Risotto alla Milanese* (see pages 97-98).

Serve with the same wine you have used in cooking: Pinot Grigio or a really good Verdicchio.

NOTE

If you have individual little marrow spoons, place one next to each plate. If you have only one, pass it around to your guests. It is perfectly proper to share the spoon.

Stinco di Vitello alla Vicentina

Veal shank the Vicenza way

Serves 4 to 6

1 2-3 pound veal shank
3 tablespoons oil
1 cup dry white wine
1 cup water
Salt and freshly ground black pepper
1 tablespoon vinegar
1 bay leaf
2 carrots
1 onion, chopped
2 stalks of celery

Preheat the oven to 350°. Veal shank is the leg of veal that is used for *ossobuco* but it is left in 1 piece instead of being cut up into 3 pieces. Dry the veal shank with a paper towel. Veal is naturally moist and tends to be watery if it is not patted dry before cooking. Heat the oil in a large skillet, and, when hot, place the veal shank in the pan. Brown the shank on all sides. When the meat is golden, add the wine and allow to evaporate. Transfer the shank to a Dutch oven or a crockery baking dish. Add water, salt and pepper, vinegar, bay leaf, and the vegetables. If any oil is left in the skillet, add it to the meat. Cover and place in the preheated oven. Roast for about 2 hours. Turn

the veal shank once or twice during the cooking time; no basting is needed. When done, place the veal shank on a warmed platter, strain the gravy, and serve separately in a gravy boat. Surround the veal shank with mashed potatoes or a green vegetable.

The veal shank should be carved lengthwise into long thin slices. If you have the time, cook the shank a day ahead and refrigerate. When ready to serve, remove the fat, carve the meat while cold (which makes carving much easier), and place the slices back on the bone. Tie lightly with a string, and place again in the baking dish. Place in a preheated oven (400°) for 10 minutes. Remove the string before serving. The veal shank will look whole and as if it hadn't been carved at all. This is a very elegant dish.

Veal shank should be eaten with a dry white wine. As always, it should be the same wine you have used in cooking. A Pinot Grigio would go very well, or a Tocai from the Friuli. They are both quite fruity. If no Italian wines are available, a California Chablis or a Pinot Chardonnay may be used.

 Vitello alle Olive

Veal with olives

Serves 4

1 pound filet of veal or a piece cut from the leg,
   ¾-inch thick
2 tablespoons butter
2 tablespoons oil
1 cup black Italian or Greek olives, pitted and
   chopped coarsely
Salt
Black pepper, freshly ground

Remove any bone or membrane from the meat. Cut it into strips about ¾-inch wide. You should have julienne strips of veal.

Melt the butter in a large skillet over high heat and add the olive pieces. Stir with a wooden spoon. The butter and oil should absorb the flavor of the olives.

Add the veal strips and cook rapidly, turning the meat and stirring it constantly. The veal must be cooked through but should not dry out. Add salt and stir; sprinkle with pepper.

Serve the dish in the skillet in which it was cooked, if it is attractive, or transfer the meat and olives to a platter. If you use a platter, make sure the dish has been warmed first.

When we had this dish in Italy, we drank a Pinot Bianco with it and that wine was just fruity enough not to be outdone by the olives. Pinot Bianco might be hard to get in this country and a Durello would go equally well, as would a Castel Chiuro Bianco.

NOTE

This dish may be partially prepared in advance. You can sauté the olives earlier and then reheat the mixture before adding the veal strips. This is a simple and delicious dish. It has only 1 drawback: good veal is very expensive. For this preparation, the veal must be the very best.

 Saltimbocca

Small veal rolls

Serves 6

6 slices veal scaloppine
6 slices lean prosciutto
16 leaves fresh sage
Black pepper, freshly ground
1 tablespoon flour
6 tablespoons butter
½ cup dry white wine
Salt

Place the slices of veal between 2 sheets of wax paper and flatten with wooden mallet (flat side) until very thin. Remove bits of skin around the edges, if any. Cut each slice into pieces of about 3 inches by 3. Cut the *prosciutto* into pieces of the same size as the veal.

Place a small piece of sage on each piece of veal (easy on the sage). Add a little pepper, place the piece of *prosciutto* on top, and roll the veal, *prosciutto*-side inside. Secure with a toothpick.

Spread flour on a working surface and roll the veal rolls to coat lightly.

Melt the butter in a large skillet and add the veal rolls. If the skillet is not large enough to hold them all without touching one another, cook a few rolls at a time and add more butter as needed. No foods should be crowded but veal is particularly sensitive and requires privacy. When all the rolls are golden on all sides, add the wine, cover, and simmer until veal is done (about 10 to 15 minutes, depending on the thickness of the veal).

Taste the sauce and add salt if desired. When *Saltimbocca* are done, remove the toothpicks, place on a hot platter, and serve immediately.

Serve with buttered spinach or any vegetable that wouldn't clash with the taste of sage in the veal.

The wine used in cooking the veal should be the one served with it: a Pinot Grigio would be a good choice.

NOTE

There is hardly a family, let alone a restaurant, that doesn't have its special version of Saltimbocca. If you order one in a restaurant, be sure you know what their intention is. I was once served a slice of veal (chop?) covered with stringy mozzarella. Saltimbocca, indeed! Saltimbocca, literally translated, means "it jumps into the mouth." That one didn't.

Scaloppine di Vitello al Limone

Scaloppine of veal with lemon

Serves 6

2 pounds veal scaloppine
3 tablespoons flour (approximately)
3 tablespoons butter
3 tablespoons oil
3 tablespoons lemon juice
1 tablespoon capers, chopped (optional)
Salt and freshly ground black pepper

Remove remaining bits of white skin from the meat. Place the slices between 2 layers of wax paper. With a wooden mallet, beat until the veal is very thin, about ⅓ inch.

Spread the flour on a wooden or marble surface, place the veal slices on the flour, turning and coating the veal on both sides. Shake well to remove excess flour.

Melt the butter in a large skillet, then add the oil. While the butter heats (but does not get brown), make small incisions into the edges of the veal slices using a sharp knife. These cuts will prevent the meat from curling when it cooks.

When the butter-oil mixture is very hot, place the veal slices into the skillet 2 or 3 slices at a time. Leave plenty of space between the slices. If the meat is crowded, it won't brown properly. Move the slices with a spatula to avoid sticking. When browned on one side, turn with a spatula and brown on the other side. Pierce the meat with a fork to determine if it is done. The exact cooking time depends on the quality of the meat and the thinness of the slices. Remove the browned slices to a warmed platter. When all the slices are done, add the lemon juice to the butter-oil mixture remaining in the pan. If the mixture has been almost all absorbed, add a few tablespoons of water. (If the meat has been cooked rapidly enough this should not be necessary.) Add salt and pepper. If capers are to be used, don't add as much salt as you normally would; capers are salty. Stirring rapidly, scrape up all the bits of brown crust and blend with the lemon juice. Pour the mixture over the veal. The veal slices should be well soaked but not swimming in gravy. If desired, sprinkle the capers over the meat.

Serve very hot with mashed potatoes or creamed spinach or any vegetable of your liking. Avoid heavily flavored vegetables such as broccoli or brussels sprouts; their tastes tend to overpower the delicate flavor of the veal.

We also don't like the veal to be surrounded by potatoes or vegetables. The gravy tends to run into them and its flavor gets lost. Serve the meat on a platter and the accompanying vegetable in a separate bowl. If the platter looks too empty, put a sprig of parsley on both ends or garnish with slices of lemon.

Veal is a very delicate meat and should be served with a delicate white wine: a Lugana, a Pinot Grigio, or a light Pinot Chardonnay.

Scaloppine di Vitello al Prezzemolo
(Scaloppine Cont l'Erborinn)

Scaloppine of veal with parsley

Serves 6

12 thin veal scaloppine (about 1 ½ pounds)
2 tablespoons flour
½ stick butter

Salt
½ cup broth
½ cup dry white wine
Juice of ½ lemon
1 teaspoon capers, finely chopped (optional)
3 tablespoons parsley, finely chopped

Place the *scaloppine* between 2 sheets of wax paper and beat with a wooden mallet (flat side) or a rolling pin. When *scaloppine* are as thin as possible, make small incisions in the edges of each slice to keep them from curling when cooked.

Spread the flour on a working surface and coat the *scaloppine* very lightly. Melt most of the butter in a skillet (leaving about 1 tablespoon for later use). When the butter is hot, but not brown, place the *scaloppine* in the skillet without crowding. Sauté, uncovered, turning as soon as edges seem golden. Add salt depending on whether you intend to use capers or not. Capers are quite salty so if you include them, use less salt.

Place the cooked slices of veal on a warmed platter, arranged as you wish to serve them. Keep warm.

Pour the broth into the skillet, reduce the heat, and with a wooden spoon, scrape up the bits of meat and butter that might have stuck to the skillet. Add the wine, the lemon juice, the chopped capers (if desired), the remaining butter, and finally the chopped parsley. Mix very briefly and pour over meat.

I find that this dish is best when served by itself. The sauce would only lose flavor if a vegetable were added. It should, however, be accompanied by a wine: a Soave di Verona, for instance. You will, of course, use the same wine in cooking.

NOTE

This is a typical dish of the Milanese cuisine. "Erborinn" is the word for parsley in Milanese dialect.

Should the veal your butcher has be a little darker pink than you would like it to be, soak the scaloppine in 2 cups of milk for about 1 hour. Pat dry and then proceed as described above. I find that the milk helps tenderize the veal.

Scaloppine di Vitello al Marsala

Scaloppine of veal with Marsala

Serves 6

2 pounds scaloppine
3 tablespoons butter
3 tablespoons oil
3 tablespoons flour (approximately)
½ cup dry Marsala
Salt and freshly ground black pepper

Remove any pieces of white skin from the meat. Between 2 layers of wax paper, place the slices one at a time and beat with a wooden mallet to about a ⅓-inch thickness. With a short, sharp knife, make small incisions in the edges of the slices. This will prevent the meat from curling when it cooks. On a flat surface spread the flour evenly and place the slices on the flour. Turn to coat; when both sides are coated, shake the slices one at a time to remove any excess flour.

In a large skillet, melt the butter and add the oil. Get the skillet very hot. Place 2 or 3 slices of meat in the skillet. There should be plenty of space between slices. If the meat is crowded, it won't brown properly and the juice will get watery. Sauté quickly, moving the meat with a spatula to prevent it from sticking. After about 3 minutes, one side should be brown. Turn the slices with a spatula and brown the other sides. Test with a fork to see if they are done. The exact cooking time depends upon the quality of the meat and the thickness of the slices. Transfer the slices to a warmed platter and continue cooking the rest of the meat. Place the slices neatly in the center of the platter, overlapping slightly. When all slices are done, add the Marsala to the skillet, scraping up all brown particles that might be clinging to the bottom of the skillet. Taste the sauce before salting, then add as much salt and pepper as desired. Pour evenly over all slices.

Serve with mashed potatoes or creamed spinach but in separate dishes. If sauce runs into the potatoes it will lose some of its flavor.

Marsala is a sturdy wine from Sicily. This particular veal dish should therefore be accompanied by a fruitier wine than you would normally serve with veal. Sicily itself produces 2 white wines, available in this country, that would do your palate proud: Corvo Bianco, from the region near Palermo, and Etna Bianco, obviously from near Mount Etna. They vary from 12½% to 14% alcohol and can hold their own no matter how much Marsala you put in your *scaloppine.*

 # Scaloppine di Vitello con Fontina

Scaloppine of veal with fontina

Serves 6

1 pound veal scaloppine, thinly sliced
2 cups milk
2 tablespoons flour
5 tablespoons butter
¼ pound fontina cheese, thinly sliced
¼ cup dry white wine
Salt

Have the butcher cut the *scaloppine* as thin as possible. If you buy the meat packaged at a market, try to see that there are not too many bits of whitish skin (this veal is rarely satisfactory). Also be sure that the meat is actually cut into slices, not into oblong chunks.

Pour the milk into a bowl and soak the veal for at least a couple of hours. The veal can soak longer, even overnight in the refrigerator, if desired. Remove the veal from the milk and pat the slices dry with paper towels. Place the veal slices on a sheet of wax paper. With a sharp knife, cut off any bits of white skin and then make little incisions along the edges. This will make sure that the meat doesn't curl around the edges when you fry it. Place a second sheet of wax paper on top, moistened with cold water, and beat with a wooden mallet (flat side) or a rolling pin until meat is paper thin.

Spread the flour on a sheet of paper and coat the meat very lightly. Heat the butter in a large skillet, but be sure it is large enough to hold the slices without overlapping them. When the butter is hot, but not brown, reduce the heat and sauté the veal. Turn the slices when the edges begin to turn golden.

Cover each slice of veal with 1 slice of *fontina*. When all are covered, sprinkle a little white wine over them. Let evaporate (1-2 minutes), then turn off the heat and let the *scaloppine* stand, covered, for a minute.

Heat a platter large enough to hold the veal slices without overlapping. Place the veal slices on the platter and sprinkle with salt when ready to serve.

Serve this dish with *Sedani di Verona* (see page 280) or buttered spinach.

The wine offered should be the same wine you have used in cooking: Soave or a Pinot Grigio would be a good choice.

NOTE

No matter how small the quantity of wine is you use in cooking, it should be good wine. You have spent so much money on the meat, you have spent so much time trimming it, don't spoil it with so-called cooking wine. Also make sure you get real fontina.

Scaloppine di Vitello con Mozzarella

Scaloppine of veal with mozzarella

Serves 6

12 slices veal scaloppine
2 cups milk
6 tablespoons butter
1 teaspoon dried oregano
12 thin slices of mozzarella
Salt and freshly ground black pepper

Have the butcher slice the veal as thin as possible. Then, when you get home, soak the meat in milk for a couple of hours. Then place the slices between 2 sheets of wax paper and beat with wooden mallet (flat side) until paper thin. With a very sharp knife, make small incisions into the edges of the meat here and there to prevent it from curling when it cooks.

Place a little of the butter in skillet and heat to melting but do not let it brown. Add as many slices of veal as can comfortably be placed side by side. Don't overlap. Over high heat, brown the slices on one side, turn, and brown on other side. The cooking time should be about 1 minute per side, according to thickness of meat. Place the browned meat in an ovenproof dish and keep warm while you cook remaining slices, adding a little butter whenever needed.

Sprinkle a little oregano over each slice, remembering that oregano is a powerful herb. Salt to taste and place a thin slice of *mozzarella* over each slice. Place under the broiler for 3 to 5 minutes or until the *mozzarella* melts. Sprinkle freshly ground black pepper over the meat and serve.

Serve a green vegetable with the *scaloppine.* And, if you want something starchy and filling, boiled potatoes or even buttered rice.

Everybody knows that veal requires a white wine. A Pinot Grigio will go well with the *scaloppine.* Consider, however, the addition of cheese to the veal and try a Bardolino, a little cooler than room temperature, and see if you don't prefer it.

Cotoletta alla Milanese, I

Veal cutlet Milanese

Serves 4

4 veal cutlets with bone, each about ½-inch thick
1 whole egg
1 cup breadcrumbs
1 stick butter
Salt (coarse salt, if available)
Lemon wedges

Have the butcher beat the meat slightly. Better still, if you have a cleaver, beat it yourself. Italian gourmets have argued about the ideal thickness of the *cotoletta*. The consensus is that the meat should be just a little thinner than the bone it is attached to.

Cut the edges of the meat in several places with a very sharp knife to keep it from curling up while frying.

Beat the egg and coat the cutlets (1 at a time) well with egg and then with the breadcrumbs. Press the breadcrumbs into the meat with the palm of your hand, so that they cling well and won't fall off while sautéing.

Melt the butter in a heavy skillet over medium heat and fry the cutlets 1 at a time, allowing plenty of space around each cutlet. Don't move the cutlets while they are frying, or the crust will stick to the skillet. Turn carefully when edges begin to brown, but not before. When both sides are brown, reduce the heat to allow the inside to cook. Allow about 6 to 7 minutes over low heat. Remove from skillet and salt. If the salt is added while the cutlets are cooking, the humidity produced by the salt would break the crust.

Place the cutlet on a warmed platter and keep warm while the others are frying. Slip paper curls over each bone and serve garnished with lemon wedges. (The paper curls nowadays are just a decoration. They used to be a necessity when people used their fingers rather than forks.)

Cotolette alla Milanese should be accompanied by a dry white wine, like most veal dishes. There are, however, those who feel that the breadcrust requires a light red wine. Try both and stick to the one you like best. A gentle Bardolino would seem most appropriate.

Cotoletta alla Milanese, II

Flatten the veal cutlet as in above recipe and cut the edges. Melt 2 tablespoons of butter in a skillet and coat the cutlets in butter, then in breadcrumbs as described above, then dip in beaten egg and finally again in breadcrumbs.

Fry as in preceding recipe, 1 cutlet at a time, allowing plenty of space around it.

Cotoletta alla Milanese, III

Prepare cutlets as in preceding recipe. Mix ½ cup of grated Parmesan cheese with ½ cup of breadcrumbs. Dip cutlets (1 at a time) in beaten egg, then coat with cheese-and-breadcrumb mixture, pressing breadcrumbs into meat as described in first recipe. Fry as described above.

The cheese makes for a richer tasting crust.

Spezzattino di Vitello

Veal stew

Serves 6 to 8

2 pounds leg of veal, cubed
1 tablespoon flour
2 tablespoons butter
2 slices lean bacon, coarsely chopped
1 cup dry white wine
1 small onion, thinly sliced
1 stalk of celery, coarsely chopped
1 medium-sized carrot, coarsely chopped
Salt and freshly ground black pepper

The meat should not be too lean. A little fat and cartilage add flavor to the stew. Pieces should be about 1-inch thick.

Sprinkle the veal lightly with flour. Melt the butter in a heavy skillet. Add the bacon. When the bacon is slightly brown, add the onion. Allow the onion to get dark blonde. Remove the onion. Add the meat and stir rapidly because the cartilage sticks easily to the bottom of the pan. Turn the meat until lightly browned on all sides. Reduce the heat and add the wine. When the wine is almost all absorbed, add the celery and carrot. Cover and simmer for about 1 hour. Keep heat very low and stir occasionally. If the stew should seem too dry, add a little water or broth. But if the lid is tight enough, no additional liquid should be needed. Add salt and pepper shortly before removing the meat from the stove. If the bacon is slightly salty, very little salt should be needed.

Serve with steamed rice or mashed potatoes.

As a rule, veal should be accompanied by white wine. We are not adamant about this. If your palate reacts more happily to a light red wine, there is no reason not to listen to it. The exception is veal dishes where the wine is used in the preparation of the dish. It has to be white wine and it should be the same wine you drink. *Spezzattino di Vitello* will be happy with a Soave, the light pale golden wine from Verona, or a Verdicchio from near Ancona. And maybe you can find a Lugana, dry and cheerful, and produced on the southern tip of Lake Garda. Be careful with Lugana: it darkens with age. When it is at its best it's almost flaxen colored.

Spezzattino di Vitello al Pomodoro

Veal stew with tomato

Serves 6

2 tablespoons butter
1 slice lean bacon, chopped
1 small onion, sliced
3 leaves fresh sage or ½ teaspoon dried
2 pounds leg of veal, cubed (about 1-square inch)
1 large ripe tomato, seeded and chopped coarsely, or 1 teaspoon tomato paste, diluted in a little water
1 cup dry white wine
Salt and freshly ground black pepper

Melt the butter in a heavy skillet. Add the bacon, onion, and sage. Sauté the onion until golden. Remove both the onion and the sage but reserve. (If onion and fresh sage are allowed to cook too long, they add a bitter taste to meat. If dried sage is used, add it once the meat starts to brown). Add the meat. Stir rapidly with wooden spoon because the cartilage sticks easily to the pan. Add the tomatoes to the meat. Stir. Cover and simmer for about 30 minutes. Stir every 10 minutes or so. After 30 minutes, add the wine, onion, and sage. (Or, if dried sage is used, this is the time to add it). Simmer, covered with heavy lid, for another 30 minutes. Add salt and pepper when almost done.

Spezzattino di Vitello should be accompanied by a dry white wine. The preceding recipe calls for wine in preparing the dish. Use a good dry white wine and serve the same wine with your meal. A Soave, a Verdicchio, or a dry Frascati should go very well. There are, however, those who like a light red wine with veal. Red wine, no matter how light, in a *Spezzattino* just doesn't work.

 ## Spezzattino di Vitello al Limone di Maria

Maria's veal stew with lemon

Serves 6

2 pounds lean veal stew meat, cubed
1 stick butter
½ cup dry white wine
1 tablespoon flour
2 cups broth, chicken or beef
2 large carrots, cut into bite-sized pieces
2 medium potatoes, peeled and cut into bite-sized
    pieces
Salt and freshly ground black pepper
Juice of 1 large lemon (1 oz.)
Rind of ½ lemon, grated (optional)

Remove all bits of membrane or tendon from the meat. Melt the butter in a skillet large enough to hold the meat in 1 layer with a little room to spare. Add the meat and cook quickly over high heat. Stir with a wooden spoon and brown the veal on all sides. After about 6 or 7 minutes, add the wine and allow it to evaporate. Reduce the heat to medium.

Place the flour in a sieve and shake it over the meat so that the flour is evenly distributed but barely coats the meat. Stir with the wooden spoon until the flour is dissolved in the liquid.

Add 1 cup of broth. Add the carrots and cover very briefly. Uncover and stir so that neither the meat nor carrots stick to the bottom. As the liquid evaporates, add more broth. After about 5 minutes, add the potatoes. Cover, then continue to stir occasionally.

If the veal is of a tender quality, 30 or 35 minutes cooking time should be sufficient. Test it with a fork; if the meat seems less than tender, add more broth and continue cooking. When the meat is ready and the carrots and potatoes are done, the liquid should be almost all absorbed as well. At this point, add a little salt and pepper to taste. Add the lemon juice and stir briskly. Taste the cooking liquid. If a slightly more bitter taste is desired, add the grated lemon peel.

This veal dish requires a rather fruity wine. A Pinot Grigio would be perfect.

NOTE

This dish is the invention of a great cook named Maria. Although she gave us this recipe, the idea of the lemon rind is our addition, since the carrots tend to make the gravy a little sweet. With or without the lemon rind, it is a very happy alternative to all the veal stews.

Beef
Manzo

Two regions of Italy claim to have the best beef: Tuscany and the Piedmont. Both claims are justified. The *Bistecca alla Fiorentina* is as unequalled as is the *Bugì*, or boiled beef of the Piedmont.

Italians attach great importance to the difference between *bue* or ox meat and *manzo*, which is closer to American beef. The ox should not be older than about 4 years. For boiled beef or roasts, both *bue* and *manzo* are used. For filets, Italians prefer ox meat. It is also said that tongue, smoked or otherwise, is better from that animal.

Whether you use ox or beef, the fat in which the roast is first browned should be very hot before you place the meat in it. The hot fat seals the juices in the meat. The pan in which a roast is cooked should have sides that are higher than the piece of meat. When turning the roast to brown all sides, 2 spatulas should be used. The meat should never be pierced with a fork while it is cooking. The hole made by a fork allows the precious juices to escape.

As for boiled beef (a dish far more popular in Italy than in the United States), the water should be boiling vigorously before you put the meat into it. Once the water has started boiling again, cover the pot, lower the heat, and simmer without disturbing it. Every time you poke it to see if it is done, you waste precious juices.

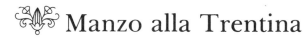 ## Manzo alla Trentina

Braised beef the Trento way

Serves 6

1 2-pound lean top round or bottom round roast
2 sprigs rosemary or 1 teaspoon dried
2 tablespoons flour
½ stick butter
⅓ cup wine vinegar
2 cups milk

2 bay leaves
½ teaspoon peppercorns
1 cup beef broth, homemade or canned
Salt

Wash the meat and pat it dry with a paper towel. Tie the roast as tightly as possible if it has not already been tied by your butcher. (If you have bought it tied, wash it carefully, being sure not to disturb the string.) If you have sprigs of fresh rosemary, stick them between the string and the meat. If you are using dried rosemary, reserve for later.

Spread the flour on a flat surface and place the meat in the flour, turning it on all sides until it is coated evenly and lightly.

Place the butter in your roasting pan and melt but don't brown. Place the floured meat in the butter and brown it on all sides over high heat. Add the vinegar and allow to evaporate, still over high heat. At this point, pour the milk over the meat and reduce the heat to medium. Add the bay leaves and peppercorns (and rosemary, if you use dried). Simmer slowly. When the meat looks dry, add the broth. The exact cooking time can't be given because it depends on the quality of the meat, but it is approximately 45 minutes. If in doubt, cook a little longer. When the meat is done (test with fork), add a little salt. Place the roast on a warmed platter. Strain the cooking liquid through a sieve and immediately pour the sauce over the meat. There won't be much gravy because most of the liquid will have been absorbed. Serve with buttered brussels sprouts or buttered celery root.

Serve a good red wine with this dish — a rather sturdy one. A wine from the Valtellina would go very well. You have the choice among several: a Sassella or a Grumello or an Inferno would go equally well.

NOTE

This is a dish from the extreme north of Italy. Trento is a town about as far north as you can go. The Austrian influence is quite evident because of the milk, just as the Austrians feel the Italian influence when they cook with wine.

Manzo Stufato alla Friulana

Pot roast, Friuli style

Serves 8

1 3-pound lean top round roast
5 leaves fresh sage or 1 teaspoon dried

(continued)

3 tablespoons butter
3 tablespoons oil
2 tablespoons salt pork, chopped
1 large carrot, coarsely chopped
1 stalk of celery, coarsely chopped
Salt and freshly ground black pepper
2 bay leaves
1 tablespoon juniper berries (optional)
1 glass dry red wine
Water

Remove any fat or tendon from the outside of the meat, and wipe it with wet paper towels; pat dry. With a small sharp knife, make small incisions in various places and insert sage leaves. The meat should not be *too* fresh and it should be at room temperature.

In a pot not much bigger than the meat, heat the butter and oil, then add the salt pork. As soon as the salt pork is partially rendered, add the chopped carrot and celery. When the vegetables are wilted, add the meat. Brown on all sides. Add salt, pepper, bay leaves, and juniper berries, if desired. Reduce heat and add the wine. Add water until the meat is almost completely covered. Place a heavy lid on saucepan, then place an iron or other heavy weight on top. Simmer over low heat for 2 hours without uncovering. After 2 hours, pierce the meat with a fork. If it doesn't seem tender enough, cover again and cook for another 30 minutes. Remove the meat from the pot and place on a hot platter. Let stand for 10 minutes before slicing but don't allow it to get cold. Meanwhile, pour the cooking liquid through a sieve. Slice the meat, then pour the gravy over the sliced meat or serve separately in a gravy boat.

Serve with mashed potatoes or with a soft *polenta* (see page 81).

A Merlot, a red wine from the Friuli region, would go best with this typical Friuli dish. If not available, a Valpolicella or Amarone from Lake Garda would go well.

 Manzo al Limone

Beef with lemon

Serves 6 to 8

2 tablespoons butter
2 tablespoons oil
1 3-pound lean eye round or top sirloin roast

6 cups water
2 teaspoons coarse salt
½ cup olive oil
Juice of 1 large lemon
2 hard-boiled eggs
4 gherkins
Black pepper, freshly ground

Melt the butter in a skillet and add the oil. Wash the meat and pat it dry with paper towels. When the butter-oil mixture is hot, add the meat and brown on all sides over high heat but don't allow the meat to get too dark. In a large saucepan, bring the water to a strong boil, add 1 teaspoon of the salt, then add the meat. Reduce the heat to medium and cook for about 1½ hours, turning the roast now and then. Skim frequently. When the meat feels tender when pierced with a fork, place it on a wooden plank and sprinkle it with remaining teaspoon of salt. Cool for a few minutes, then slice as thin as possible. Arrange the slices on a platter, overlapping a little.

Beat the olive oil and lemon juice until well blended. Pour this mixture over the meat, decorate with slices of hard-boiled eggs and gherkins, and let stand for at least 2 hours before serving. Serve at room temperature. The meat should not be refrigerated but if for some reason this becomes necessary, cover with wax paper and then tightly with aluminum foil to prevent the meat from getting dry. Remove it from the refrigerator at least 1 hour before serving.

This is an ideal summer luncheon dish, but if you want good broth from your boiled meat, this recipe won't do it because the broth will have a burned taste from the brown outside of the meat. The meat, however, will be very tasty because the browning seals in the juices.

Like all beef this should be served with a red wine. The lemon, however, will not mix too well with wine, and a truly great wine will be wasted. A young Chianti would be a happy companion for this dish.

 Manzo Bollito

Boiled beef

Serves 6 to 8

2 quarts water
2 teaspoons coarse salt

(continued)

1 3-pound lean eye round or top sirloin roast
2 carrots
2 stalks of celery
2 leeks

Bring the water to a strong boil in a pot that will just hold the meat and the vegetables. Add 1 teaspoon of the salt. Add meat. Add the vegetables to the meat and cook over medium heat. After 30 minutes, remove the vegetables and keep warm on a platter; continue to cook the meat for another hour. When done, place in the center of platter with the vegetables and sprinkle with the remaining coarse salt. Serve with *Salsa di Rafano* (see page 24).

This is a sturdy dish and will go well with a sturdy wine like a Barolo from Piedmont or a Gattinara, also from Piedmont.

NOTE

Boiled beef is the specialty of Piedmont and Lombardy. The horseradish sauce comes from the Friuli and Trieste and is of Austrian origin. In Trieste it is called Salsa di Cren (from the German Kren), whereas it is called Salsa di Rafano in other parts of Italy.

Bollito Misto

Mixed boiled meats and vegetables

Serves 12

1 cotechino (optional)
Water
1 teaspoon coarse salt
1 2-pound eye round or bottom round roast
3 carrots
3 stalks of celery
1 large white onion
½ head cabbage
2 pounds veal filet
1 calf's head (optional)
1 calf's tongue
1 3-pound chicken

Soak the *cotechino* in cold water overnight.

Bring the water to a boil in a large pot. Add salt to the water then add the vegetables. When the water returns to a strong boil, add the beef. Reduce the heat and cook covered for about 1 hour. Add the veal and the calf's head, tongue, and *cotechino*. Wash the chicken, remove the tips of the wings, then add it to the pot.

Cook this mixture of meats for about 1 hour longer. When done, place all the meats onto a large warmed platter and all the vegetables on another. Cover each with a little of the broth (a ladleful for each platter) to prevent the meats and vegetables from drying out. Sprinkle coarse salt over the meats. Serve immediately, accompanied by a *Salsa Verde* (see pages 23-24) or a *Salsa al Rafano* (see page 24).

This is a magnificent dish, not hard to prepare but expensive. It requires a magnificent wine from the Piedmont: a Barolo or a Gattinara.

NOTE

Readers who have been served this dish in Italy in fine restaurants might be familiar with those impressive carts that are brought to your table. With the meats in their broth on one side and the cutting board on the other, the headwaiter deftly carves the meats and cuts the vegetables to present to you on individual plates. It need not always be so. One of Venice' great hostesses serves it in what seems to me the perfect manner. The meats are sliced in the kitchen; the chickens are carved there too. The meats are then placed in neat rows in deep baking dishes and almost covered with the broth. Guests help themselves to whatever meats they choose. There is no need to eat the calf's head if you don't want to, nor do you have to try the cotechino (although I recommend it). Place a couple of hot trays on a buffet or in the center of your dining room table and put your platters or baking dishes on top. Served in either manner, it is a festive dish. But don't prepare it for just a few people. If you use small quantities of meats the Bollito won't be good and if you use the given quantities for a small group, you will eat leftovers forever.

Bollito Misto Sbagliato

Boiled meats that were a mistake

Serves 4

2 quarts water
1 1½-pound eye round roast
2 chicken legs with thighs
1 chicken breast

(continued)

2 carrots
2 stalks of celery
¼ head cabbage
Salt
Salsa de Rafano (see page 24)

This was going to be my version of *Bollito Misto*, the marvelous mixture of boiled meats for which the Italian cuisine is famous. It was my version because my very American husband doesn't like calf's head or *cotechino*. He likes chicken legs, I love the breast and we both like beef. The vegetables are all for me.

I had brought the water to a boil in a large pot. I then added the meat, chicken, vegetables, and salt. When the pot had been on the stove for about 30 minutes, uncovered and over medium heat, I went to look at my favorite TV program. When it ended, I foresaw disaster! I had left the pot on the stove for an entire hour without ever checking the liquid.

There wasn't any! I barely arrived in time to save the meat and fowl from burning. What I found in the pot was a sort of stew, a mixture of meat and vegetables. Everything was so overcooked that it was unthinkable to add broth and try to bring it back to life again.

Feeling very guilty I heaped everything onto a warmed platter, removing chicken bones here and there wherever I saw any.

I had prepared a horseradish sauce and brought it to the table in a separate little dish. I said nothing. My husband said nothing. We looked at each other only after we had eaten the first couple of bites of one of the best meals we ever had.

The meats had retained all the juices, the vegetables had added their tastes. I don't advocate this dish for an elegant dinner but all it lacked was looks.

Serve this with an excellent bottle of Valpolicella.

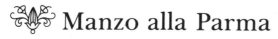 # Manzo alla Parma

Beef, Parma style

Serves 6

3 tablespoons butter
3 tablespoons oil

(continued)

1 carrot, coarsely chopped
1 stalk of celery, coarsely chopped
1 small onion, coarsely chopped
5 slices of lean uncooked roast of beef, about 1
    pound
Salt and freshly ground black pepper
2 tablespoons salse di pomodoro (see page
    20), dissolved in 2 cups dry red wine

Melt the butter in a skillet, add the oil, then the vegetables. When the onion is transparent, add the slices of meat. Avoid heaping one on top of the other and keep them as separated from one another as possible. Turn the slices with a fork 2 or 3 times. When they are easily pierced with a fork, add salt, pepper, tomato sauce, and wine. Cover and simmer over low heat until the meat is done. As an alternative, you could also transfer the contents of the skillet to a Dutch oven or baking dish and continue cooking either on top of the stove or in the oven. The exact cooking time depends on the quality of meat you use; average is about 45 minutes.

Transfer the slices to a hot platter, strain the gravy, and pour it over the meat.

The wine served with the dish should be the same as used in cooking. A Chianti would go very well.

Fettine di Manzo Saporite

Tasty slices of beef

Serves 4

1 pound sliced beef (use bottom round or
    sandwich steaks that aren't good enough to
    broil)
2 tablespoons flour
1 stick butter
2 slices (about 4 oz.) pancetta (if unavailable,
    use salt pork), diced
1 young onion, thinly sliced
2 bay leaves
¼ cup dry red wine
¼ cup wine vinegar
1 cup beef broth
Salt and freshly ground black pepper

Place the slices of beef between 2 sheets of wax paper and beat with a wooden mallet (use flat side) or a rolling pin until as flat as possible. Spread the flour on a wooden surface and coat the meat lightly.

Melt the butter in a large skillet, then add the *pancetta* and onion. When the *pancetta* and onion are brown, remove with a slotted spoon. Discard the onion but reserve the *pancetta* for later use.

Place the meat in the skillet, being careful not to have the slices too close together. Brown the meat on both sides over high heat. Add the bay leaves, wine, and vinegar. Cook over high heat, uncovered, for about 3 minutes, allowing the liquid to evaporate and moving the slices around with a spatula to avoid sticking.

Add the broth and the *pancetta*, reduce the heat, cover, and simmer for about 1 hour (longer if the meat seems quite tough). Test the meat with a fork to determine if it is done. Taste the cooking liquid and add salt and pepper if needed.

Serve this dish with boiled potatoes. The wine should be a Barbera or a Barbaresco.

NOTE

This is a good way to prepare a cut of beef you are unsure of or for an occasion when you don't want to spend a lot of money on an expensive cut.

 # Spezzattino di Manzo Semplice

Beef stew the simple way

Serves 6

1 2-pound chuck roast
2 fresh bay leaves
½ teaspoon peppercorns
1 teaspoon rosemary
2 cups dry red wine
3 tablespoons butter
2 small carrots, coarsely chopped
3 stalks of celery, coarsely chopped
1 small onion, coarsely chopped
Salt

Cube the meat into bite-sized pieces. Discard any stringy tendons and gristle. Place the cubes in a bowl, add the bay leaves, peppercorns, and rosemary. Add the wine, being sure the meat is entirely covered. Let stand for at least 1 hour, more if desired. When ready to use, remove the meat from the wine and pat it dry with a paper towel.

Preheat the oven to 350°. Melt the butter in a very large skillet. Add the meat and stir to prevent sticking and to make sure all the meat is browned evenly on all sides. Cook for about 10 minutes. Transfer the meat to an ovenproof dish. Strain the wine marinade through a sieve and pour it over the meat. Cover and place baking dish in the center of the preheated oven.

Place the skillet in which the meat has been browned back on the heat, then add the vegetables to any juice that is left in the skillet. There should be enough butter and juice from the meat left to sauté the vegetables *al dente*, or for about 10 minutes. Add salt to the vegetables.

When the meat has been in the oven for about 30 minutes, add the vegetables to the baking dish. Check the liquid: there should be plenty left, but if not, add some broth. Place the lid back on the casserole, put the dish back in the oven, and continue to bake for 1 hour more. The exact cooking time depends upon the tenderness of the meat. Check your meat 1 hour after you have added the vegetables: it should be tender (test with a fork) and the wine should be almost totally evaporated. If the meat looks as if it needs a little more cooking and the wine is gone, add ½ cup more and place the dish back in the oven for another 30 minutes. Taste and add salt if needed.

The wine used in cooking should be a robust Barbera or Gattinara. If either one is too heavy for your taste, a Chianti will do very well. The same wine should, of course, be drunk with the meat.

NOTE

This is a dish for either lazy or very busy people. It requires almost no attention. After you have soaked the meat, then sautéed the vegetables and added them to the meat, it takes care of itself. In addition, the meat may be prepared ahead of time and reheated when you want to serve it. Finally, it is ideal on a buffet because it is good even when it is not piping hot. However, if you want to reheat it, there is no problem. Add a spoonful of wine and place the dish in a hot oven for a couple of minutes. Other stews, whose sauces are not based on wine but on butter or oil, either dry out if reheated or have to have some more butter added to them, which sometimes makes them too greasy.

Spezzattino di Manzo

Beef stew

Serves 6

3 tablespoons butter
⅓ cup salt pork, diced
1 small onion, finely chopped
1 2-pound eye round or top round roast
1 tablespoon flour
1 cup dry red wine
1 stalk of celery, sliced
1 medium carrot, sliced
Salt and freshly ground black pepper

Melt the butter in a skillet. Add the salt pork, then the onion. When the onion is transparent and slightly golden, remove but don't discard. Cut the meat into cubes of about 1½ inches. Spread the flour on a board and coat the meat lightly. Add the meat to the pan and brown on all sides, stirring frequently so that the meat won't stick to the pan. Add the wine and let it boil away. Add the carrot and celery to the meat, then add the reserved onion. Salt to taste and add pepper. Cover and simmer over very low heat for an hour or an hour and a half, depending on the tenderness of the meat. Stir frequently and add a little water or broth if needed.

This dish requires a sturdy red wine. Depending on how festive the occasion is, you might want to serve a noble Barolo or a Gattinara. You should use the same wine to cook the meat.

Spezzattino di Manzo con Funghi

Beef stew with mushrooms

Serves 6

3 tablespoons butter
2 slices salt pork, about ¼-inch thick, cubed
1 small onion, thinly sliced
1 2-pound eye round or top round roast
1 tablespoon flour

⅓ cup imported dried mushrooms
1 cup water
Salt and freshly ground black pepper

Melt the butter in a skillet and add the salt pork. When the fat begins to show color, add the onion. Allow onion to yellow but do not brown it. Remove the onion but don't discard. Cut the meat into 1½-inch cubes. Spread the flour on a board and coat the meat lightly. Place the meat in the skillet. Brown the meat on all sides, stirring frequently to prevent sticking. When meat is browned, reduce the heat, cover, and simmer for 1 hour. Stir occasionally to prevent sticking. If the meat gets too dry, add a few spoonfuls of water or broth.

Soak the mushrooms in a cup of water for about ½ hour. When the meat is almost done, add the reserved onion and the mushrooms along with the water in which they have been soaked. Taste the juice, add salt and pepper to taste, and simmer for another 15 minutes. There should be very little gravy.

A good dry wine should be the companion of this tasty dish — one of the many great wines from the Piedmont. A Barolo would make it festive but also a Barbera or a Barbaresco would do well.

Spezzattino di Manzo al Barolo

Beef stew with Barolo wine

Serves 4 to 5

1 2-pound top round or eye round roast
1 stalk of celery, coarsely chopped
1 carrot, coarsely chopped
2 bay leaves (fresh bay laurel, if you can find it)
Pinch of thyme
½ teaspoon peppercorns
½ teaspoon juniper berries
2 cups Barolo wine
3 tablespoons butter
2 slices (about 4 oz.) pancetta or salt pork,
   chopped
1 small onion, chopped
2 tablespoons flour
Salt

Have the butcher cube the meat or do it yourself. The cubes should be about 2 inches thick. Remove any bits of gristle or tough tendons. Wash the meat, pat it dry, and place it in a large bowl. Add the celery and carrot and the spices, then the wine. The meat should be covered. Let stand overnight in a cool place but don't refrigerate.

The next day remove the meat from the marinade and drain on a paper towel.

Heat the butter in a large skillet and add both the *pancetta* and the onion. While the onion cooks, spread the flour on a board and roll the meat cubes in it. The meat should be lightly coated. Add the meat cubes to the pan and brown over high heat, uncovered, stirring frequently to keep the meat from sticking to the skillet.

When the meat is browned on all sides, pour the marinade over it. Reduce the heat and simmer, covered, but uncover frequently to stir. The exact cooking time can't be given because it depends on the tenderness of the meat; approximately 2 hours.

When done, remove the meat from the skillet using a slotted spoon. Keep warm. Pour the marinade through a sieve. Discard the bay leaves, peppercorns, and juniper berries. Taste and add salt. Put the wine and vegetables in a blender, run the motor for 30 seconds, then pour this sauce over the meat. Serve with boiled potatoes.

People might question why a noble wine like a Barolo should be used in cooking. The answer is that its taste is inimitable. The same Barolo should be drunk with the *Spezzattino*, of course.

Bistecca alla Fiorentina Classica

Classic Florentine steak

Serves 4

2 large T-bone steaks, about 1-inch thick
Black pepper, freshly ground
Coarse salt

People who believe in the classic *Fiorentina* frown upon marinating the meat in oil or doing anything to it but having the meat at room temperature. It should be cooked on an open fire of wood or charcoal. Keep in mind, however, that the *Bistecca Fiorentina* in Italy comes from a younger animal than we use in this country and is therefore more tender than the meat we get here.

You might, at times, have been baffled in Italy when you read the right-hand column of restaurant menus and found "S.G." instead of a price. It means *secondo grandezza* or *according to size*. A *Fiorentina* may weigh anywhere from 1 to 2 pounds.

Have your fire very hot. Put your grill over it and let it get red hot. Place your meat on the grill and, as soon as this side is seared by the grill, turn it over. Sprinkle a little pepper on the seared side. Repeat the turning as often as you wish if you want your meat well done. Sprinkle coarse salt on the steak when serving.

Serve this steak with a fine old Chianti (make sure you choose one that ages well). Personally I suggest not serving any vegetable with it. The *Fiorentina* should not be allowed to get cold. Eat it, by itself, while it is hot and have a salad afterwards.

NOTE

I suggest using T-bone steak. I have tried sirloin and found it less than satisfactory, but I have also used a thick slice of top round, after keeping it for a couple of days in a cool place (but not in the refrigerator). I know that this sounds terrible to American ears, but the meat was tender and delicious. There must be readers who still remember the days when we didn't refrigerate everything, from bread and meat to fruit and vegetables.

Costata Fiorentina alla Martellini

Steak Fiorentina the Martellini way

Serves 4

2 T-bone steaks about 1-inch thick, or 1 large
   sirloin
½ cup olive oil
1 teaspoon black pepper, freshly ground
Fresh bay leaves
Coarse salt

Place the steaks in a dish large enough to hold them side by side. Pour the oil over them and sprinkle with pepper. Let stand for a couple of hours. Turn and sprinkle pepper on the other side. Let stand for another hour.

Place a large iron skillet over high heat and cover the bottom with fresh bay leaves. When they are so hot that they smoke, place the steaks on top, cook

until done on one side, turn and cook on the other side. Place on a serving platter and sprinkle coarse salt over them.

Serve these steaks with a fine old Chianti. Be sure you know what wine you are choosing or get advice from someone who knows. Only very good Chiantis age well.

NOTE

I call this recipe alla Martellini because the Martellinis are an old family in Siena. Their villa is surrounded by laurel hedges. It was Mrs. Martellini who taught me how to cook steaks when you don't have a charcoal fire. What if you also don't have fresh bay laurel? I have tried a thick layer of dried bay leaves and, although it wasn't the same thing, it was acceptable.

With both T-bone or sirloin steaks make sure you remove most of the fat. The Bistecca Fiorentina is much leaner than American beef.

Filetto di Bue Sotto Coperta

Filet of beef under a blanket

Serves 6

6 slices of filet of beef, about 1½ pounds
2 tablespoons flour
3 tablespoons butter
Salt and freshly ground black pepper
2 ripe tomatoes, sliced and drained of water
½ teaspoon oregano (optional)
1 tablespoon oil
6 thin slices of fontina cheese, about ¼ pound

Trim the filet slices, then beat them lightly with a wooden mallet. Spread the flour on a wooden board. Place the meat on the flour, a slice at a time; turn and shake so that only the flour that sticks to the meat remains.

Melt the butter in a large skillet, it should be hot but not brown. Place the meat slices in the skillet and sauté. The slices should not overlap or even touch. If the skillet is not large enough, sauté the meat in 2 installments. Turn the slices when done on one side and sauté on the other side. The cooking time will be according to how well done you prefer your meat— approximately 10 minutes. Salt meat when almost done, then add the pepper.

Preheat the oven to 375°. Place the slices in an ovenproof dish. Cover each slice of meat with a slice of tomato. Sprinkle the tomatoes with oregano, if desired. Pour a few drops of oil over each slice, cover with the slices of cheese and place in the preheated oven for about 10 minutes. Either serve in the baking dish or preheat a large platter and transfer slices. Serve very hot.

The filet with its blanket requires a noble wine: a Barolo or a Gattinara. Both come from the region of Piemonte, which is also the home of *fontina* cheese.

NOTE

This dish was named by a cook who was an important person in my childhood. The "blanket" is, of course, the slice of fontina, which might be replaced by Swiss cheese if fontina is not available; the taste will, however, be quite different.

Some people might object to doing anything to filet of beef. The meat is so expensive it should not be tampered with. The answer to this objection is that, whereas filet is very tender, it is not very tasty. Also, the tomato and cheese make a pound of meat go a long way. Finally, it is a delicious dish.

 # Filetti di Bue al Tartufo

Filet of beef with truffles

Serves 6

6 slices of filet of beef, each about ½-inch thick
1 tablespoon flour
3 tablespoons butter
Salt and freshly ground black pepper
⅓ cup dry Marsala
1 small white truffle, cut into 6 slices
Salt and pepper to taste

The slices should all be the same size, taken from the center of the filet. Sprinkle the flour on a wooden board and coat the filets lightly on both sides. Melt the butter in a large iron skillet, big enough to hold the filets without overlapping. Sauté the slices, then turn, add salt and pepper, and cook on other side until done (medium rare requires about 3 minutes each side). When they are done, sprinkle some of the Marsala over them and move the steaks to a hot platter. With the rest of the Marsala, deglaze the pan, scraping up all particles of meat from the skillet with a wooden spoon. Pour the sauce over the filets.

Place the truffle slices in the centers of the filet slices, 1 truffle slice for each piece of meat and handling each slice of truffle as if it were gold (which it is).

Serve this very hot with mashed potatoes or creamed spinach. This elegant dish requires an elegant wine: a Barolo, a fine Gattinara.

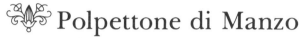 Polpettone di Manzo

Beef meat loaf

Serves 6

2 pounds chopped sirloin or filet
1½ teaspoons salt
Black pepper, freshly ground
1 small onion
1 whole egg
1 tablespoon light cream (optional)
1 tablespoon oil
1 tablespoon butter

Place the meat in a bowl and add salt and pepper. Mix thoroughly. Place the onion in a food processor and purée completely (about 10 seconds with the sharp blade). If you don't own a processor, grate the onion very fine. Add it to the meat and mix with a wooden spoon. Add the egg and the cream. At this point, forget about using the wooden spoon. Mix the ingredients with your bare hands; it is the only way to make sure that all the ingredients are evenly mixed.

Preheat the oven to 350°. Oil a roasting pan, tilting it to make sure the bottom is coated. Shape the meat into a loaf. This is the only difficult part of the operation. The surface of the loaf has to be completely smooth without any little holes or cracks where the juices could escape. Smooth every crack carefully with your fingers while holding the loaf as you would a baby to avoid the forming of new cracks.

Place the loaf in the center of the baking pan and, once again, go over the surface with your hands to smooth every possible opening. Place the pan in the center of the oven and bake for 20 minutes. Open the oven and coat the surface of the loaf with butter. This is really only a cosmetic touch to make the loaf shiny. Bake for another 15 minutes if you want the loaf rare, bake 20 minutes longer if you want it medium, and 25 minutes longer for well done.

This meat loaf (or a glorified version of it) may be served hot or at room temperature. If the loaf is served hot, it may be accompanied by sautéed mushrooms, a green vegetable, or roasted potatoes.

This dish is every bit as glamorous as a filet of beef and requires a glamorous wine: a Barolo, or a Gattinara from the Piedmont, or a Castel Chiuro from Valtellina.

NOTE

I frequently serve this meat loaf for dinners or buffets. I always make 2: one rare, the other medium, to please the taste of all guests. I put a small flag in the rare one so that guests can tell them apart.

This dish has a story. When Andrea Dodi applied for a job as chef in a private home, he was asked to prepare a dish his prospective employers could take to the country for the weekend. It would give them a chance to find out how good he was. He said he would prepare a meat loaf. His employers were not impressed. There is no glory to a meat loaf, they thought, and besides everyone can make it. He prepared it anyway. The next day he got a call from the country, "You are hired!" was the message. That was 20 years ago.

Tortino di Manzo e Patate

Beef and potato pie

Serves 4 to 6

4 tablespoons butter
2 tablespoons chives, finely chopped
3 large potatoes, boiled and sliced
2 hard-boiled eggs, sliced (optional)
Salt and freshly ground black pepper
1 pound leftover boiled beef, cubed

This is a dish to prepare when you have cooked too much boiled beef or *Bollito Misto* and have some meat left over. Both the meat and the potatoes should be cold. If eggs are to be used, they too should be cold.

Melt the butter in a skillet about 9 inches in diameter. Add the chives and sauté for a couple of minutes. Add the potatoes and the eggs. Add salt and

pepper to taste. (Add quite a bit of both; eggs and potatoes are bland.) Then add the meat, but be sure any bits of fat are removed. Mix all ingredients well and flatten with a spatula. Cook for about 10 minutes over high heat. If desired, turn the mixture by placing a plate on top, turning the skillet upside down rapidly, and sliding the potato-meat mixture back on the skillet to cook on the other side. I find that turning it makes it a little too dry for my taste. When finished, just turn it upside down onto a platter so that the browned side is on top. Serve accompanied by a salad.

This is a dish from the very north of Italy. I have first encountered it in the Alto Adige, with the Dolomites looking on as we were eating. Of the wines produced in that region I prefer the whites. But, obviously, a red would go better with this dish. There is a Cabernet I got very friendly with. It is just heavy enough to go with beef and ages surprisingly well.

NOTE

This Tortino may be made with other leftovers, particularly with bits of ham that are no longer beautiful enough to be sliced elegantly. Chicken and veal, however, are a little too dry.

Lamb
Pork and Sausages
Variety Meats

Lamb *agnello*

Italians like their lamb young and tender. It is eaten mostly around the Easter holidays, not so much for religious reasons or tradition, but because it is the time of year when lamb is at its best. Friuli, the incredibly beautiful region between Venice and Trieste, is known for especially tender lamb. The best recipes in this section are, in fact, *Agnello Friulano*, or Lamb Friuli Style.

It occurs to me that all these lamb recipes are prepared without garlic. Somehow, young and tender lamb with its delicate flavor doesn't seem to need any garlic. Mature lamb is another story. If you are cooking a mature leg of lamb, rub it with garlic before cooking it. Place 1 clove of uncrushed garlic in the pan where you melt the butter for *Spezzattino di Agnello* (Lamb Stew) and remove it when you start browning the meat. I say this only because there are people who feel that lamb without garlic is heresy. It is not always so. If you use horseradish in the *Agnello Friulano*, please don't use garlic; the 2 would fight one another.

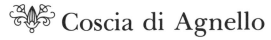 ## Coscia di Agnello

Roast leg of lamb

Serves 6 to 8

1 5-6 pound leg of lamb
2 tablespoons salt
1 teaspoon black pepper, freshly ground

(continued)

1 teaspoon thyme
¼ cup fresh tarragon or 1 tablespoon dried
2 carrots, peeled and coarsely chopped
2 stalks of celery, coarsely chopped
1 large onion
3 cups of dry white wine

Preheat the oven to 325°. Wipe the leg of lamb with wet paper towels, but don't wash it. Dry it thoroughly. Mix the salt, pepper, thyme, and dried tarragon (if that is what you are using). Rub the surface of the lamb with the seasoning mixture. Place the meat in the center of a roasting pan not much larger than the meat. If fresh tarragon is used, sprinkle it over the meat. Pour 1 cup of dry white wine over the meat. Place the pan in the center of the oven. Don't cover. Check after 15 minutes. If the meat seems dry, add another cup of wine. There should be about 1 cup of juice in the pan at all times.

The lamb should roast for approximately 3 hours. If a meat thermometer is used, roast until 175° on the thermometer.

When done, place the meat on a warmed platter. Remove any fat from the surface of the pan juices. Pour the juices with all the herbs into a blender. Blend at high speed for about 1 minute.

Let the meat stand for at least 15 minutes before slicing. Serve the slices surrounded with the vegetables. Place the sauce, very hot, in a separate gravy boat or pour it over the slices.

Lamb may be accompanied by either red or white wine. Since this particular recipe calls for white wine in its preparation, white wine should be served with it. In fact, serve the same wine as used in cooking.

Costolettine di Agnello Fritte

Fried chops of baby lamb

Serves 4

8 small lamb chops, either rib or loin
2 whole eggs
1 teaspoon butter
3 tablespoons very fine breadcrumbs of white
    bread only
Oil or shortening such as Crisco

1 teaspoon salt
White pepper
Lemon wedges

Place the chops between 2 sheets of wax paper, moisten the top piece with cold water, and beat gently with a wooden mallet. The meat should be about ¼-inch thick.

Beat the eggs lightly with a wire whisk or a fork. Melt the butter and add it to the beaten eggs. Mix the breadcrumbs with the salt and a pinch of white pepper.

Heat the oil or shortening in a saucepan. When a few drops of water sprinkled on surface sizzle, the oil is hot enough.

Cover the chops with breadcrumbs on both sides, dip them in the egg-butter mixture, and then again in the breadcrumbs. Use your hands to make the crumbs stick to the meat. Lower the chops carefully into the hot oil and fry until golden.

Place the chops in the center of a warmed platter. Surround them with lemon wedges and serve with buttered spinach in a separate bowl.

Serve these chops with a good Bardolino, a little cooler than room temperature.

NOTE

These little chops may also be served cold for a buffet dinner, or as appetizers with drinks. In this case, the little bone should be wrapped with a small piece of aluminum foil so they can be picked up easily and so no forks are needed.

Agnello Friulano

Lamb, Friuli style

Serves 6

1 stick + 1 tablespoon butter
1 onion, chopped
2 pounds lamb cut from the leg, cubed
½ teaspoon fresh thyme leaves or ¼ teaspoon dried
3 bay leaves
1 cup broth, chicken or beef
3 tablespoons wine vinegar

(continued)

Salt and freshly ground black pepper
1 tablespoon grated horseradish (optional)
2 tablespoons parsley, finely chopped

Melt the stick of butter in a large skillet. Add the onion. When the onion is translucent and light blonde, but not brown, add the meat and stir. Add the thyme and bay leaves and brown the meat rapidly over high heat. As soon as it gets a little color, add the broth and vinegar. Reduce the heat and simmer for about 40 minutes or until the meat is tender.

Remove the meat from the skillet, place on a hot platter, and keep warm. Taste the cooking liquid and add salt and pepper if needed. Remove the bay leaves.

In a small saucepan, melt the tablespoon of butter, then add the horseradish, if desired, and the parsley. Pour the cooking liquid over the meat, then top with the butter-parsley-horseradish mixture and serve immediately.

Serve with buttered green peas and boiled potatoes. Friuli, the region where this recipe comes from, provides the best wine to serve with it: a bright red Merlot.

 # Spezzattino di Agnello Friulano

Lamb stew, Friuli style

Serves 8

5 tablespoons butter
1 medium onion, sliced
2 bay leaves
Pinch of thyme
1 teaspoon peppercorns
1 3-pound leg of lamb, cubed
2 anchovy filets, coarsely chopped
1 tablespoon vinegar
½ cup broth, preferably beef
4 tablespoons parsley, finely chopped

Melt 3 tablespoons of butter in a large iron skillet, add the onion and sauté until wilted. Add the bay leaves, thyme, and peppercorns. Add the meat and brown lightly over high heat. Reduce the heat, add the anchovies, vinegar, and broth a little at a time. Stir frequently to prevent meat

from sticking to the bottom of the skillet. Simmer gently for 30 to 40 minutes until done.

When the meat is done, place it on a warmed platter. The platter should be fairly deep in the center. Remove the bay leaves and pour the liquid over the meat. Melt 2 tablespoons of butter, add the chopped parsley, and pour over the meat. The butter must be piping hot. Serve immediately with mashed potatoes.

Either a fruity white or a light red wine may be served with this lamb.

Spezzattino di Agnello all'Uovo

Lamb stew with eggs

Serves 8

3 tablespoons butter
3 tablespoons oil
1 3-pound leg of lamb, cubed
⅓ cup dry white wine or 2 tablespoons wine vinegar
Salt and freshly ground black pepper
2 tablespoons parsley, finely chopped
3 whole eggs

Heat the butter and oil in a skillet large enough to hold the meat in 1 layer. When the butter and oil are very hot, add the meat and brown rapidly over high heat. Stir frequently to avoid sticking. Add the wine or vinegar. Taste and add salt and pepper. The cooking time varies according to the tenderness of the meat.

After 20 minutes, pierce the meat with a fork: if it seems a little tough, add a little more wine, cover, and simmer over low heat (this should not be necessary if the meat is tender enough). If the meat seems done, add the parsley and stir. There should be about ½ cup of liquid in the skillet. If the meat seems dry, add a little broth.

Beat the eggs lightly in a bowl. Remove the meat from the heat and immediately pour the eggs over it. The meat should be hot enough to cook the eggs without hardening them. Serve immediately with boiled potatoes or steamed rice.

Either red or white wine may be served with this lamb, provided it be dry. Follow your taste and preference.

Pork and Sausages   *maiale e salsiccie*

Italians are not really enthusiastic pork eaters, inspite of their love for *prosciutto*, both *cotto* and *crudo*. *Prosciutto cotto* is boiled ham and *prosciutto crudo* is raw, or cured, ham. Aside from *prosciutto*, salami, and sausage, however, Italians will also eat roast pork and occasionally pork chops. The chapter on pork, therefore, is a very short one: the *Arista Toscana* and the *Salsiccia all'Aceto* are two recipes that alone would warrant a chapter.

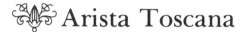 Arista Toscana

Loin of pork, Tuscan style

Serves 6 to 8

1 3-pound loin of pork roast, bone removed
2 small sprigs fresh rosemary or 1 teaspoon dried
1 clove garlic, slivered
1 teaspoon coarse salt
½ teaspoon freshly ground black pepper

Preheat the oven to 375°. Wipe the meat with a wet paper towel. Pat dry. Place on a flat surface. Place the sprigs of rosemary in the center of meat, placing one sprig below the other or sprinkle the dried rosemary over the center of the meat. Close both sides of meat over the center and tie. Make small incisions into the meat and place the garlic slivers inside. Be sure to make the incisions in various parts of the meat and not too close together.

Mix salt and pepper together and sprinkle liberally over meat. Place the meat in roasting pan and place the pan in the center of the oven. Cook for about 2 hours, turning the meat frequently and basting it with its own juices. Serve hot with potatoes or a green vegetable. If you don't mind the rich flavor, the vegetables may be cooked in the pork juices in the pan where the meat is roasting.

Serve with a good Chianti Classico or, for special occasions, with a fine Brunello di Montalcino.

NOTE

Arista is an ancient recipe. The name comes from the Greek Aristos, *meaning excellent. In the 15th and 16th centuries, the meat was cooked on a spit. It is still the best method for the lucky ones who own one.*

Arista may be served cold, accompanied by mostarda, the Italian mixed fruit, sweet and sharp, sold in jars in most Italian groceries, or in food departments of department stores. Mostarda is the specialty of the city of Cremona and is an acquired taste for most people.

 Arrosto di Maiale all'Acqua

Roast loin of pork

Serves 6

1½-pound pork loin roast, bone removed
1 sprig fresh rosemary or ½ teaspoon dried
5 leaves fresh sage or ½ teaspoon dried
   (optional)
½ clove garlic
Salt and freshly ground black pepper
Water

Wipe the meat with a wet paper towel. Mix the herbs together and place them in the center of the meat. Roll the meat and tie it as you would a sausage. Place the meat in a saucepan not much larger than the meat. Add the garlic, then sprinkle salt and pepper over the meat. Cover with cold water and cook uncovered over medium heat for 1½ hours. Check now and then. If the water is evaporating too quickly, lower heat. If after 1½ hours water is left, increase the heat and cook until all water has disappeared. The meat should then be surrounded only by its own fat. Turn the meat and brown on all sides. Remove the garlic. Place the pork on warmed platter. If desired, add a little broth to the fat in the saucepan and make a gravy to serve with the meat. Be careful, though, because the gravy will be quite rich. The meat, on the other hand, should be quite juicy and should require no gravy.

Serve with mashed potatoes or with sautéed spinach or both. Serve with one of the red wines of Valtellina: Inferno, Sassella, or Grumello. If not available, a young Chianti would be a good companion for this roast, which is less rich than other pork roasts.

Braciole di Maiale al Limone

Pork chops with lemon

Serves 6

6 pork chops
½ cup olive oil
Juice of 1 lemon
1 clove garlic, sliced
Black pepper, freshly ground
Salt
2 tablespoons parsley, finely chopped (optional)
3 tablespoons broth (optional)

Place the chops between 2 sheets of wax paper, moisten the one on top with cold water, and beat lightly with a wooden mallet. They will be as tender as veal.

Mix the oil and lemon together and marinate the chops for about 1 hour. Remove the chops from the oil and reserve. Heat the marinade then add the garlic but don't brown it. When the oil is very hot, add the pork chops. Sprinkle with pepper. Brown well on both sides. Remove the garlic, turn heat to medium, cover, and cook until done, about 15 minutes. (Remember that pork has to be very well done.)

Before serving, add salt to taste. Sprinkle the parsley over each chop, if desired. Serve very hot with mashed potatoes or sautéed spinach.

If desired, add the broth to the skillet, scrape together the particles of meat, and make a sauce to pour over the chops. Personally, I prefer the chops rather dry. The pork is a rich meat without any added gravy.

A sturdy red wine is required. The choice depends on how festive the rest of the meal is. For an informal dinner, a young Chianti would be fine. If you want to splurge, a Barolo would be excellent.

Polpettone di Maiale e Vitello

Pork and veal loaf

Serves 6

½ pound chopped pork
½ pound chopped veal

¼ pound prosciutto (fat removed), ground
2 whole eggs
1 teaspoon Italian spices (see page 14)
Salt
2 tablespoons oil

Preheat the oven to 375°. Knead the meat together with your hands without pressing too hard. Add the eggs, the spices, and the salt. Shape into a loaf, being careful to seal the surface where the juices might escape. The surface must be totally smooth.

Oil a baking pan that is not much longer than your loaf (the sides of the pan should not be higher than 1½ inches). Place the loaf in the center and, with your fingers, oil the surface. Place the pan in the center of the oven and bake for 45 minutes. (Ovens vary. If you have a slow oven, make it 50 minutes. The pork has to be well done.) This loaf may be served hot or cold. If you serve it cold, it should be accompanied by a salad with a mustard dressing (see pages 27-28). If you serve it hot you might like to serve it with a *Salsa di Capperi* (see page 27). Hot or cold, Valpolicella from Lake Garda will go well with it.

NOTE

There are packages of ground beef-veal-pork ready at some supermarkets. If you buy one of those, discard the beef and keep for other uses. I much prefer to buy the veal and the pork and to grind them myself. The butcher might be reluctant to grind the pork for you because the law requires that he then clean the meat grinder. If you have a food processor, grind all the meat, including the prosciutto, using the sharp blade. Run the motor for about 10 seconds and you will have the desired consistency (if you run it longer, instead of a meat loaf, you will have a paté).

 Pasticcio di Carne

Meat loaf

Serves 10

6 slices lean bacon
10 slices white Italian bread, each slice about
  ¾-inch thick
Water
1 pound veal shoulder or similar cut, ground
1 pound pork shoulder or similar cut, ground

(continued)

1 large onion, finely grated
2 whole eggs
½ cup heavy cream
1 teaspoon salt
½ teaspoon black pepper, freshly ground
½ teaspoon thyme
½ teaspoon nutmeg, freshly grated

Preheat the oven to 325°. Line an 8-inch bowl (about 4 to 5 inches deep) with 6 slices of bacon, placing one narrow end in the center of bowl, and making it cling to the sides until it reaches the rim. When 6 slices are in place they should form a sort of star.

Soak the bread slices in water for about 15 minutes, then squeeze very well. Mix together the ground meats, then add the soaked bread slices. Add the onion to the meat mixture. Add the eggs, one at a time, blending in the first before adding the second. Add the cream, salt, pepper, and spices. Work very well with your hands for at least 5 minutes, but 10 is better.

Fill the mold with the mixture, making sure that no empty spaces remain. Flatten the surface with the back of a spoon. Place the mold in a large pan. Add water to the pan. The water should be at least 2 inches deep. Place the pan with the mold in the preheated oven and bake for 2½ hours.

Remove from the oven and cool. There should be a thick edge of fat (bacon and pork) all around the *Pasticcio*. Remove as much of it as you deem necessary. Loosen the mold all around the edges with a sharp knife. When ready to serve, place a round platter on top, rapidly turn upside down, and remove the mold. It will unmold very easily because the bacon strips hold the mixture together.

Kept in the refrigerator, this dish will last a couple of days. Let stand at room temperature for one hour before serving. Decorate with watercress or green bean salad all around.

This is a very rich dish and requires a red wine with some authority. A Castel Chiuro from Valtellina would be just right.

NOTE

I once made this Pasticcio for a party that didn't materialize. I asked myself "why not?" and put it in the freezer, never expecting it to survive. It did, beautifully, for about 2 weeks.

✿ Prosciutto alla Milanese

Boiled ham, Milanese style

Serves 4

2 slices of ham steak, about ⅓-inch thick
4 tablespoons butter
1 whole egg, beaten
3 tablespoons breadcrumbs
Lemon wedges (optional)
A few sprigs parsley (optional)

Cut each slice of ham in half. Each half slice should weigh about ¼ pound.
Heat 2 tablespoons of butter in a skillet wide enough to hold 2 ham slices. Dip the ham into the egg then into the breadcrumbs, using your hands to make the crumbs stick to both sides of the meat. Sauté in the butter on both sides, turning carefully. When done, place the slices on a warmed platter. Add the remaining butter to the skillet and sauté the remaining slices of ham.

Arrange on a platter with lemon wedges and fresh parsley, if desired.

The wine to serve with this is a Bardolino from Lake Garda, or an Amarone from the same region.

NOTE

I don't think that this is an old recipe as I can't find it in any old manuscript. It is probably the result of the soaring price of veal in Italy (or anywhere). Whatever its origin, it is a delicious dish. It might be served with Carciofi alla Milanese (see page 273).

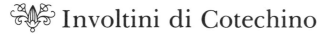

✿ Involtini di Cotechino

Wrapped cotechino

Serves 6

½ cup imported dried mushrooms
Water
1 cotechino, about ½ pound
½ pound veal scaloppine
1 tablespoon flour

(continued)

2 tablespoons butter
2 slices (about 3 oz.) prosciutto, coarsely chopped
½ small onion, sliced
1 stalk of celery, coarsely chopped
2 cups warm water

Soak the mushrooms in a little water and let stand for about 30 minutes. Take the skin off the *cotechino*, being careful not to break the sausage. Beat the slices of veal with a cleaver until very thin and as large as possible. Lay the meat flat on a board so that it forms one sheet. Place the *cotechino* in the center of the meat.

Squeeze the water out of the mushrooms and place the mushrooms around the *cotechino*. Wrap the meat around it and tie it with a piece of string as you would a sausage. Coat lightly with flour.

Melt the butter in a skillet, add the *prosciutto*. Add the onion and celery. When the onion is translucent, carefully place the wrapped *cotechino* in the center of the skillet. Add 2 cups of water (the *cotechino* should be half covered) and simmer, uncovered, over very low heat for about 2 hours. Should the water evaporate, add a few spoonfuls, but be careful not to make the sauce too watery. At the end of the cooking time, the sauce should have the consistency of a regular sauce for pasta (for which it is eminently suited).

Serve the *cotechino* hot, sliced, surrounded by mashed potatoes or *Spinaci all'Olio* (see pages 293-94). Save the cooking liquid for another purpose.

This is a dish from the region of Emilia. Nevertheless, I suggest a wine from the Piedmont with it: a Barolo or a Gattinara. The dish is majestic and requires a majestic wine.

NOTE

Cotechino is a special kind of spicy sausage, available in most Italian communities. It is usually served boiled, either by itself, or as part of a Bollito Misto, the great classic dish of a mixture of boiled meats. The wrapped cotechino is a very rich dish that doesn't require a great deal of work and produces stupendous results.

 Involtino di Salsiccie

Wrapped sausages

Serves 4

4 slices veal scaloppine (about 6 oz.)
4 links sweet Italian sausage

1 teaspoon flour
1 tablespoon butter
½ small onion, sliced
1 stalk of celery, coarsely chopped
1 cup warm water

Place the slices of veal between 2 sheets of wax paper, moisten the top one with cold water, and beat with a cleaver or a mallet (the flat side of the mallet) until very thin. Carefully remove the skin from the sausage links and place one sausage in the center of each slice of meat. Wrap carefully with a string and coat lightly with flour.

Heat the butter in a skillet large enough to hold the 4 sausage links side by side without touching each other. Add the onion to the butter, then add the celery. Cook the onion until transparent. Carefully add the wrapped sausage links and enough water to half cover the sausages. Reduce the heat and simmer for about ½ hour, turning the sausages once.

Serve one *involtino* per person, with mashed potatoes or a green vegetable, accompanied by a red wine: Dolcetto or a Merlot.

Salsiccia all'Aceto

Sausages with vinegar

Serves 4

1 small slice pancetta or salt pork
4 links of sweet Italian sausage
1 clove garlic, crushed
4 tablespoons strong vinegar

Rub a skillet with the *pancetta* or salt pork. This serves only to keep the sausages from sticking. Heat the skillet and add sausage links. Add garlic. Move the sausages with a fork to prevent them from sticking. When they start oozing fat, turn them frequently. Remove garlic. Sprinkle vinegar over the sausages, turning them while doing so. Continue cooking over high heat until the skin of the sausages is golden and slightly wrinkled.

Total cooking time is between 15 and 20 minutes depending on the thickness of the sausages.

Serve with *polenta* (see page 81), accompanied by a Merlot from Friuli or, if unavailable, a Valpolicella. The latter should be slightly cooled.

Variety Meats *interiora*

Variety meats are cuts from the inside of an animal rather than the outside. For the Venetians, they are an acquired taste, with the exception of calf's liver. Venetians seem to be born with a taste and desire for *Fegato alla Veneziana*, or Liver, Venetian Style. But even without onions, liver is a well-liked dish in Italy and is hardly ever missing from a menu.

Kidneys are another matter; one either likes them very much or not at all. The combination of liver and kidneys, broiled or *al burro* (sautéed in butter), appears frequently on menus, but just as frequently people will ask for *solo fegato, senza rognoni* — just liver, without kidneys.

When Italians love kidneys, they love them a lot . . . and a lot of them! I had admired those enormous portions of *Rognoni alla Veneziana*, cooked with Marsala and served sprinkled with parsley, which is a specialty of a restaurant about 30 miles east of Venice. But then one day I ordered them — a whole deep dish full. I ate them . . . all of them, with the result that I couldn't look a kidney in the face for quite a while. Happily that period is over and I can again enjoy them.

There seems to be a lesson in my experience. No variety meat should be eaten in large quantities. Nor should anything else, for that matter, but kidneys, brains, or sweetbreads can easily become what we call in Italian *stucchevoli*, or slightly sickening.

But, until you overeat, these cuts are more tempting in Italy than anywhere else. The reason seems to be that Italian veal is superb. Italian calves are slaughtered at a very early age, which accounts for their pale pink tenderness. One only has to stop in at an Italian butcher store and see the color of the calf's liver to know that it is true.

I have omitted the common recipes, like fried liver or broiled kidneys, simply because they are obvious. And, in case you should be wondering what Marsala wine is doing in a Venetian recipe, please keep in mind that the Republic of Venice was in contact with Sicily (as it was with Greece and with what is now southern Italy, where the use of oil originated) from time immemorial. That's where we got the Marsala habit, although actually it is not used very much in Venetian cooking.

Animelle al Prosciutto

Sweetbreads sautéed with prosciutto

Serves 4 to 5

1 ½ pounds sweetbreads
Water
2 tablespoons butter
2 slices of prosciutto
1 teaspoon salt
Black pepper, freshly ground
1 cup broth, chicken or beef
1 teaspoon flour

Soak the sweetbreads in cold water for 1 hour. Change water once or twice during that period.

Remove the sweetbreads from the water and place them in a saucepan with boiling water. Boil for a couple of minutes. (The cold water will keep them white, the boiling water will permit you to peel them.) Remove the sweetbreads from the boiling water, rinse them under cold water, and remove the skin. Cut the sweetbreads into bite-sized pieces.

Melt the butter in a saucepan, but don't brown. Chop the *prosciutto* in a food processor, using the sharp blade. Run the motor for 30 seconds or less; the *prosciutto* should not be chopped too finely. Add the *prosciutto* to the butter and sauté. When the fat of the *prosciutto* is translucent, add the sweetbreads. Season with salt and pepper. Cover and cook, for a couple of minutes. Stir, turning the sweetbreads to make sure they cook evenly. Add a couple of tablespoons broth, cover, and cook for another 8 to 10 minutes. The total cooking time should be about 10 to 15 minutes, depending on the size of the sweetbread pieces. When they are done, place on a warmed platter and keep warm.

Remove the *prosciutto*-butter mixture from the heat and stir in the flour. Add a little broth and put the pan back onto the low heat. Cook until the liquid is reduced to the desired thickness: it should not be too liquid and not too thick. Pour the sauce over the sweetbreads and serve immediately. Serve with sautéed mushrooms or buttered peas or both.

Serve with a dry white wine. Sweetbreads are a delicate dish and require a delicate wine. A Lugana from Lake Garda or a good Soave from the same region would be perfect.

NOTE

Many cooks hesitate making sweetbreads because they feel that they are difficult to prepare or not appetizing to handle. Keep sweetbreads in cold water and they will stay appetizingly white. Blanch them in hot water and the skin will come off with ease.

Imported Italian prosciutto seems hard to come by these days. American prosciutto, although not adequate for other purposes, is satisfactory for this.

 Animelle con Funghi

Sweetbreads with mushrooms

Serves 4 to 6

1 pound sweetbreads
1 quart water
1 cup (tightly packed) fresh sliced mushrooms
4 tablespoons butter
⅓ cup broth, chicken or beef
⅓ cup light cream
Salt and freshly ground black pepper
2 tablespoons lemon juice
2 tablespoons parsley, chopped

Soak the sweetbreads in cold water for 1 hour. Change the water once or twice during that period.

In another saucepan bring water to a boil and dip the sweetbreads in it. The skin should come off easily. Cut into bite-sized pieces.

Clean the mushrooms; if necessary, peel them. Slice both caps and stems after removing all sandy parts.

Melt the butter in a skillet, add the mushrooms, cover, and cook over high heat for about 3 minutes. That's the way to cook them if you want them to stay white. Add the sweetbreads and cook over medium heat for about 10 minutes, turning them frequently. Move the sweetbreads to a warmed platter and keep warm while you prepare the sauce.

Add the cream to the butter-broth mixture in the skillet. Taste and add salt and pepper. Add the lemon juice and, using a spatula, scrape up all particles that have stuck to the bottom of the skillet. Add the parsley and cook for a few seconds. Pour the mixture over the sweetbreads and serve at once with no other dishes. Rice or any other starch would dilute the delicate taste of the dish.

A good white wine, like a really good Soave di Verona would go well with this dish, as would a Pinot Grigio or a Durello (the latter is still hard to find but is getting more popular in this country; in Italy it already is popular).

 Animelle con Piselli

Sweetbreads with green peas

Serves 6

1 ½ pounds sweetbreads
1 quart water
½ stick butter
3-4 tiny young onions or 1 medium-sized leek
1 cup small fresh green peas, cooked or canned
Salt and freshly ground black pepper
1 cup broth, chicken or beef
1 tablespoon parsley, finely chopped

Soak the sweetbreads in cold water for 1 hour. Change the water once or twice during that period.

Bring fresh water to a boil in a saucepan. Place the sweetbreads on a slotted spoon and dip the spoon into the boiling water until they are submerged. Remove almost immediately; the skin should come off easily.

Depending on the thickness of the sweetbreads, cut them into pieces or slices. The pieces shouldn't be thicker than ½ to ¾ inches.

Melt the butter in a skillet. If onions are very small, add them whole to the butter, otherwise cut them in half. If leek is used, chop it coarsely then add it to the skillet. Don't brown. Add the sweetbreads and sauté over high heat until pale golden. Add the peas (if you are using canned peas, also add the canning liquid — it contains the best part of the taste). Season with salt and pepper. After about 10 minutes, add a little broth. Continue cooking for about 15 minutes. Whenever the sweetbreads seem dry, add a little broth. A couple of minutes before removing from stove, add the parsley. Mix and serve immediately.

Sweetbreads are not everybody's taste. But those who like them like them a lot. I belong to those.

A Pinot Grigio, dry, white, and slightly fruity, or a Durello from the region near Vicenza, would be ideal wines with this delicate dish.

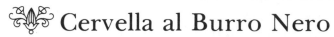 Cervella al Burro Nero

Calf's brains with browned butter

Serves 4

1 pound calf's brains
Water
1 cup dry white wine
6 tablespoons butter
Salt and freshly ground black pepper
1 tablespoon parsley, finely chopped
1 tablespoon small capers packed in vinegar,
    drained

Place the brains in a colander and rinse under cold running water for several minutes. If the skin doesn't come off easily, dip the brains briefly into hot water. Peel. Bring water to a boil in a sauce pan not much larger than the brains. Add ⅓ cup of the wine to the water. Add the brains and cook over medium heat for about 10 minutes. Drain and place on a warmed platter. Keep warm while you prepare the butter.

Melt the butter in a skillet and heat until quite brown. Add the remaining wine and the salt and pepper. Cook for 5 minutes over medium heat (the liquid should not evaporate). Add the brains to the butter turning them once or twice in the pan. Sprinkle with parsley and serve immediately, placing the brains in the center of the platter. Pour the browned butter over the brains then sprinkle the capers over them as you serve them.

The wine used in cooking should be served with this dish: a Pinot Grigio, a Durello, or maybe a white Venegazù.

NOTE

Brains, like sweetbreads, are not everybody's dish. They are mine, passionately so. But I like to cook them myself, not only because I like to make sure that they are perfectly fresh (on hot days it is one of the most dangerous dishes to order in a restaurant you don't trust completely), but also because most cooks use vinegar instead of wine and I find the smell of hot vinegar unpleasant. If the brains seem too bland, squeeze a little lemon over them.

 # Fegatini di Pollo con l'Uva

Chicken livers with grapes

Serves 4 to 5

½ cup small white seedless grapes or ⅓ cup
   raisins
1 pound chicken livers
1 stick butter
Salt and freshly ground black pepper
½ cup dry white wine

If raisins are used, soak them in warm water while you prepare the livers. Clean the chicken livers carefully. Cut the larger ones in half. Heat the butter in a skillet large enough so that the livers won't be crowded. Add the livers to the butter when it is very hot but not brown.

Drain and add the raisins to livers or, if grapes are used, add these to the livers. Season with salt and pepper, then stir carefully to avoid crushing the grapes. Add the wine and cook over medium heat until done or until no blood is visible when you press the livers with a wooden spoon. Serve immediately.

A chicken liver dish, as with any other meal, traditionally calls for red wine. This particular dish, however, is cooked with white wine and should therefore be accompanied by a white wine. It should not be too dry because it would make the grapes taste too sweet. A Pinot Grigio would be a very good choice. If, however, you want to stick to red, I would suggest a Merlot from the Friuli, a region near Venice, slightly to the east of the city.

NOTE

   This is a Venetian dish (Figadini con L'Ua in Venetian dialect). An Oriental influence is obvious, as is the case in many Venetian dishes whose origins go back to the 15th and 16th centuries.

 # Fegato alla Milanese

Calf's liver, Milanese style

Serves 4

1 pound calf's liver
½ cup breadcrumbs
1 whole egg, beaten

(continued)

3 tablespoons butter
Coarse salt
Juice of ½ lemon

Slice the liver into the desired thickness, depending upon how well done you prefer it. Cut the slices thin if you like your liver well done: ⅓-inch thickness for slightly pinkish liver. Remove all tendons and membrane.

Spread the breadcrumbs on a working surface. Dip the liver into the beaten egg, then into the breadcrumbs, pressing the crumbs to the meat with your hands to make sure they will cling.

Melt the butter in a skillet over high heat. Sauté a couple of liver slices at a time so they have plenty of space between them. Turn the slices with a spatula; they should be golden on both sides.

Arrange the slices on a warmed, oblong platter. At the moment of serving, sprinkle a little salt over each slice and then a few drops of lemon juice.

The liver should be served immediately because it gets tough. It is usually served with boiled potatoes and spinach sautéed in oil. A Bardolino, or a Valpolicella, both from Lake Garda, are fragrant red wines that would go well with liver.

 # Fegato alla Veneziana

Calf's liver, Venetian style

Serves 4

3 tablespoons butter
3 tablespoons oil
2 large white onions, thinly sliced
1 pound calf's liver
1 tablespoon parsley, finely chopped
Salt and freshly ground black pepper
3 tablespoons broth (optional)
3 tablespoons vinegar (optional)

Melt the butter in a pan or skillet, then add the oil. Don't brown. Add the onions and cook over very low heat until they are wilted and pale blonde. Don't brown the onion.

Cut the liver into thin slivers, removing membrane and veins. Add the

liver to the onions and cook rapidly over high heat (cooking time is 5 to 6 minutes depending on thickness of slices), stirring and turning with a wooden spoon. One minute before removing the liver from the pan, add the parsley, salt and pepper, broth (if needed because liver seems too dry), and vinegar, if desired. Serve at once, with *polenta* (see page 81) or boiled potatoes.

This dish is as Venetian as Saint Mark's square. It requires a wine from the region around Venice: a Merlot from the Friuli, or a Valpolicella from nearby Lake Garda. Keep in mind that no grapes grow in Venice!

Fegato di Vitello alla Vicentina

Calf's liver, Vicenza style

Serves 4

3 tablespoons butter
3 tablespoons oil
2 or 3 large white onions, thinly sliced
1 cup dry white wine
1 pound calf's liver
Juice of ½ lemon
Salt and freshly ground black pepper

Melt the butter in a skillet or heatproof pan large enough to hold the liver in 1 layer. Add the oil and heat.
Add the onions to the pan and cook over very low heat until wilted and light blonde. Add the wine. Remove the membrane and veins from the liver and cut into thin slivers. Add it to the butter-oil-wine mixture and increase the heat, keeping in mind that liver cooks in 5 minutes and has to be eaten immediately. Cook over high heat, stirring with a wooden spoon. One minute before removing from heat, add lemon juice, salt, and pepper. Serve immediately.

Usually I would suggest a light red wine with liver, but this recipe calls for white wine in cooking and the same wine should be served with the dish. Try one of the dry whites with which the Veneto is so rich: a Soave or a Durello, if available. It is worth making an effort to find this wine. It is gay and lively like a spring day in Vicenza.

Rognoni d'Agnello

Lamb kidneys

Serves 6

6 lamb kidneys
¼ cup imported dried mushrooms
¼ cup hot water
2 tablespoons oil
2 tablespoons butter
¼ cup dry Marsala wine
1 tablespoon wine vinegar
Salt and freshly ground black pepper

Remove the membrane from the kidneys along with the center vein. Cut each in half lengthwise. Soak the mushrooms in the hot water and let stand until soft (approximately 5 minutes).

Heat the oil and sauté the kidneys very quickly over high heat, 2 minutes each side. Remove and place on a warmed platter. Add butter to the oil in the pan and add the mushrooms with their water. Simmer and add the Marsala and vinegar. Taste and add salt and pepper. Simmer the mixture until the liquid is reduced to 2 tablespoons. Pour over the warm kidneys and serve immediately.

Serve this with steamed rice or boiled potatoes. A Valpolicella from the region of Lake Garda will enhance this dish.

NOTE

Never add the kidneys to the sauce. Kidneys should cook as little as possible because they harden easily.

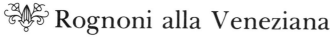

Rognoni alla Veneziana

Kidneys, Venetian style

Serves 6

2 cups water
½ cup vinegar
1 pound veal kidneys
1 tablespoon flour

½ *stick butter*
1 *scallion, chopped*
Salt and freshly ground black pepper
Pinch of nutmeg, freshly grated
1 *cup broth*
½ *cup dry Marsala wine*
1 *tablespoon parsley, finely chopped*

Pour the water into a bowl and add the vinegar. Soak the kidneys in this mixture for at least 1 hour. Remove, dry, and slice the kidneys. Remove the center vein if the butcher has not already done so. Spread the flour on a flat surface and coat the kidneys lightly.

Melt the butter in a skillet, add the scallion, then the salt, pepper, and nutmeg. Place the kidneys in the pan. Cook over high heat for about 6 to 8 minutes, stirring frequently so that all slices are cooked evenly; add a little broth when they seem to get dry. Don't overcook because the kidneys tend to get tough. When done, add the Marsala and let it evaporate. Sprinkle the parsley over the kidneys, stir and serve immediately.

Serve this with boiled potatoes or even only with good bread. It is best not to serve any vegetables that will interfere with the taste of the kidneys.

The kidneys and the Marsala require a red wine with authority: a Castel Chiuro from Valtellina would be an excellent choice.

NOTE

I have said repeatedly that the wine used in cooking should also be served with the dish. In this case this is obviously not possible. No one can drink Marsala while eating kidneys. It is used in cooking to add its unique almondlike flavor to the dish.

 # Rognoni di Vitello al Cognac

Veal kidneys with Cognac

Serves 4 to 5

1 ½ *pounds veal kidneys*
2 *tablespoons butter*
2 *tablespoons olive oil*
3 *tablespoons Cognac or brandy*
¼ *cup broth*
Salt and freshly ground black pepper
2 *tablespoons parsley, finely chopped*

Clean the kidneys, removing membrane, fat, and center vein. Slice the kidneys crosswise.

Heat the butter and oil in a skillet large enough to hold the kidney slices without overlapping too much. Add the kidney slices and stir rapidly over high heat, turning the slices quickly. After about 5 minutes, add the Cognac or brandy. Stir and add as much broth as needed to keep the slices moist (approximately ¼ cup but you might need even less). Add salt and pepper, stir, and add the parsley a minute or so before the kidneys are done. Parsley, like kidneys, should cook as little as possible.

Serve with steamed rice or mashed potatoes. The kidneys being veal would require a white wine, but I personally feel that kidneys have a richer taste than veal. If a white wine is served, it should be a fruity one, like a Pinot Grigio. Personally I would prefer a Bardolino. In any case, the wine should not overpower the taste of the Cognac.

Vegetables and Salads

Vegetables

Italians don't like to eat vegetables out of season. They wait impatiently for the first tender peas, the first ripe tomatoes. All these firsts are called *primizie* and are considered great delicacies, which they are. However, in recent years in Italy as in this country, most vegetables are available the year round, artificially grown in hothouses, or even kept in storage from previous seasons. Many Italians ignore them, however. They say they are tasteless (which they are) and less nutritious (which they might be).

Meat is expensive in Italy, and large families can't afford to have it frequently. So meats are served on great occasions and vegetables — baked, fried, stuffed, with sauces, or steamed and lavishly seasoned with olive oil — frequently take the place of meat or fish.

The ways of preparing vegetables are almost endless. Some of the following recipes are classic ones, others are specialties of certain restaurants, family recipes, or recent additions to the Italian gastronomic heritage.

The special emphasis on asparagus is because I have lived in the Piedmont and have paid several visits to Santena, the center of the Land of the Asparagus. I have tasted asparagus in every shape and form, I think.

I remember one dinner quite vividly. We used to say to the owner *faccia lei*, meaning, serve whatever you choose. It started with the most tender parts of the asparagus cut into bite-sized pieces, served cold with a sauce made of olive oil and lemon juice with a little fresh pepper. This was followed by asparagus soup — not the creamed variety we are so used to, but a clear chicken broth with quantities of green asparagus tips floating in it. Fresh Parmesan was served on the side. The third course was a marvelous plate of *Asparagi al Burro e Parmigiano* (see page 275), followed by *Asparagi alla Milanese*. The asparagus orgy ended with *Asparagi fritti* (see pages 276-77), when he reluctantly brought us chunks of Parmesan to nibble with our fruit.

You would think that, after that experience, we wouldn't want to look at asparagus for a while, but no! A week or so later we repeated the

performance, more or less. This time in Albenga, the center of the fruit and vegetable producing coast of Liguria on the Mediterranean.

The asparagus of Albenga are probably the most famous in Europe and are exported in quantity. They are beautiful looking asparagus that any asparagus lover dreams of but, at the risk of making enemies among the "*conoscitori,*" the experts, I find them less tasty than the much less known Santena variety.

And then there are the bright green and comparatively skinny asparagus of Lombardy. Their flavor is almost a perfume and their taste totally different from either the Santena or the Albenga variety. We mention all this to say that the same vegetable, grown in different parts of Italy, can be totally different in taste and appearance. Soil? Climate? Both. Italy is long and thin as a country and it covers a large area.

Incidentally, both Santena and Albenga are well worth a visit if you are on a gourmet tour of Italy. Albenga also produces famous and glorious peaches and the most delicious tiny artichokes, whereas Santena wouldn't even admit that they eat any vegetable other than asparagus.

 # Fondi di Carciofi al Tegame

Artichoke hearts in a skillet

Serves 6

4 large artichokes
Juice of ½ lemon
Salt and freshly ground black pepper
1 cup of broth, chicken or beef
1 clove of garlic
1 tablespoon parsley, finely chopped
2 tablespoons oil (optional)

Artichoke hearts is a misleading expression. *Fondi di carciofi* are actually the whole bottom of the artichoke, with the stems and hard outer leaves removed. Remove the choke as well and cut the artichokes into 4 or 6 pieces. Place in a skillet large enough for the artichoke pieces not to pile on top of one another. Add the lemon juice, salt, and pepper and cover with broth. Bring to a boil. Cover and simmer for 5 minutes. Add the garlic clove and parsley. Stir and continue to cook over medium heat, this time completely

uncovered, for a couple of minutes, or until the broth is almost completely absorbed. The artichokes should be tender and easily pierced with a fork.

Add the oil to the pan and cook for 2 or 3 minutes longer. The total cooking time for the artichokes should be not more than 10 minutes. Serve with roast meat or fowl.

Artichokes will kill any wine; try it if you don't believe it. The taste of artichokes does funny things to your palate. But, if you serve them with meat or fowl, the meats will dictate the choice of your wine. Just make sure you don't drink it after you eat a piece of artichoke.

Carciofi alla Milanese

Artichokes, Milanese style

Serves 4 to 6

4 large artichokes
1 lemon
Water
Salt
2 whole eggs, beaten
4 tablespoons breadcrumbs
6 tablespoons butter

Prepare this dish only when artichokes are in season. They should be firm and green, not flecked with brown spots.

Remove the stems and outer leaves, as well as the sharp tops of the leaves. Cut the lemon in half and rub the artichokes all over with it. Fill a saucepan with water, drop the artichokes in, and add a lemon half while you prepare the other artichokes.

Cut the artichokes into slices about ¼-inch thick. Remove the choke from each slice. Salt the water then add a few drops of lemon. Bring the water to a boil and cook the artichokes until tender (about 7 to 8 minutes, depending upon the freshness of the artichokes). Drain well. Dip the slices of artichokes into the beaten egg, then into the breadcrumbs. Heat the butter in a skillet wide enough to hold the artichokes in 1 layer. If they are crowded, they won't brown properly. Sauté until golden. Serve as accompaniment to a roast or breaded veal cutlets.

No wine should be drunk with artichokes. Their taste will alter the taste of any wine and make it seem sweet. If they are served with meat, take a sip of wine while eating the meat, not after tasting the artichokes.

Carciofi Ripieni con Funghi

Artichokes stuffed with mushrooms

Serves 6

6 large artichokes
Water
1 lemon, cut in half
1 ½ cups fresh mushrooms
2 tablespoons butter
½ cup olive oil
½ cup Parmesan cheese, freshly grated

Remove the outer leaves of the artichokes. Stop removing leaves only when all the dark ones have been discarded. Trim off about 1 inch from top. Cut off the stems and trim the bases so that the artichokes can stand up. Rub them all over with the lemon half.

Fill a saucepan with water and add the other lemon half. The saucepan should be large enough for the artichokes to float and not to be on top of one another. Boil for 15 to 20 minutes or until the bases can be pierced easily with a fork. Remove the artichokes from the water and let cool. Open the centers with your hands and remove the chokes, called *barba* (beard) in Italian. With a teaspoon, make a well in the centers of the artichokes.

Preheat the oven to 400°. Rub the mushrooms with a wet towel but don't wash them unless you have to. If the caps are very dark, peel them. Remove the ends of the stems if they are sandy. Place the mushrooms in a food processor and run the motor for 30 to 40 seconds. The mushrooms should be finely chopped but not puréed.

Melt the butter in a skillet, add the mushrooms, and cook, covered, over very high heat for about 5 minutes. Uncover and continue cooking over high heat until the liquid has all been absorbed.

With 1 tablespoon of oil, coat a large pan. Place the artichokes in the pan side by side. Fill the artichokes with the mushrooms then pour the remaining oil evenly over the surface. Sprinkle with Parmesan. Bake for about 25 minutes. If you want the tops to be darker, place the pan briefly under the broiler before serving.

If artichokes are served as a first course, no wine should be served with them. Artichokes have a strange effect on tastebuds: they make everything taste sweet. If artichokes are served as accompaniment to a meat course, the meat dictates the wine to be served. We can only hope that no one will take a sip of wine while his or her mouth is full of artichoke.

 # Asparagi al Burro e Parmigiano

Asparagus with butter and Parmesan

Serves 6

2 pounds fresh asparagus
Salt
½ cup Parmesan cheese, freshly grated
1 stick butter

Cut the tough parts of the stems off the asparagus. Scrape but don't peel the asparagus. Cut them all to a uniform length. Cook vertically in an asparagus cooker or steam horizontally in a long narrow pan. Salt, cover, and cook until the asparagus are done but still quite firm.

Place the asparagus on a long platter with half the stems going one way, the other half reversed; the tips should meet in the center. Sprinkle Parmesan cheese over the center and over the edible parts of the asparagus, leaving only the tail ends uncovered.

Melt the butter and brown it in the pan. Pour it over the Parmesan while still very hot; it should melt the cheese slightly. Serve very hot as a first course, 5 or 6 per person, on individual dishes.

Serve with a light dry wine: a Bardolino or a Valpolicella.

NOTE

I say to leave the tail ends uncovered, meaning they should have no butter or cheese on them. Italians believe that it is perfectly proper to pick up asparagus with your fingers, eat the tender part, and place the end back on your plate. As with most things in life, it depends on how you do it. If you gesture while you eat and spray your neighbor, or even if you let the butter run down your forearm, you are better off using a fork and cutting off the tender parts. But you will miss so much of the taste.

 # Asparagi alla Milanese

Asparagus, Milan style

Serves 6

2 pounds fresh asparagus
½ cup Parmesan cheese, freshly grated
4 tablespoons butter

(continued)

6 whole eggs
Butter to fry the eggs

Clean and cook asparagus as for the preceding recipe. Melt the butter and brown it in the pan.

Place the cooked asparagus on individual plates, cover the tops with Parmesan cheese, and pour a little browned butter over each portion.

Melt the remaining butter in a pan. Fry eggs sunny side up in a very shallow frying pan so that they slide out without breaking. Place 1 egg on each portion of asparagus, pour a little of the butter from the pan over each, and serve very hot.

A Chiaretto del Garda, light red and fruity, is the best companion for this dish.

NOTE

The reason for the lesser amount of browned butter as compared to the preceding recipe is that the eggs are fried in butter; you add that butter to the asparagus.

 Asparagi Fritti

Fried asparagus

Serves 4 to 6

1 pound fresh asparagus
1½ cups oil
1 cup breadcrumbs, finely ground
1 whole egg, beaten
Salt

Cut off the hard parts of the asparagus, making quite sure that the portions that are left are totally edible. They should all be the same length. That length depends upon the quality of the asparagus — about 4 inches.

Scrape off the thorny little leaves below the tip, but don't peel your asparagus. Wash in cold water until no trace of sand is left. Dry on a paper towel.

Heat the oil in a large skillet. The oil should be deeper in the pan than the thickest part of the asparagus. While the oil heats, spread the breadcrumbs on

a working surface. Sprinkle a few drops of water into the oil; when they sizzle, the oil is hot enough. Dip the asparagus, one by one, into the beaten egg and roll in the breadcrumbs. Put a few asparagus in the oil at a time. They, like all other foods, don't like to be crowded. Turn them with a slotted spatula when they are golden. When both sides are done (about 1 minute each side), lift them out with the spatula and drain on a paper towel. Sprinkle a little salt on them while they are hot.

Serve as accompaniment to roast meat or fowl, or with a plain omelette. Avoid serving them with dishes with sauces or gravies. One of the delights of this dish is the crispness of the asparagus. The choice of wine depends, of course, on the main dish for your meal.

 # Broccoli "Strascinati" all'Olio d'Oliva

"Dragged" broccoli with olive oil

Serves 4

1 pound fresh broccoli
½ cup olive oil
1 clove of garlic
Salt and freshly ground black pepper

Cut off the tough parts of the stems and remove any tough outer leaves. Cut the tender portions of the stems lengthwise and separate the tops into bite-sized florets. Wash and drain well.

Pour the oil into a large skillet wide enough to hold the broccoli parts without piling them on top of one another. Heat the oil and add the garlic clove over high heat. As soon as the garlic is blonde, remove and discard. Add the broccoli pieces to the oil, mixing gently with a wooden spoon. Reduce the heat and add salt and pepper. Cover and simmer over very low heat until done. Check every now and then and add a little water if needed. The exact cooking time can't be given because it depends upon the thickness of the broccoli; it should be approximately 20 minutes. Test with a fork to make sure they are done. Serve as accompaniment to roasted meat or fowl.

NOTE

Keep in mind that broccoli in Italy are less beautiful and less thick than in the United States, but they tend to be more flavorful. At times you find wild broccoli or mustard greens in the market. They lend themselves to the same preparation.

When I started writing this book I wondered where that funny name of "dragged" came from. My only explanation is that, in order not to break up the broccoli, you don't stir them as you would carrots or other vegetables but you "drag" them with a wooden spoon from one side of the skillet to the other.

 # Cavolfiore con Salsa di Acciughe

Cauliflower with anchovy sauce

Serves 6

1 medium-sized cauliflower
Water
Salt
½ cup olive oil
1 clove of garlic, crushed (optional)
8 anchovy filets
Black pepper, freshly ground
3 tablespoons chopped parsley

Remove the outer leaves from the cauliflower, as well as the tough part of the stem. Wash under running water. Make a cross-shaped incision in the remaining part of the stem (this is the old-fashioned way of cooking cauliflower: it is supposed to make the stem tender).

In a saucepan that isn't much larger than the cauliflower, bring the water to a boil. Add salt. Add the cauliflower and cook, uncovered, until tender but not mushy. The cooking time will vary depending upon the size of the cauliflower, but it will be about 20 minutes.

When the cauliflower is almost done, heat the oil in a saucepan; add the crushed garlic, if desired. Add the anchovies and, stirring with a wooden spoon, dissolve the anchovies in the oil. Add pepper to taste.

Remove the cooked cauliflower from the water and place it on a warmed platter. Add the chopped parsley to the oil and then almost immediately (parsley gets bitter if it cooks too long) pour the mixture over the cauliflower and serve very hot, either with a meat or fish dish.

Crostata di Cavolfiore e Riso

Cauliflower and rice casserole

Serves 6

1 medium-sized cauliflower
1 quart water
Salt
1 cup rice, preferably Italian
½ stick + 1 tablespoon butter
1 small onion, chopped
Black pepper, freshly ground
½ cup Parmesan cheese, freshly grated
1 cup besciamella (see pages 22-23)

Discard the stem and all tough outer leaves of the cauliflower. Bring the water to a boil in a saucepan that is quite a bit larger than the cauliflower. Add salt and cook the cauliflower until almost done; about 15 minutes, depending on the size of the cauliflower. Remove from the water with a pair of slotted spoons and place on a warmed platter.

Bring the water in which cauliflower has cooked to a boil again and add the rice. Stir rapidly and cook until done but still firm (about 20 minutes, depending on the quality of the rice). Bite 1 kernel: it has to be quite firm between your teeth but it must not taste raw. Drain the rice and place in a bowl. Add 4 tablespoons of butter. Mix.

Preheat the oven to 400°. Melt 4 tablespoons of butter in a large skillet, add the chopped onion, and sauté until golden but not brown. Add the buttered rice and mix well. Add salt if needed; remember, though, that the rice was cooked in salted water. Add pepper and Parmesan, reserving 1 tablespoon of grated cheese for later use.

With 1 tablespoon of butter grease an 8-inch baking or soufflé dish. Make a layer of rice, followed by a layer of *besciamella* and a layer of cauliflower, using only the tender parts of the vegetable. Continue to make layers until all the rice and cauliflower have been used up. The top layer has to be *besciamella*. Sprinkle the top with the rest of the Parmesan and place in preheated oven. Remove as soon as the top is golden, about 20 minutes.

If the *Crostata* is used as a course by itself, a light red wine should be served with it. If it is used to accompany a meat dish, the meat will dictate the choice of wine.

Sedani di Verona al Burro e Formaggio

Celery root with butter and Parmesan

Serves 6

2 or 3 large celery roots
Water
Salt
Juice of ½ lemon
4 tablespoons butter
4 tablespoons Parmesan cheese, freshly grated

Wash the celery roots and peel them, using a very sharp small knife. Celery roots have an uneven surface. Use the knife to remove dark spots. Bring the water to a boil in a large saucepan, add the salt and the lemon juice. Place the roots in the boiling water and cook until tender — about 15 to 20 minutes, depending on the size of the roots. When done, let cool and slice into pieces about ⅓-inch thick.

Melt the butter in a skillet, add the celery slices, and sauté briefly for 3 to 4 minutes, or until the slices are well coated with butter; don't overcook. Sprinkle Parmesan over the celery slices and serve as an accompaniment to meat or fowl.

NOTE

Celery roots are called Celery of Verona because that is the city where they were first appreciated. They are now a popular dish, particularly in northern Italy. In the United States, celery roots have really not come into their own. If they are served at all, they are usually served raw, cut into thin strips and served as celery remoulade. It is about time some attention were paid to these delicious roots.

 Sformato di Cicoria

Chicory mold

Serves 4 to 6

2 medium-sized heads of chicory
Salt

*3 slices white or whole wheat bread (no rye, nor
   bread with caraway seeds)*
½ cup chicken broth
3 whole eggs
Black pepper, freshly ground
3 hard-boiled eggs, halved lengthwise
½ teaspoon nutmeg, freshly grated
½ cup Parmesan cheese, freshly grated

Preheat the oven to 350°. Cut or tear the chicory leaves into 1- to 2-inch pieces, using all the green leaves of the chicory. If there are small tender white leaves in the center, set these aside and reserve for a salad.

Boil the chicory in slightly salted water for about 10 minutes. Let cool. When the chicory is cool enough to handle, squeeze out the water, taking a little chicory at a time. When as much water as possible has been removed, purée in a food mill. If you have a food processor use the sharp blade and run the motor for about 2 to 4 seconds.

Soak slices of bread in the check broth until quite mushy. Add these to the chicory and mix well with a wooden spoon until blended. Add the 3 uncooked eggs to the chicory mixture and mix well. Add salt, pepper, nutmeg, and most of the Parmesan, reserving 1 spoonful for later use.

Generously butter an 8-inch soufié dish. Make a layer of chicory mixture using half the mix. Arrange the hard-boiled egg halves in a circle over the chicory mixture. Cover with the remaining chicory. Sprinkle with the remaining Parmesan. Place the soufflé dish in the center of oven and bake for 40 minutes.

Let stand for about 10 minutes, then unmold onto a platter. If you prefer, *Sformato* may be served as is without unmolding. If you choose to unmold it, cheese should be sprinkled over surface after unmolding.

This *Sformato* is delicious hot or cold and may be served as first course, for a picnic, or as an accompaniment to a main course. If it is served by itself, either a Merlot, a Valpolicella, or a Bardolino (if your preference is for red wines) may be served with it. If you serve it on a hot summer day and prefer a cold glass of white, a Soave or a Pinot Grigio would go equally well. In other words, stick to a light dry wine and stay away from a heavy wine that might overpower the dish.

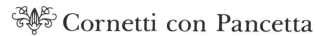 Cornetti con Pancetta

Green beans with pancetta

Serves 6

1 pound fresh green beans
Water
Salt
¾ (tightly packed) pancetta or salt pork, diced
1 small onion, chopped
⅓ cup olive oil

Cornetti are a special type of short thin bean; the equivalent in this country are the long beans, available in Oriental food stores. The long beans, however, are much longer than the Italian *cornetti* and have to be cut 3 or 4 times into 3-inch segments. The texture is exactly the same and they are equally tasty.

Remove the tips of the long beans, cut to desired length, and wash. Bring water to a boil, add salt, then the beans. Boil until beans are almost done. Bite into 1; it should be cooked *al dente*. Drain and reserve.

Place the *pancetta* in a large skillet and brown lightly. Add the onion to the pan. When the onion is translucent, add the oil and fry a couple of minutes longer. Add the beans and mix well with a wooden spoon. Taste again and add salt if necessary. Serve as accompaniment to a roast of veal or beef.

NOTE

This recipe sounds like a lot of bother with special ingredients, what with the pancetta and the long beans. But, once you take the trouble looking, you will be surprised how easy it is to find both of them. Pancetta is available in most Italian groceries or butcher stores and even in some markets.

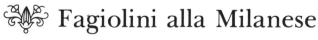 Fagiolini alla Milanese

Green beans, Milanese style

Serves 4

1 pound fresh green beans
Salt
Water

1 whole egg, beaten
3 tablespoons light cream
Black pepper, freshly ground
1 tablespoon Parmesan cheese, freshly grated
Juice of ½ lemon

Be sure your beans are fresh; they should snap sharply when you break off the ends. Wash them, then boil, uncovered, in a lot of salted water. Drain very well by pouring the contents of the pot into a colander, then place the colander with the beans into the empty pot and place the pot back on the stove with the heat turned off. There will be enough heat left to dry the beans but not so much as to burn the pot or the colander.

In a bowl, place the beaten egg, the cream, salt, and pepper and beat until well blended. Add the grated Parmesan, beat again, and then add the lemon juice. Beat a little longer, then pour the mixture over the beans, stirring continuously as you pour. They should be evenly coated. Quickly cook, stirring, for a minute or less. Serve hot. If desired, serve a little grated Parmesan with the vegetable, to be sprinkled over it at the moment of eating.

NOTE

The beans may, of course, be boiled ahead of time. Be sure not to overcook them. The cooking time depends upon size of the beans. Figure approximately 10 to 15 minutes, taking into account that the beans you buy in U.S. markets are usually quite mature. If you can find long beans, available in Oriental food stores, cut them to the desired length and boil for about 7 to 8 minutes.

I have added this egg-cream-cheese mixture to boiled spinach and found it very good. Make sure the spinach is dry or the result will be watery.

 Fagiolini al Buro

Green beans sautéed in butter

Serves 6

2 pounds fresh green beans
2 quarts water
Salt
3 tablespoons butter
1 tablespoon parsley (optional)

Wash the beans and snap off the ends. Remove any strings. In a large kettle bring the water to a boil and add the salt. When the water is boiling vigorously, add the beans. The beans should be cooked in plenty of water. Cook until done; they should be tender but not mushy. The cooking time depends on the size and freshness of the beans. The average cooking time is about 15 minutes. Drain.

Heat the butter in a skillet but don't allow it to brown. Add the beans and mix well so that all are well coated. Cook for about 5 more minutes. Just before removing them from the heat, add salt and the parsley, if desired. The parsley should never cook for more than a minute because it tends to become bitter.

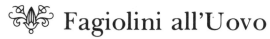 ## Fagiolini all'Uovo

Green beans with eggs

Serves 6

1 pound fresh green beans
Water
Salt
2 tablespoons oil
2 tablespoons butter
1 small onion, thinly sliced
½ teaspoon oregano
2 egg yolks
Juice of ½ lemon

Wash the beans. Snap off the ends and remove the strings, if they have any. Bring the water to a boil in a large kettle and add salt. The beans should always be boiled in plenty of water. The cooking time depends on the size of the beans; average time is 15 minutes.

While the beans are cooking, heat the oil and butter in a skillet. Add the onion slices. Cook the onion until blonde but not brown. Drain the beans and add them to the pan. Cook for about 5 minutes over low heat. The onion must not burn.

After 5 minutes, add the oregano. Beat the egg yolks with the lemon juice. Remove the beans from the burner and quickly mix in the beaten egg. Mix and serve as soon as yolks have been absorbed.

Fagiolini Fritti

Green beans deep fried

Serves 6

1 pound fresh green beans
Water
Salt
2 whole eggs, lightly beaten
½ cup flour
Oil for deep frying
1 teaspoon coarse salt

Wash the beans and snap off both ends, removing strings if there are any. Bring the water to a strong boil, add salt, and then add the beans. Cook until tender. The cooking time depends upon the freshness and size of the beans — approximately 15 minutes. Drain.

Dip 3 or 4 beans in the beaten egg, holding them together like a little bunch, then dip them in flour. Heat the oil in a deep saucepan. If you have an oil thermometer, heat the oil to 450°; if not, heat the oil until a couple of drops of water will sizzle when sprinkled on the surface. Lower the beans into the oil with a slotted spoon. Fry until golden. Remove with the slotted spoon and place on a paper towel. Sprinkle with salt and serve very hot on a heated platter.

This is an unusual dish. Deep-fried green beans are not only pretty but also delicious. They must be eaten while they are crisp. Serve around a roast or a roasted fowl. Don't place them around a meat course with gravy since they would get soggy.

NOTE

Frying oil may be reused provided it is used only to fry vegetables. Oil that has been used to fry fish would produce disastrous results if used for beans. Keep oil refrigerated between uses.

 # Fagiolini al Pomodoro

Green beans with tomatoes

Serves 6

1 pound fresh green beans
Water

(continued)

Salt
1 can (16 oz.) whole tomatoes or 3 large ripe
   peeled fresh ones
½ cup olive oil
1 tablespoon chopped fresh basil or ½ teaspoon
   dried
½ teaspoon oregano
½ teaspoon granulated sugar (optional)

Wash the beans and snap off the ends. Bring the water to a boil and add the salt and beans. Cook the beans until not quite done — approximately 10 minutes. Drain.

Cut the tomatoes into wedges. Heat the oil in a large skillet, add the tomato wedges, crush lightly with a fork, and allow to wilt over high heat. (If canned tomatoes are used, add both the tomatoes and the canning liquid to the skillet). Cook for a couple of minutes, then add the cooked beans. Mix well. Place a lid on the skillet and reduce the heat. Add the basil and oregano. Add salt and sugar if desired. Simmer for at least 30 minutes. Remove the lid every now and then to see if the liquid has been absorbed. If needed, add a little broth, but usually, the liquid from the tomatoes will be sufficient to cover the beans. The beans should look shrivelled when done and the tomatoes should be totally dry.

NOTE

If you have a home garden or have access to one, pick the beans when they are very small (2 or 3 inches long). They are then tender enough to be cooked only in the liquid of the tomatoes without boiling them first. These young beans are indeed a delicacy. If you buy the beans in a market, make sure they break when you bend them and that their color is bright green. If there are Oriental food stores in your neighborhood try their long beans. They are about 15 inches long and have to be cut to about 4- or 5-inch segments. They come actually closest to Italian beans as they have only very small seeds inside.

 Sformato di Fagiolini

Green bean mold

Serves 4 to 6

1 pound fresh green beans, or 2 packages (9 oz.)
   each, frozen
1 teaspoon salt

3 large potatoes
½ cup + 1 teaspoon olive oil
5 large leaves fresh basil or 1 teaspoon dried
½ teaspoon oregano
½ teaspoon freshly ground black pepper
⅓ cup breadcrumbs
½ cup + 1 tablespoon Parmesan cheese, freshly
   grated

Preheat the oven to 350°. Remove the ends from the beans. Bring the water to a boil, add the salt, then the beans. Boil until tender or almost overcooked. Drain well and chop finely but don't purée.

Boil and peel the potatoes. While they are still hot, mash them rather coarsely using a potato masher. Mix with the chopped beans and put the pot back on the stove (low heat) to remove all remaining moisture. When the mixture is dry, add ½ cup of the oil and ½ cup of the Parmesan. Mix well. Add basil, oregano, salt, and pepper. Blend together.

Oil a 6-inch mold and coat with breadcrumbs, making sure that the surface is evenly coated. Fill the mold with the bean and potato mixture. Press down well to remove any holes. Sprinkle the remaining Parmesan on top and place in preheated oven. Bake for 40 minutes, or until the Parmesan is golden. Remove from the oven and let cool for a few minutes.

Place a round platter over the mold and turn quickly. Serves either as a first course or as an accompanient to a meat course.

NOTE

The Sformato may be served hot or cold. If desired, serve Salsa di Pomodoro (see page 20) with it. Or the top of the mold may be lightly covered with additional grated cheese.

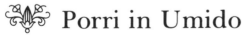 Porri in Umido

Stewed leeks

Serves 4

10 medium-sized leeks
1 quart broth, beef or chicken
4 tablespoons butter
2 tablespoons flour
3 tablespoons light cream

(continued)

Salt and freshly ground black pepper
Juice of ½ lemon

The leeks should be fresh and firm. If you buy them by the bunch and there are a couple that are very thick, cut them in half lengthwise. Clean the leeks and cut off the green tops as well as the roots.

Bring the broth to a boil and place the leeks gently into the pan without bending or breaking them. Cook for 3 to 4 minutes. Remove the leeks with a slotted spoon or spatula. Reserve the broth.

In a skillet large enough to hold leeks in 1 layer, melt half the butter, then add the flour and mix thoroughly until the butter is light brown. Add 2 cups of the reserved broth and blend together, being sure to smooth out any lumps. Add the leeks and then the cream. Reduce the heat. Taste the sauce and add salt if necessary (the broth is salty). Add pepper. Cover and simmer gently for about 20 minutes or until the leeks are done to your taste. Personally I prefer them firm.

Place the leeks on a warmed platter. Add the remaining butter to the skillet along with the lemon juice. Mix well and pour over the leeks. Serve very hot, either as first course or with a meat course.

 # Lenticchie

Lentils

Serves 6

1 cup dried lentils
Water
2 slices pancetta or salt pork, about ¼-inch
* thick, chopped*
1 medium-sized onion, chopped
1 clove of garlic
2 tablespoons tomato paste
2 cups water
½ teaspoon salt
Black pepper, freshly ground

Soak the lentils overnight in a bowl of water. Drain and rinse.

Melt the *pancetta* in a saucepan. Add the onion and sauté until golden. Add the garlic, tomato paste, and lentils. Add the water and bring to a boil. Simmer over low heat for 25 to 30 minutes. Taste and add salt and

pepper. Remove the garlic. If the mixture is too dry for your taste, add a little water or broth.

Serve as accompaniment to *Cotechino* (a special sausage-type of Italian meat). Lentils go equally well with roasts of beef or Polish sausages.

 ## Piselli allo Zucchero

Peas with sugar

Serves 6

2 tablespoons butter
1 tablespoon oil
1 pound green peas, shelled
1 cup water
1 teaspoon sugar
Salt

Melt the butter in a saucepan and add the oil. When the oil and butter are hot, add the peas. Sauté briefly, stirring.
Add the water, sugar, and salt. Cook, stirring, over very high heat for about 2 minutes. When the peas begin to look shrivelled, reduce the heat and cook until the liquid is evaporated. If the peas are young, they will be done. If you have used more mature peas, then add additional liquid and cook a little longer until done.

NOTE

This traditional Milanese recipe requires young peas. In Italy, in the spring, the peas are tiny and sweet. In this country, peas never seem to reach the markets when they are at their best.

 ## Patate alla Veneziana

Potatoes, Venetian style

Serves 4 to 6

2 pounds potatoes
4 tablespoons butter
4 tablespoons olive oil

(continued)

1 small onion, sliced
½ teaspoon dried rosemary
Salt and freshly ground black pepper

Wash the potatoes and peel them. Remove any dark spots. Cut the potatoes into 1-inch cubes.

Melt the butter in a large skillet and add the oil. Sauté the onion slices until blonde but not burned. Add the potato cubes and fry over medium heat, stirring frequently. Add the rosemary and salt. Continue cooking and add a little pepper. The exact cooking time cannot be given because it depends on the quality of the potatoes — approximately 20 minutes. Taste a small piece to determine if it is done. If so, remove from the pan and serve as accompaniment to roast meats and fowl.

NOTE

For this recipe, use mature potatoes with heavier skins rather than new potatoes.

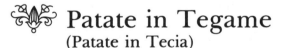 ## Patate in Tegame
(Patate in Tecia)

Potatoes in a skillet

Serves 6

Water
Salt and freshly ground black pepper
2 pounds potatoes
2 tablespoons lard
1 small white onion, sliced
⅓ cup strong broth, beef or chicken

Bring the water to a boil, add salt, and boil the potatoes. Let cool so they can easily be handled. Peel and cut into slices ⅓-inch thick or less.

Melt the lard in a skillet, add the sliced onion, and cook, stirring every now and then, until the onion is golden (don't allow it to brown). Add the potato slices and cook over medium to high heat. Add salt and pepper. When the lard is absorbed, add the broth. Flatten the potato slices with a slotted spatula and cook until golden. Turn the potatoes with the spatula, flatten again, and cook until slightly golden on the other side. Serve as an accompaniment to meat.

NOTE

Patate in Tecia *means "Potatoes in a Skillet" in Triestine dialect. I first tasted this dish on a ship going from Venice down to the Dalmatian coast. These potatoes tasted unlike any other. The waiter explained to me that only a Triestino could cook them and that the water in which they were boiled had to come from Trieste. I find that New York water is perfectly adequate, but the potatoes used have to be mature and round. Baking potatoes won't do, nor will new potatoes.*

 # Torta di Patate
(Tortel)

Potato tart

Serves 4

2 large potatoes
1 whole egg
1 teaspoon salt
Black pepper, freshly ground
Pinch nutmeg, freshly grated
2 tablespoons flour
2 tablespoons milk
½ cup + 2 tablespoons Parmesan cheese, freshly
  grated
2 tablespoons oil

Preheat the oven to 400°. Peel and grate 2 large raw potatoes. The gratings should make about 2 cups. Place the potatoes in a bowl, add the egg, salt, pepper, and nutmeg. Mix. Add the flour a little at a time, alternating with a little milk, and mixing carefully to avoid lumps. Add ½ cup Parmesan cheese. Mix again. The mixture should not be too solid.

Oil a 9-inch pie pan and spread the potato mixture evenly to a thickness of about ½-inch. Sprinkle the rest of the Parmesan on top.

Bake the potato tart for about 40 minutes, or until the top and bottom have a golden crust. This may be served hot with a salad, or cut into wedges and served hot or cold with drinks.

NOTE

This is definitely a regional dish. The name "Tortel" comes from the region around Trento. "Tart" is the best translation we could find but it does not convey the special quality of this very simple dish.

 # Zucca Ripiena

Stuffed pumpkin

Serves 6

1 medium-sized pumpkin, about 6-7 pounds
Salt
2 tablespoons butter
Spezzatino di Manzo for 6 people (see
   page 238)
1 pound potatoes
Water

Preheat the oven to 350°. Choose a pumpkin that hasn't been picked weeks before. With a sharp knife, cut a slice off the top. With a spoon, remove all the seeds from the inside. Salt the cavity and place the butter inside. Replace the top of the pumpkin and wrap the entire pumpkin in aluminum foil as tightly as possible. Place in the preheated oven and bake for 2 hours or until tender.

While the pumpkin is baking, prepare the *Spezzatino di Manzo*. Shortly before both the *Spezzatino* and pumpkin are done, boil the potatoes in salted water. When they are done, peel and cut into chunks. Place the potatoes in the blender. Remove the pumpkin from the oven and scoop out the pulp. Add this to the blender. If the mixture is too dry to make the blender work, add a couple of tablespoons of water. Run the blender at low speed for 30 seconds.

Place the mixture from the blender in a saucepan and cook over low heat, stirring until the liquid is absorbed and the mixture is firm.

Take the top off the pumpkin and place the *Spezzatino* inside. Replace the lid and serve very hot, accompanied by the potato-pumpkin mixture.

NOTE

   The pumpkin will only serve as a bowl to hold the Spezzatino and should not be eaten.

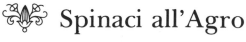 # Spinaci all'Agro

Spinach with lemon

Serves 6

2 pounds fresh spinach
Salt

Juice of 1 lemon
½ cup olive oil
Black pepper, freshly ground (optional)

Spinach is one of the most popular vegetables in Italy. There are 2 ways to cook it and Italians have very strong feelings about the way they prefer. One way is to remove the hardest part of the stems, then wash the leaves very well, changing the water 2 or 3 times. Put them to boil in a pot with only the water that clings to the leaves.

The other way is to wash the leaves and boil the spinach for quite a while (about 15 minutes) in a lot of water. Both schools of thought agree on removing the hard stems and on cleaning the leaves very well.

I have always preferred the first version. It is true, however, that people who are allergic to spinach find that the second method provides fewer problems. Whatever way you choose, cook the spinach, let cool, then squeeze the water out with your hands, taking a handful of spinach at a time.

Place the spinach in a bowl. Place a pinch of salt in a spoon, dissolve it with a bit of lemon juice, then pour it over the spinach. Add the rest of the juice, add the oil, mix well, and serve at room temperature or even lukewarm. If you have to refrigerate the spinach, let it stand at room temperature for an hour before serving. Add pepper if desired.

 Spinaci all'Olio

Spinach with oil

Serves 6

2 pounds fresh spinach
Salt
½ cup olive oil

Remove the tough parts of the stems and wash the spinach in lukewarm water, changing the water 2 or 3 times until all the sand is removed. Cook the spinach as described in the previous recipe. Whichever method you use, add a pinch of salt at the beginning of the cooking. When the spinach is done, let it cool, then take a fistful at a time and squeeze out the water.

Place the spinach in a skillet, separate it with a fork, then add the oil. Cook over medium heat letting the spinach absorb the oil. Stir to prevent any sticking. Taste, and if additional salt is desired, add before serving. If desired, sprinkle a little Parmesan cheese over spinach before serving. Serve hot with any roast meat or fowl.

NOTE

Some people like this spinach cooked until the edges almost turn brown.

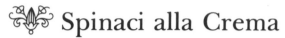 Spinaci alla Crema

Spinach with cream

Serves 6

2 pounds fresh spinach
3 tablespoons butter
1 tablespoon flour
1 cup heavy cream
1 cup broth, chicken or beef
Pinch of nutmeg, freshly grated
Salt

This is my version of creamed spinach.
Wash the spinach well in lukewarm water, changing the water 2 or 3 times until all the sand is gone. Remove the tough parts of the stems, and cook as described on page 293. Drain and let cool. With your hands, squeeze the spinach, a fistful at a time, until all the water is gone. Chop the spinach or run it through an electric chopping machine, but not through a blender. The spinach should be chopped, not puréed.

Melt 2 tablespoons of butter in a saucepan, and add the spinach. Cook for about 5 minutes until the butter has been absorbed. Remove from heat and sprinkle with flour, mixing it well to avoid any lumps. Add the cream, broth, and nutmeg. Mix and taste the mixture. If salt is needed, add it at this time. Put the saucepan back on the stove and cook over medium heat until the spinach bubbles. Reduce the heat and simmer for another 5 minutes or until the liquid has been absorbed. Before serving, add the remaining butter. Serve with roast meat or poultry.

 # Spinaci alla Milanese

Spinach, Milanese style

Serves 6

2 pounds fresh spinach
3 tablespoons butter
⅓ cup pine nuts
Salt and freshly ground black pepper
Pinch of nutmeg, freshly grated

Discard the tough stems of the spinach and wash the leaves in luke-warm water, changing the water 2 or 3 times until all the sand is removed. Cook the spinach as described on page 293.

Remove the spinach from the water and run it briefly under cold water. With your hands, squeeze the water out of the spinach. Melt the butter in a saucepan, add the spinach, and mix until well coated with butter. Add the pine nuts. Taste, and if more salt is needed, add it along with pepper and nutmeg. Cook for about 5 minutes. Serve hot.

NOTE

I have tried all sorts of nuts instead of pine nuts since they are not always readily available. Pecans, a nut unknown to Italians, seem to come closest to that taste.

 # Spinaci con Uova

Spinach with eggs

Serves 6

2 pounds fresh spinach
4 tablespoons butter
6 eggs
1 cup besciamella (see pages 22-23)
Pinch of nutmeg, freshly grated
Salt and freshly ground black pepper
½ cup Parmesan cheese (optional)

Preheat the oven to 400°. Wash the spinach carefully. Remove any hard stems and then cook the leaves without adding any water. Stir while cooking. After 6 to 7 minues, remove from the heat. Let cool. As soon as it is cool enough to handle, take a fistful at a time and squeeze with your hands to get the water out. Chop with a *mezzaluna,* or use a vegetable chopper, but don't use a blender. In a saucepan, melt 3 tablespoons of butter, add the spinach, and cook for 5 minutes.

Butter a round baking dish with ½ tablespoon butter. Pour the chopped spinach into the dish and flatten it with a spatula. Carefully break the eggs, one at a time into the dish, forming a ring over the spinach.

Make a rather stiff *besciamella.* Add nutmeg, salt, and pepper. Mix. With a spoon, cover each egg with *besciamella,* being careful not to let the sauce cover the spinach. Sprinkle the eggs with Parmesan, if desired. Dot the eggs with the remaining butter. Bake in a preheated oven until the eggs are done to your taste—about 5 minutes—and then place briefly under the broiler for another 5 minutes. Serve with roast meats.

 # Polpettone Primaverile

Springtime spinach loaf

Serves 6

2 pounds fresh spinach
Water
1 can (6 ½ oz.) tuna packed in oil, drained
6 anchovy filets, chopped
½ cup breadcrumbs
3 whole eggs
½ cup Parmesan cheese, freshly grated
Pinch of nutmeg
Salt and freshly ground black pepper
⅓ cup olive oil
2 tablespoons lemon juice
2 hard-boiled eggs

Wash the spinach carefully in lukewarm water. When all the sand has been removed, cook the spinach, covered, in a deep pan without any additional water. Remove the lid every now and then to make sure the liquid has not evaporated completely. Don't overcook: 6 or 7 minutes should be sufficient. Drain and let cool.

Take a little spinach, squeeze it between your hands until the water is completely gone. Continue until all the spinach is dry. Chop the spinach with the tuna but do not use a blender. Add the anchovies to the mixture. Add the breadcrumbs and the whole eggs, one at a time. If the mixture seems too moist to handle after you have added 2 eggs, omit the white of the third egg (or add more breadcrumbs). Add Parmesan cheese and the nutmeg and pepper. Taste the mixture before salting. Remember, both the Parmesan and the anchovies are salty. Blend all ingredients thoroughly.

Bring the water to a boil in a heatproof casserole. Place the mixture on a flat surface, preferably marble, and shape it as you would a meatloaf. It will be somewhat softer than a meatloaf but is should be easy to handle. Wrap the loaf in cheesecloth, knot the cloth at both ends, and place the loaf in the casserole with the boiling water. Cover and cook over medium heat for about 30 minutes. The ends of the cheesecloth should hang over the rim of the casserole so that the loaf can be removed easily from the pan.

When done, remove and let cool. Unwrap and place the loaf on a long platter. When the loaf is completely cold, slice it with a very sharp knife and arrange the slices so that they overlap slightly. Beat the olive oil and lemon juice together and pour the mixture over the slices.

Put the hard-boiled eggs in a small sieve and press them through until both whites and yolks come out in small drops. Cover the slices with the egg sprinklings. The platter should look like a spring lawn (that is where the dish gets its name). Allow to stand for a couple of hours before serving. Serve as a separate course with a dry, light white wine: a Soave or a Lugana.

NOTE

I usually say that cheese and fish don't mix and I still say so. In this recipe the spinach is the main ingredient and spinach and cheese mix very well indeed.

 # Pomodori al Forno

Baked tomatoes

Serves 6

6 ripe medium-sized tomatoes
6 tablespoons olive oil
Salt and freshly ground black pepper
1 clove of garlic
6 leaves fresh basil or 1 teaspoon dried
3 tablespoons parsley, finely chopped

Preheat the oven to 400°. The tomatoes should be ripe but firm. Wash and cut in half horizontally.

Oil a baking pan and place the 12 tomato halves side by side. They should be close enough so they don't topple over. Sprinkle with salt and pepper.

Chop the garlic with the basil. Sprinkle the garlic-basil mixture over the tomatoes. Pour the remaining oil over them, using a spoon so that all the tomatoes are coated evenly. Bake for about 20 minutes. Remove from the oven briefly and sprinkle the parsley over the tomatoes. Bake for another 5 minutes. The tomatoes should be wilted and their juice should have evaporated.

Place around a roast, a meat loaf, or a roasted chicken. These baked tomatoes are also delicious chilled, served as a first course on a bed of lettuce or a bed of cold steamed rice, lightly seasoned with salt, pepper, and oil. The wine to be served could be a Coronata, from the region near Genoa, the same city this recipe comes from. It is a particularly attractive summer dish.

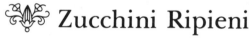 Zucchini Ripieni

Stuffed zucchini

Serves 4

4 medium-sized zucchini
Salt
1 tablespoon chopped fresh basil or ½ teaspoon
* dried*
1 cup besciamella (see pages 22-23)
½ cup Parmesan cheese
1 whole egg, beaten
Pinch of nutmeg, freshly grated
Black pepper, freshly ground
1 tablespoon oil
⅓ cup breadcrumbs

Preheat the oven to 375°. When buying zucchini, choose carefully. The skin should be glossy. Pinch the blossom end: if it feels soft, avoid them because when they are cooked, they will taste bitter.

Boil the zucchini in slightly salted water for 5 to 6 minutes. The zucchini should still be firm. Let cool and cut lengthwise.

With a spoon, scoop out some of the pulp, being careful not to cut into the shell. Chop the pulp very fine, then add the chopped basil. Place the pulp in a bowl. Add the *besciamella,* Parmesan, egg, nutmeg, and pepper. Taste before adding salt. The zucchini are bland, but the Parmesan is quite salty. Stuff the zucchini shells with the mixture. Oil a baking dish and arrange the stuffed zucchini side by side. Sprinkle breadcrumbs over the top. Bake for 20 minutes, or until the edges curl slightly. Place under the broiler for about 3 minutes to brown the tops lightly.

Serve these zucchini hot or cold; they are also delicious the next day.

Zucchini Grattugiati

Grated zucchini

Serves 6

3 medium-sized zucchini
1 teaspoon salt
½ cup oil
Pinch of nutmeg, freshly grated
2 tablespoons parsley, finely chopped

When buying the zucchini, make sure the tips are firm and the skins are bright green and shiny. If the tips are even only slightly soft, the zucchini are not fresh and will have a bitter taste. For this recipe the zucchini should be at least 2 inches in diameter.

Wash the zucchini then grate them into a bowl using the large holes on your grater. Add the salt and let stand for at least 30 minutes. Take a fistful of grated zucchini at a time and squeeze with both hands. Depending upon the size of the zucchini you will squeeze out ½ to 1 cup of water.

Heat the oil in a skillet. When it is very hot, add the grated zucchini and spread them with a wooden spoon. Use a rather large skillet: the more space, the better. Whatever water is still left in them will now evaporate. Taste and if all the salt has gone out with the water, add salt to taste. Add nutmeg. Stir and when all the liquid is absorbed, add the parsley. Cook for about 1 minute longer. The cooking time should be about 7 to 8 minutes.

Serve with a roast or roasted fowl or steak. Avoid a meat dish with sauce because it would destroy the taste of the zucchini.

 Zucchini al Forno

Baked zucchini

Serves 6

8 medium-sized zucchini
Salt
¾ cup + 1 tablespoon oil
3 tablespoons breadcrumbs
½ cup flour
2 tablespoons fresh basil, chopped
2 tablespoons Parmesan cheese
Black pepper, freshly ground

Preheat the oven to 375°. When buying the zucchini make sure their skins are shiny and the tips are firm when you squeeze them. If the tips are soft, the zucchini will be bitter.

Wash the zucchini and slice them into thin rounds. Sprinkle salt over them and let stand for 30 minutes to make them lose their water. With 1 tablespoon of oil, coat a 10-inch ovenproof casserole and sprinkle the bottom and sides with breadcrumbs. Pat the zucchini slices dry using a paper towel. Make a layer of slices covering the bottom of the casserole. Sprinkle flour over them, followed by a trickle of oil. Dot with basil. Cover with another layer of zucchini. Repeat as before until all the zucchini are used up. Sprinkle the Parmesan cheese over the top and pepper, if desired. Bake for about 45 minutes. If done, a fork should go into zucchini easily.

NOTE

This recipe is the invention of a truly great gourmet of my acquaintance. It sounds improbable: all that raw flour and the uncooked zucchini. It is absolutely delicious, provided you learn how to use the flour. There shouldn't be a layer of flour between the layers of zucchini, but a sprinkling.

Zucchini Trifolati

Zucchini, truffle style

Serves 4 to 6

1 pound small zucchini
1 teaspoon fresh oregano or ½ teaspoon dried

Salt
½ cup oil
3 tablespoon chopped parsley
Black pepper, freshly ground

This dish is called "truffle style" only because the zucchini should be cut as thin as you would cut a truffle.

The zucchini should not be longer than about 7 inches. When choosing them, pinch the tips slightly: if they are soft, avoid them. The zucchini should be hard and shiny.

Cut the zucchini into round slices using a sharp knife or a slicer. The slices should be about ⅛th of an inch thick. Sprinkle with salt and let stand for about 30 minutes. Pat dry with a paper towel.

Heat the oil in a large skillet and add the zucchini slices. They should overlap as little as possible. Cook over high heat, moving the slices delicately with a spatula. When the edges are blonde, turn the zucchini and add the parsley. Reduce the heat and add the oregano. Taste and add salt if needed. Add pepper. When the slices are transparent and slightly golden, they are done. They should not be cooked until they are mushy. The total cooking time should be about 10 minutes.

Serve hot as vegetable with a meat course or as first course.

 Rostissana

Serves 4 to 5

1 large onion
1 large bell pepper, yellow or red
½ cup olive oil
6 medium-sized zucchini
Salt and freshly ground black pepper
½ cup Parmesan cheese, freshly grated
   (optional)

This is a specialty of Piacenza, Dodi's hometown.

Cut the onion and pepper into thin strips (no need to peel pepper first). Heat the oil in a skillet, and add the onion and pepper. Sauté for a couple of minutes over medium heat until wilted.

Cut the zucchini into thin rounds, using either a hand slicer or your food processor. Add these slices to the onion-pepper mixture. Add salt and pepper. Cook over very low heat for about 20 minutes, or a little less if you like your vegetables *al dente*. Stir every now and then.

If desired, add half the Parmesan just before removing pan from the heat and mix. Place the vegetables in a serving bowl and sprinkle the remaining Parmesan on top.

NOTE

This is a very old recipe and has been, for many years, the terror of Italian children, who hate it. When they grow up they like it. The Parmesan is a modern addition to the recipe.

Salads

 Insalata di Cavolini di Bruxelles e Indivia Belga

Brussels sprouts and belgian endive

Serves 4 to 5

10-12 fresh brussels sprouts
Water
1 teaspoon salt
2 thick heads belgian endive
½ teaspoon black pepper, freshly ground

For the dressing:
½ teaspoon salt
3 tablespoons wine vinegar
1 teaspoon prepared mustard (optional)
⅓ cup olive oil

Cut the stems off the brussels sprouts and remove the outer leaves. They usually are tough and yellowed. Wash them under cold running water. Bring the water to a boil in a moderately large saucepan, add the salt, and then add the brussels sprouts. Cook, uncovered, over high heat for 8 to 9

minutes, according to the size of the sprouts. They should be done, but not too soft. Rinse immediately under cold water and let cool.

Clean the endive, remove any dark spots, and cut horizontally into 1-inch pieces.

To prepare the dressing, place the salt in the bottom of a bowl. Add the vinegar and mix to dissolve the salt. Add mustard, if desired. Add the oil and mix very well until totally blended.

Add the brussels sprouts to the bowl with the dressing. If some of the sprouts seem too large, cut them in half. Let them stand in the dressing for 10 minutes. Add the endive and toss well. Sprinkle some little black pepper over the top and serve.

NOTE

The amounts given may, of course, be doubled. A large bowl of the salad looks glamorous and tastes delicious. Some might ask what all these Belgian ingredients are doing in an Italian salad. Both brussels sprouts and belgian endive are very popular in northern Italy, particularly in the winter when few fresh vegetables are in season.

Insalata di Citrioli

Cucumber salad

Serves 4

2 large cucumbers, peeled and sliced thin
Salt
¼ cup olive oil
Pinch of paprika (optional)

Sprinkle the cucumber slices liberally with salt. Place the slices in a deep dish, cover with an inverted deep dish, and place a weight on top. Let stand for at least 1 hour.

Pour off the water shed by the cucumbers. Season with oil, place in a serving bowl, and sprinkle with paprika, if desired.

NOTE

I shall never forget the surprise I had when I came to this country and found myself confronted with slices of cucumber, sometimes not even peeled, hard to digest, and almost tasteless. I had always eaten cucumber salad as described above, with all the bitterness gone out of it. The paprika on top is of Austrian origin, although I first encountered it in Trieste.

Melanzane Marinate

Marinated eggplant

Serves 8

6 medium-sized eggplants, no longer than 7
   inches
Salt
½ cup of lard or shortening, such as Crisco
1 clove garlic
10 leaves fresh sage or 1 teaspoon dried
½ cup wine vinegar

Wash the eggplants, remove the stems, and cut into slices lengthwise. The slices should be ¼-inch thick or less. Place the slices on a platter and sprinkle with salt (coarse, if possible). Cover with a deep dish, bottom-side on the eggplants. Place a weight on it so that it presses down on the eggplant slices. Let stand for about 30 minutes. When you remove the weighted dish the eggplants will have lost their bitter water and will be slightly limp. Pat dry with a paper towel.

Melt a tablespoon of lard in a skillet and heat until very hot. Crush the clove of garlic and add it to the hot fat. Fry 3 or 4 slices of eggplant at a time. They should not overlap and should have a little breathing space between them. When they are golden on one side, turn with a spatula and fry on other side until done. Drain the fried slices on a paper towel and continue to fry the remaining slices, adding lard as needed.

Discard the garlic. When all the slices are done, place them in a bowl in layers, putting a couple of leaves of sage between each layer or sprinkle with a little dried sage. Pour the vinegar over the eggplant slices. Place a lid on the bowl and let stand in a cool place for about 24 hours. Serve at room temperature with cold meats.

Fagiolini all'Agro

Green beans with oil and lemon

Serves 6

2 pounds green beans
Water

Salt
Juice of 1 large lemon
½ cup olive oil
1 scallion (optional)

Wash the beans and snap off the ends. Bring plenty of water to a boil in a large kettle. Add salt then add the beans. Boil until tender but not overdone. When you pick one up with your fingers it should not go limp. The cooking time depends upon the freshness and age of the beans—average cooking time is 15 minutes.

Drain and let cool. Place the beans in a bowl. Pour the juice of the lemon over the beans and mix. Add the oil and mix again. If a scallion is to be used, chop it very fine and sprinkle it over the beans. Let stand for about 10 minutes before serving.

NOTE

There is a marvelous word in Italian — insaporire, *meaning to absorb the flavor. It takes the beans a while. Give them a chance.*

 ## Insalata di Cavolo Nero

Red cabbage salad

Serves 6

1 medium-sized head of red cabbage, about 1 to
*   1 ½ pounds*
3 hard-boiled eggs
Salt and freshly ground black pepper
½ cup black olives, pitted and coarsely chopped
1 can (6 ½ oz.) tuna packed in olive oil
½ cup olive oil

Shred the cabbage as you would for coleslaw. If you have a food processor, remove the hard core at the bottom of the cabbage, cut the head into wedges and feed them into the tube, one wedge at a time. Use the shredder and run the motor for about 2 seconds per wedge.

Place the shredded cabbage in a bowl, add the eggs, salt, and pepper. Mix well.

Add the olives to the cabbage, then the tuna. Break up the tuna with a fork and mix well. Add the olive oil. If the mixture seems too rich for your taste, reduce the quantity of oil. Let stand for at least 1 hour before serving.

This dish may be served as first course on a hot summer day. If desired, place lettuce leaves on individual small plates and heap the cabbage mixture on top. Garnish with a slice of hard-boiled egg or a whole olive. Or, leave the salad in its bowl and serve it with cold meats.

NOTE

In Italy this is called Cavolo Nero or black cabbage. In this country, it is called red cabbage. The Germans call it Rotkraut. In reality, it is purple.

I am not sure about the origins of this dish but I tasted it for the first time in Friuli. Since then, I found that a Friulano restaurant in New York City serves it as part of its antipasto.

 # Insalata di Riso

Rice salad

Serves 5 to 6

2 quarts water
1 teaspoon salt
1 cup long grain or Italian rice
1 can (6½ oz.) tuna
4 hard-boiled eggs
⅓ cup olive oil
2 tablespoons capers, packed in brine or salt
1 teaspoon powdered mustard (optional)
Black pepper, freshly ground
1 can (8 oz.) tiny peas

Bring the water to a vigorous boil and add the salt. Boil rice until done. While the rice cooks, empty the can of tuna into a deep bowl and break it up with a fork. Bite a grain of the rice: it should be firm and not mushy. When done, drain the rice in a colander and run hot water over it. Place the colander on top of the pot where the rice has been cooked. Place the pot on the stove over low heat for just a few seconds. The heat will dry the rice.

Pour the rice immediately over the tuna and mix. The hot rice will almost absorb the tuna. Cut the eggs into round slices and add to the rice-tuna mixture. Add a little of the oil and mix. Add the capers. (If salted capers are used rinse lightly in cold water.) If mustard is used, dissolve it in a little water and add it to the rice; mix. Taste the mixture and if more salt is needed add it as well as some freshly ground pepper. Add the rest of the oil and mix well. Add the peas and mix gently because the peas easily get mashed.

Keep the salad in a cool place for at least one hour but don't refrigerate it. Mix again lightly before serving.

This is an ideal dish for a cold luncheon or as part of a cold buffet. It should be accompanied by a cold dry white wine.

NOTE

For most rice dishes we prefer the Italian rice, sold in small canvas bags. For this dish, however, long-grain rice may be used. The exact cooking time can not be given because it varies according to the quality of the rice. It should be 20 minutes or less.

 # Insalata Mista Cotta

Salad of mixed cooked vegetables

Serves 4

4 fresh zucchini, not longer than 4 to 5 inches
Water
1 cup, tightly packed boiled spinach, squeezed dry
4 small very young pink beets
1 cup young fresh green beans
Salt and freshly ground black pepper
2 tablespoons wine vinegar
½ cup olive oil

Wash the zucchini. Scrape off any rough spots but don't peel. Bring water to a boil and add the whole zucchini. Boil for 5 to 6 minutes, according to size. If you can stick a fork in easily they are done. Remove the zucchini from the water, let cool, and slice into pieces ⅓-inch thick. The spinach should be cooked and the water squeezed out with your hands. Wash and boil the beets in water until tender; about 10 minutes. Let cool, peel, and slice. The slices should be the same thickness as the zucchini.

Cook the beans, then cut them into bite-sized pieces. Place the vegetables in a bowl and separate them with a fork. Place the desired amount of salt and pepper in a serving spoon. Fill the spoon with the vinegar, and with a fork, stir to dissolve the salt in the spoon. Pour over the vegetables. Holding the cruet about 10 inches above the bowl, pour a thin stream of olive oil over everything. Taste and, if you want more sharpness, add more vinegar. The taste of these fresh young vegetables is so delicate that a little vinegar will go a long way. Mix very well and serve as a first course or after a meat course.

NOTE

You can make your own variations, of course. Some people like to add a boiled potato, some add fave, or kidney beans. Finally, some people like what is known as Insalata Cotta e Cruda, meaning a mixture of cooked vegetables and raw greens (provided the latter are very tender leaves).

Desserts

Italians are not sweet eaters; not on working days, anyway. This is understandably so. A meal that starts with a marvelously rich *polenta* dish and continues with either fish or meat (or both) can hardly end with a rich dessert.

In a restaurant Italians might ask for *una punta di formaggio* at the end of a meal, or *frutta fresca;* a small piece of cheese, that is, or fresh fruit. *Il Carrello di Dolci* (the dessert cart) is rarely spectacular.

On Sundays and holidays you will see men, women, and children slowly walking home from church, carefully carrying a white cardboard box tied with white string. It contains *le paste* — the pastries that will be eaten at the end of Sunday luncheon. They were bought in a pastry shop and they are, usually, excellent. They are not homemade.

It is really only since I began living and entertaining in this country that I have started making desserts or have even begun being concerned with them. When I lived in Italy, fruit and cheese was our dessert most every day. Desserts were served at the end of formal dinners (or luncheons) only. In the fall, it changed to fresh walnuts. And I mean *fresh*. We would crack the outer shell and then peel the nut until it came out white, bare, and sweet. We ate them with bread and they were delicious, provided you didn't eat too many nuts. There is an old Genoese saying *"Pan e nos mangiar de spos; nos e pan mangiar de can."* This means "bread with nuts is a dish fit for a bride; nuts with a little bread is a dish fit for dogs." Whatever they might think in Genoa, we ate a lot of nuts. And sometimes nuts with celery.

Italian-born hostesses, who live and entertain in this country, have a repertory of desserts. I have collected a few, added my own, as well as the more obvious Italian desserts like the ever-present *zabaglione*.

Ices and ice creams are popular in Italy. They are rarely homemade, but are frequently "doctored up" in the home and served after dinner.

Lemon sherbet with a tablespoon of Creme de Menthe poured over each individual serving or a spoonful of Framboise or Poire instead of Creme de Menthe makes a marvelous end to a meal. One of the great things about Italy and the Italians is that they adopt good things wherever they find them and make them their own. It was in Milan that I first tasted a marvelous vanilla ice cream covered with a healthy jigger of Bourbon.

Some of the cakes, like the *Torta di Castagne* would not be served at the end of a meal in Italy but more likely with tea or coffee in the afternoon. Teatime is not an exclusively British custom. In some Italian households *si prende il thé* after 5 o'clock.

Budino Dolce di Pangrattato

Bread pudding

Serves 8 to 10

1 quart milk
¾ cup very fine homemade breadcrumbs
5 whole eggs, separated
6 generous tablespoons sugar
Rind of ½ lemon, grated
½ cup raisins

Put the milk in a saucepan (milk should be at room temperature). Add the breadcrumbs and soak for about 6 hours.

Preheat the oven to 400°. Beat the egg yolks with the sugar until pale yellow. Add the lemon rind. (Be careful not to grate the white part which is bitter.) Beat the whites until stiff. Add the yolks to the breadcrumbs and blend. Add the whites a little at a time, folding them in with a rubber spatula.

Generously butter a 10-inch mold, making sure that all the inside is equally coated. Fill with the mixture and sprinkle the raisins on top. Don't stir; the raisins will sink into the mixture.

Bake in a preheated oven for 1 hour or until done. A fine knife, when inserted, should come out clean. Cool for a few minutes before unmolding. Serve warm.

Budino di Savoiardi e Cioccolato

Chocolate and ladyfingers pudding

Serves 6 to 8

1 quart milk
½ cup sugar
18 ladyfingers, broken into pieces

4 squares semisweet chocolate, broken into small
  pieces
4 eggs
1 teaspoon vanilla extract

Preheat the oven to 375°. Butter a 9-inch round cake pan then sprinkle with sugar.

Bring the milk to a boil. Add the sugar and ladyfingers. Put in the chocolate. (If you have a food processor, break the chocolate into 1-inch pieces, feed the pieces into the tube, and run the motor for about 15 seconds, using sharp blade). Simmer for about 10 minutes, stirring every now and then. The mixture should be fairly thick. Allow to rest and cool.

Beat the eggs as you would for an omelette, using a fork or a wire whisk. When the milk mixture is cool, add the vanilla extract and the beaten eggs. Mix well until totally blended.

Fill a roasting pan with water. Pour the chocolate mixture into the greased and sugared cake pan. Place cake pan into the roasting pan and bake for 1 hour or until done.

Allow the pudding to settle completely before unmolding. Better still, place it in the refrigerator for a couple of hours. Unmold onto a round platter.

NOTE

This dessert is particularly attractive to busy hostesses because it may be prepared a day ahead. If you want to make it richer or more glamorous, you may serve whipped cream in a separate bowl. But, as for taste, it is delicious the way it is.

 # Latte Fritto

Fried milk

Serves 8 to 10

1 quart milk
¾ cup flour
8 whole eggs
Peel of 1 lemon, finely grated
8 tablespoons sugar
Oil or shortening such as Crisco

(continued)

*3 tablespoons fine breadcrumbs, made from
  white bread only*
2 tablespoons confectioners' sugar

Have the milk at room temperature. Mix the milk with the flour until no lumps remain.

Place 4 eggs in a saucepan and beat with a wire whisk (or an electric mixer). Add the sugar and continue beating until eggs are frothy. Separate the remaining eggs and add the yolks to the pan. (Reserve the whites for later). Beat well. Add the lemon peel, then add the milk-flour mixture a little at a time. When all ingredients are blended, place saucepan on low heat and cook, stirring frequently, for 1 hour. When the mixture has the consistency of a thick white sauce, remove the pan from the heat. Wet a large platter (or a marble-top table) with cold water and pour the mixture onto it. Smooth the surface with the blade of a wet knife. The mixture should be about 1½ inches thick. Let it cool completely.

Beat the remaining egg whites until quite stiff. Heat the oil or shortening in a deep pot. When drops of water sprinkled on the surface of oil sizzle, the oil is hot enough for deep frying.

Cut the milk mixture, which should now be quite solid, into squares of about 1 to 1½ inches. Dip each in the egg whites, then in the breadcrumbs, making sure they are evenly coated. Deep fry until golden.

Place the squares on a warmed platter, making a pyramid. Sprinkle each layer of squares with confectioners' sugar. Serve warm.

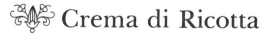 Crema di Ricotta

Cream of ricotta

Serves 6

4 eggs, separated
¾ cup granulated sugar
1 container (15 oz.) ricotta
1 ounce dark rum
Pinch of salt

Beat the yolks with the sugar until the mixture whitens. Add the *ricotta* and continue beating with a hand mixer until totally blended. In a separate bowl, beat the egg whites. Add a pinch of salt and continue to beat until quite stiff.

Add the rum to the *ricotta*-egg mixture, then fold in the beaten whites a little at a time, allowing one spoonful to be incorporated before adding the next. Fill individual dishes with the mixture and chill well before serving.

NOTE

In Italy, this dish is made with mascarpone, a bland, very rich cheese not available in this country. The ricotta sold in this country is softer than the type available in Italy and lends itself very well to this recipe. If desired, sprinkle a little powdered coffee over the top before serving.

Should the surface of the ricotta look wet when you open the container, place the contents on a paper towel and pat dry before using.

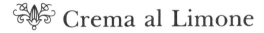 Crema al Limone

Lemon cream

Serves 6

1 pint heavy cream
Peel of ½ lemon, finely grated
½ cup sugar
Juice of ½ lemon
1 ounce brandy

Have the cream as cold as possible. Whip it with a hand mixer or a whisk until very stiff. Add the grated lemon peel and mix gently. Slowly add the sugar. Add the lemon juice and mix until well blended. If the cream should have gotten slightly liquid around the edges, whip it again for a couple of minutes. Add the brandy and mix.

Spoon the cream into individual serving dishes and refrigerate for a couple of hours. Just before serving, garnish with a small curl of lemon peel.

NOTE

This is a recipe I have tasted many times in restaurants around Lake Como. Recently a hostess in Milan served it with Bourbon whisky instead of brandy.

Zabaglione

Serves 6 to 8

½ cup sugar
6 egg yolks
Water
1 cup dry Marsala

Place the sugar and egg yolks in the upper part of a double boiler. Beat with a wire whisk until the mixture is light yellow.

Bring the water to a boil in the lower part of the double boiler. Reduce the heat and simmer the water. Place the top part with egg-sugar mixture over the simmering water. Add the Marsala and continue beating with a wire whisk. After a couple of minutes, the mixture will get foamy and begin to bubble. Continue beating until the foamy mixture clings to the whisk. *Zabaglione* must not be runny.

Spoon into small individual cups. The kind of glass you would use for fruit salad is never used in Italy. Serve cold, accompanied by ladyfingers or dry sweet crackers.

Zabaglione may be served warm if that is the way you want it, but I suggest you refrigerate it for a couple of hours. If it should have gotten too liquid, beat it with an electric mixer before serving.

NOTE

Remember that there is a difference between a double boiler and a bain-marie. (Bagno Maria in Italian. I use the French only because Americans are more familiar with it.) The former consists of a large pot placed on top of another pot where water bubbles. Water must not touch the upper pot. A bain-marie consists of two pots that fit into one another. The water boils in the bottom one and envelops the lower part of the upper pot. For this recipe you should use a double boiler.

Zabaglione con le Fragole

Zabaglione with strawberries

Serves 6 to 8

6 cups zabaglione (see above)
1 cup white wine
2 cups strawberries, hulled

Prepare a *zabaglione* as described in the preceding recipe.
Pour the wine into a deep dish. Place the strawberries in the wine and soak for 30 minutes. Turn the berries a couple of times. After 30 minutes, drain and discard the wine. The berries should now be clean.

Cut the larger berries in half and place them in the bottom of a large bowl. Pour the *zabaglione* over them and decorate the top with the smaller berries, left whole.

Zabaglione con Fragole may be served in individual bowls but it is less spectacular than the large bowl.

 # Zabaglione alla Crema

Zabaglione with whipped cream

Serves 8

6 cups zabaglione (see page 314) made with:
6 egg yolks
¾ cup sugar
1 cup dry Marsala
1 cup whipped cream

Prepare a *zabaglione* as described previously. Allow *zabaglione* to cool.
Whip the cream until very stiff. Carefully mix the *zabaglione* and cream together with a spatula, adding the cream a little at a time. This mixture may be served by itself with a little grated orange or lemon rind sprinkled on top. But it also lends itself to marvelous combinations. It may be used as topping for sliced bananas, stewed pears or peaches, or over ladyfingers, lightly soaked in a little Marsala. Just don't use over citrus fruit. They don't go together.

NOTE

We use additional sugar in this recipe because the cream is not sweetened.

 # Sformato al Caffé

Coffee brick

Serves 6 to 8

1 stick butter
⅓ cup sugar
1 egg yolk
11 ounces sweet biscuits (Social Tea or similar)
¼ cup very strong black coffee
1 pint heavy cream (optional)
1 tablespoon confectioners' sugar (optional)

The butter should be at room temperature. Place it in a bowl and add the sugar. Cream together with a wooden spoon until well blended. Add the egg yolk and continue mixing for a couple of minutes.

In a food processor, place the biscuits a few at a time into the tube and run the motor for 30 seconds, or until all the biscuits are pulverized. Continue until all the biscuits have been reduced to the consistency of heavy flour. Add the biscuits to the creamed butter and sugar a little at a time. When about half the biscuits have been absorbed, start adding the coffee a little at a time, alternating with the biscuits. When all ingredients have been blended together, they should have the consistency of a thick paste.

Line a rectangular 9″ × 5″ mold with aluminum foil. Grease the foil, being careful not to coat it too heavily. Fill the mold with the mixture, pressing hard to make sure there are no gaps or holes. Fold the aluminum foil over the top and refrigerate for at least 2 hours. If possible, refrigerate overnight.

Before serving, unmold the brick and whip the cream and sugar until very stiff. Use the whipped cream to decorate the brick by squeezing it through a tube or pastry bag.

NOTE

This is a very rich dessert. Personally, I find the cream a little too much. The brick by itself, however, looks a little bare. I like to decorate it with roasted coffee beans. With or without the cream, it should be served in very small portions.

❧ Soffiato all'Arancio Rapido

Orange soufflé

Serves 8

1 can (8 oz.) frozen orange juice
2 packets unflavored gelatine
8 large eggs, separated
¾ cup sugar
Water
12 ladyfingers
2 ounces rum or brandy
Pinch of salt
1 pint heavy cream

Fold a strip of aluminum foil to make a 4-inch collar around a 2-quart soufflé dish. Tie the collar on with a piece of string. The collar should be about 3 inches higher than the top edge of the soufflé dish.

Soften the orange juice concentrate. Pour half of it into a small saucepan and add the gelatine. Let stand. Reserve the other half of the orange juice.

Beat the egg yolks with the sugar until pale yellow. Add the reserved orange juice (without the gelatine) and beat with a hand mixer. Put some water into a large saucepan and bring water to a boil. Place the small saucepan with the gelatine and orange juice into the larger pan with the boiling water. Heat the gelatine-orange mixture to almost the boiling point but don't allow it to boil. When the gelatine is totally melted, remove the pot from the *bain-marie* and add the mixture to the egg yolks. Beat well.

Crumble the ladyfingers and place them in the soufflé dish. Add the rum and allow it to soak into the ladyfingers.

Add a pinch of salt to the egg whites and beat until quite stiff. Fold the whites into the yolks with the help of a rubber spatula. Beat the cream until quite stiff, then add it to the mixture. Pour slowly into the soufflé dish, mixing in the soaked ladyfingers.

Place the dish in the refrigerator and keep chilled for 4 to 5 hours. When ready to serve, place the soufflé dish on a plate and serve.

NOTE

This dessert may be prepared 6 to 8 hours before serving. Don't try to freeze it because the gelatine would turn gooey.

Torta di Mele e Pane

Apple and bread pie

Serves 6

10 slices white bread
1 stick butter
5 large ripe apples (McIntosh or similar variety)
½ cup orange marmalade
½ cup sugar
1 cup breadcrumbs (optional)
2 tablespoons dark rum

Preheat the oven to 375°. Remove the crust from the bread slices. Butter 5 slices on both sides. Line a 10-inch pie pan with the bread, pressing it with your fingers to cover the entire bottom of the dish.

Peel and core the apples. Slice them very thin. If you have a food processor, place pieces of apple into the feeder tube. Use the slicer and count to "One." One apple will have been sliced. Repeat the operation and it will take less than 5 seconds to slice 5 apples.

Make a layer of apple slices on top of the buttered bread, dot with orange marmalade and sprinkle liberally with sugar. Repeat with a layer of apples, then marmalade and sugar. When the apples, marmalade, and sugar have been used up, tear the remaining 5 slices of bread into bits and scatter on top. If the apples and marmalade are not toally covered, sprinkle breadcrumbs into the open spaces. Pour the rum over the top. Dot with the remaining butter and sprinkle any remaining sugar over it. Bake in the preheated oven for 40 minutes. The top should be very crisp. Serve hot.

NOTE

This is a solution for cooks who seem unable to produce a decent pie crust, or for cooks who are in a hurry.

It is also "a pie with a difference." I invented it in post-war Berlin, as the wife of the New York Times correspondent in Germany. We all got our staples from the commissary; we all served the same food. It was maddening. I simply had to have a different pie. It made a big hit and it still does.

Torta di Pesche Santo Stefano

Peach pie, Santo Stefano

Serves 8

For the pie crust:
2 ½ cups flour
2 sticks butter
5 hard-boiled egg yolks
¾ cup confectioners' sugar
Rind of 1 lemon, grated

For the filling:
6 large ripe peaches
3 tablespoons confectioners' sugar
1 ½ cup apricot or peach jam

See Illustrated Techniques, page 355.

With your fingertips, mix the butter with the flour. Strain the egg yolks through a sieve and add them to the flour-butter mixture. Add the sugar and grated lemon rind. Knead the dough with the palm of your hand, working it on a wooden or marble surface. When the dough is shiny and glistening, the butter and flour are properly blended and the dough is ready. Remember that this kind of dough (called *pasta frolla* in Italian) should not be worked too long.

Shape the dough into a ball and wrap it in wax paper. Keep it in a cool place (in the refrigerator, if you wish) until ready to use.

Peel the peaches and cut them into slices about ¼-inch thick. Place the slices in a jelly roll pan and sprinkle with sugar. Place under the broiler, not too close to the heat, and broil until golden brown. Let cool.

Remove the dough from the refrigerator and place it on your working surface. Roll out and flatten with a rolling pin to the desired thickness. Don't use a heavy hand; this type of dough crumbles easily. Sprinkle the pie pan with flour. Line it with the pie crust and bake until golden (about 20 minutes).

Remove the peach slices from the sheet: there will be about 2 tablespoons of peach juice left. Add the juice to the jam and heat until quite liquid.

Arrange the peach slices in the crust in whatever pattern you like. Glaze the top of the peaches with the melted jam and juice mixture.

NOTE

Andrea Dodi has named this pie alla Santo Stefano after a small town on the Mediterranean sea where he works in the summer, surrounded by the most wonderful peaches.

Torta di Mandorle

Almond cake

Serves 10

Water
3 cups almonds
2 tablespoons butter
1 tablespoon flour
6 whole eggs
2 cups confectioners' sugar
Peel of 1 lemon, grated
½ teaspoon vanilla extract

Preheat the oven to 350°. Blanch the almonds by bringing the water to a boil in a medium-sized saucepan, add the almonds and boil for 2 to 3 minutes. Let cool a couple of minutes and, as soon as the almonds are cool enough to handle, peel them. The skins will come off easily by just squeezing the almond at one end. Let dry on paper towels then chop as fine as possible.

Generously butter a 10-inch cake pan (possibly a springform) with a thick layer of butter, being careful that the bottom and sides are equally well coated. Dust the pan with flour. Turn the pan from side to side to make the flour cling to the entire surface, then shake to get off excess flour.

Separate the eggs and reserve the yolks for another use. Beat the whites until very stiff. When the whites are so stiff that you can turn bowl upside down and they remain in the bowl, add the sugar a little at a time, alternating with a little of the chopped almonds. Continue until all the almonds, except 1 tablespoon have been absorbed. Add the lemon peel and vanilla to the mixture, incorporating it gently into the egg whites. With a rubber spatula fill the cake pan with the mixture. Smooth the surface. Sprinkle with the remaining almonds and place the pan in a preheated oven. Bake for 40 minutes or until done. Insert a very thin knife and if knife comes out clean remove cake from oven.

Let cool for at least 30 minutes.

Coffee Brick

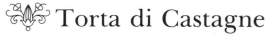 # Torta di Castagne
Chestnut cake

Serves 8 to 10

1 teaspoon butter
1 teaspoon flour
Water
1 pound fresh chestnuts
½ cup almonds
4 eggs, separated
1 cup sugar
Rind of 1 lemon, grated
1 stick butter
Few drops of vanilla extract (optional)

Preheat the oven to 350°. Coat an 8-inch cake form (preferably a springform) with butter and then dust with flour, being careful that all sides are equally coated.

Bring the water to a boil in a large kettle. With a sharp knife, make an *x* across the flat side of the chestnuts and drop them into the boiling water. Cook for about 20 minutes. When they are done, peel them and purée either through a sieve or in a blender. If a sieve is used, the chestnuts must still be warm when you push them through.

To blanch the almonds, bring water to a boil and drop almonds in. After a couple of minutes, remove and peel by simply squeezing them at one end. Chop the almonds rather fine.

In a bowl, beat the yolks with a fork. Add the sugar and grated lemon. Slowly add the butter in small pieces and blend in well. Add the almonds and the chestnut purée. Mix well.

Beat the egg whites until stiff. Fold the egg whites into the batter using a rubber spatula. Add vanilla, if desired.

Pour the chestnut mixture into the greased and floured form. Smooth the surface with the spatula. Bake for 35 to 40 minutes or until done. Insert a knife into center. If it comes out clean, the cake is done.

This cake may be served lukewarm or cold.

Torta di Cioccolata

Chocolate cake

Serves 10

1 tablespoon butter
4 tablespoons flour
8 ounces semisweet chocolate
2 sticks butter
¾ cup sugar
4 eggs, separated
Salt

Preheat the oven to 350°. Butter a 7-inch cake pan (preferably a springform) until heavily greased. Grate the chocolate into a bowl and add the flour. Mix well and set aside.

Place 2 sticks of butter in another mixing bowl and add the sugar. Add the egg yolks to the butter. Beat, either with an electric mixer or by hand, until the batter is almost white.

Add a pinch of salt to the egg whites and beat until quite stiff but not hard. The whites should have the consistency you would use for a soufflé.

Add the chocolate-flour mixture to butter-yolk mixture a little at a time until completely blended. Fold in the egg whites very gently. Pour the batter into the greased pan. Smooth the surface with a rubber spatula. Bake for 1 hour and 5 minutes or until done. Cool before unmolding. The center of this cake should be moist and almost creamy.

Focaccie

The dictionary describes a *focaccia* as "dough, flattened and baked in the oven." It is much more. In English it could be called many things: a tart, a pie, a cake, even a "Danish." It can be sweet or salted. It can be eaten for breakfast, as a snack, or as main course at a picnic.

The *focaccia* is one of the oldest traditional dishes of the Italian cuisine. The following recipe appears in no cookbook, as far as we know. We once inquired about its origin and were told: "It was simply always there."

 # La Focaccia del Re

The King's focaccia

Serves 6

2 sticks butter
½ pound honey
2 whole eggs
1 cup flour
½ cup dried figs, coarsely chopped
⅓ cup pine nuts, chopped

Preheat the oven to 375°. The butter should be at room temperature. Place it in a mixing bowl and soften with a wooden spoon. Add the honey, which should be of the liquid variety. Mix well. Beat the eggs separately and add them to the butter and honey mixture. Mix very well until all ingredients are well blended. Add the flour a little at a time, blending in to avoid lumps. Add the figs and pine nuts. The mixture should have the consistency of a soft dough.

A real *focaccia* should be baked in a rectangular dish. If not available, a 9-inch pie pan will do. Pour the dough into the pan and smooth the surface to an even thickness. Make sure the surface is even or the *focaccia* will be well done on one side and soft on the other. Place in the hot oven and bake for 40 minutes or until done. A toothpick should come out dry.

Cut the *focaccia* into wedges if a pie pan was used to bake it, or into squares if a rectangular baking dish was used.

 # Frittata di Mele

Apple frittata

Serves 4

2 extra large eggs, separated
3 tablespoons granulated sugar
Peel of 1 orange or lemon, grated
2 medium-sized apples (McIntosh or another
 firm variety)
2 tablespoons flour

1 ounce dark rum
3 tablespoons butter
1 tablespoon confectioners' sugar

Mix the egg yolks with the granulated sugar and beat well with an electric mixer or a wire whisk, until the mixture turns pale yellow. Add the orange or lemon peel and mix.

Peel and core the apples. Quarter them and cut into thin slices. If you have a food processor, feed the quartered apples into the tube, using the slicing blade. They will be sliced faster than you can look. Add the sliced apples to the yolk-sugar mixture.

Beat the whites until very stiff. Fold them into the yolks, mixing very gently and alternating with a little flour until all the flour has been absorbed. Add half the rum and mix gently.

Over high heat, melt 2 tablespoons of butter in an 8-inch skillet or omelet pan. When the butter is hot but not brown, pour the mixture into the pan. Smooth the surface with a spatula. As the edges begin to brown, reduce the heat to medium. With the spatula, push the edges to the center, at the same time lifting the edges slightly to make sure the *frittata* doesn't stick to the bottom of the pan. The reason for pushing the edges to the center is that the *frittata* should be as high as possible (at least 1 inch in the center).

When the surface is no longer liquid, place a plate on top and turn the skillet upside down.

Add the remaining butter to the skillet and slide the *frittata* back into it. Brown on the other side. The total cooking time is about 20 minutes. When done, the *frittata* should be golden on both sides and the center should be soft.

Sprinkle the top with confectioners' sugar and let cool. Before serving, sprinkle the remaining rum on top.

If desired, heat the rum before pouring it over the *frittata* and ignite.

NOTE

Igniting the rum doesn't really add to the taste of the frittata but it looks impressive.

Mele al Forno al Rum

Baked apples with rum

Serves 6

*6 large round apples (McIntosh or similar firm
    variety)*
2 ladyfingers (4 halves)
2 tablespoons butter
6 tablespoons dark rum
2 tablespoons brown sugar
½ cup water

Preheat the oven to 300°. Wash and core the apples. They should be large and flawless; they should also stand upright. Don't peel them. With a very sharp knife, make an incision all around them, about 1½ inches from the top. Don't cut too deeply into the flesh.

Butter a baking dish that will hold all 6 apples upright. Using your fingers, stuff a small piece of ladyfinger into the center of each apple. Follow with a pat of butter and close up the center with another piece of ladyfinger. The last piece should stick up in the air as if it were a leaf.

Arrange the apples in the baking dish. Spoon the rum over them so that it will penetrate into the centers of the apples. Sprinkle brown sugar over them. If you like your desserts very sweet, increase the amount of sugar.

Place the baking dish in the center of the oven. Bake for 1 hour, basting with a little water after ½ hour. The cooking time depends upon the size of the apples. When they are done, they should look wilted but not desperate. Remove from the oven and let stand for at least 30 minutes before serving.

NOTE

The first time I served these to my husband, he said "Italian? Baked apples are New England." Perhaps so, but this is a dessert of my childhood, minus the rum. When I was very good, Rosa, who was then the family cook, would insert a piece of chocolate between the piece of ladyfinger and the butter. She had never heard of New England.

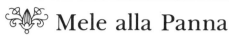

Mele alla Panna

Apples with whipped cream

Serves 4 to 6

6 large apples, preferably McIntosh
½ stick butter
½ cup sugar
½ teaspoon cinnamon (optional)
2 strips lemon peel
½ pint heavy cream
10 Amaretti di Saronno Lazzaroni (Italian almond macaroons)

Peel and core the apples. Cut into wedges (about 8 wedges per apple). Melt the butter in a large skillet. Add the apples. The apples should not be heaped on top of one another but, rather, spread out in a layer. Cook uncovered over medium heat for about 2 minutes. Add sugar, cinnamon, and lemon peel. Cook for about 3 more minutes. The apples should not be mushy but should also not be raw inside. Let cool, then arrange on individual plates.

Whip the cream (cream should be as cold as possible). Spoon the cream over the apples.

Crush the *Amaretti* in a mortar with a pestle or place the *Amaretti* in a metal bowl and put a smaller bowl on top; press hard until the *Amaretti* are crumbled but not pulverized. Sprinkle the *Amaretti* over the whipped cream. Serve at room temperature.

NOTE

Amaretti are available in almost all fancy grocery stores. If they are not available, don't try to replace them with soft macaroons but try hard oatmeal cookies. Don't expect the same result.

Fichi alla Gritti, I

Fresh figs alla Hotel Gritti

Serves 4

8 fresh ripe figs
½ ounce Kirsch

Choose 8 fresh ripe figs. They must be soft to the touch and the small opening at one end should be moist. Peel them carefully with a small sharp knife starting at the tip. Halve the figs and place them cut side up on individual serving plates, 2 figs per person. Sprinkle Kirsch over the figs and let stand a few minutes before serving.

NOTE

These are called Figs alla Gritti because it is at the Hotel Gritti in Venice that I first tasted them. We tried for a while to trace the origins of this marvelous combination and then we gave up; we were too busy eating them.

This dish requires really ripe green figs. If they are hard and the inside is somewhat like straw, forget about this recipe.

 # Fichi alla Gritti, II

Figs alla Hotel Gritti

Serves 4

16 ripe fresh figs, soft to the touch
½ cup heavy cream
1 ounce Kirsch

Peel the figs but leave them whole. Mix the cream and the Kirsch. Place the figs in a bowl (possibly glass or other transparent material) and pour the cream and Kirsch mixture over them. Toss carefully; the figs should not be mashed.

Let stand for at least 1 hour before serving. Keep in a cool place but don't refrigerate.

NOTE

We suggest serving them in a glass bowl because the figs are quite a spectacular sight. White or purple figs may be used. The only important thing is that they be ripe. They must be soft to the touch. Hard figs taste of sawdust.

This version of Figs alla Gritti is, of course, much richer than the preceding one. Personally we prefer the Kirsch alone, particularly if the figs are really ripe. But the cream does add a festive touch. And, judging from the number of people who order them, they are very popular.

Fresh Figs alla Hotel Gritti

Pesche al Vino Rosso

Peaches in red wine

Serves 6

6 ripe peaches
6 teaspoons sugar
Peel of ½ lemon (optional)
4 cups dry red wine, preferably Chianti

The peaches should be ripe but firm and, if possible, flawless. Halve the peaches, remove the stone, and cut into slices about ⅛-inch thick. Place the peach slices, unpeeled, in a deep bowl. Sprinkle with sugar. Add the lemon peel, if desired.

Cover the peaches with the wine, then cover the bowl and let stand for several hours or overnight. Don't refrigerate; just keep it in a cool place.

When you are ready to serve, divide the contents of the bowl into 6 portions, filling glass bowls first with the peach slices (remove the lemon peel first), then adding the wine in which the peaches were marinated.

NOTE

Leave out the sugar and these peaches in wine make a delicious before-or-after-dinner drink. Do this strictly during the summer months however; peaches must be in season. Canned peaches won't do at all.

 Pesche Ripiene

Stuffed peaches

Serves 6

6 ripe freestone peaches
6 Amaretti di Saronno Lazzaroni (Italian
*   almond macaroons)*
2 tablespoons sugar
3 egg yolks
½ cup light rum
Water
12 whole almonds (optional)
2 tablespoons sugar

Preheat the oven to 350°. Halve the peaches and remove the pits. With a small spoon, scoop out a little of the pulp and reserve it.

Place the *Amaretti* in a mortar and crush with a pestle or place on a flat surface, cover with a towel and crush with a rolling pin. Don't use a blender. The *Amaretti* should be reduced to crumbs, not powder. Add the sugar to the reserved peach pulp and then add this to the crumbs. Mix in the egg yolks. Fill each peach cavity with the mixture.

Coat a baking dish with butter and place the stuffed peach halves in the dish side by side. Bake for about 30 minutes. During the baking time, baste the peaches with rum.

In a saucepan, bring the water to a boil. Briefly blanch the almonds, remove them from the water and peel. When the peaches are done, decorate each half with a blanched almond.

NOTE

Some people like to dip peaches in boiling water and peel them before stuffing but there is an Italian proverb, *"peel figs for your friends and peel peaches for your enemies."* I prefer them unpeeled; also, they keep their shape much better.

Peaches may be served lukewarm or cold.

 ## Pere alla Gelatina di Frutta

Pears with currant jelly

Serves 6

6 pears, not too ripe (Bosc or other
  firm variety)
⅓ cup currant jelly
2 cups water
2 tablespoons sugar (optional)
½ ounce Amaretto liqueur (or Maraschino)

Peel the pears, leaving the stems intact. Place in a saucepan that will hold them standing up. Mix the jelly with the water and pour it over the pears. They should be covered so that only the stems poke out above the liquid. Cover and bring to a boil over very low heat. Allow to simmer for about 30 minutes.

Cool the pears in the juice, then remove the fruit and place it on a serving platter. Bring the liquid to a boil on the stove and then taste carefully. If desired, add the sugar for additional sweetness. Cook until the liquid coats a spoon. At this point, add the liqueur. Pour the liquid over the pears and let stand until cool. Don't refrigerate.

NOTE

The pears may be prepared ahead of time. If they stand overnight, scoop up the liquid and pour it over the pears again before serving. The pears should not look dry.

Pere in Forno al Rum

Pears baked with rum

Serves 6

6 *pears (Bosc or other firm variety)*
Juice of 1 lemon
2 *tablespoons brown sugar (optional)*
4 *tablespoon dark or light rum*
4 *tablespoons water*
6 *cloves*
1 *pint vanilla ice cream (optional)*

Preheat the oven to 200°. Peel, halve, and core the pears. Place them, cut side down, in a baking dish with a tight-fitting lid. The dish should not be much larger than the pear halves. Squeeze the lemon juice over them and sprinkle with sugar, if desired.

Mix the rum with water and pour over the pears. Scatter the cloves around the pears, keeping them from actually touching the fruit. Cover.

Place the baking dish in the center of the oven and bake for 1½ to 2 hours, according to the ripeness of the pears. Baste occasionally. Test with a fork to determine if they are cooked. When they are done, they will be pinkish.

Discard the cloves and let the pears cool. Serve them with their juice or place them cut side up in individual dishes and cover with a scoop of vanilla ice cream over each pear. Pour the rum-flavored liquid over the ice cream.

Pere Meringate

Pears with meringue topping

Serves 6

6 fully ripe pears (Bosc or other firm variety)
1 cup dry white wine
1 teaspoon vanilla extract
⅛ cup sugar
5 egg whites

Preheat the oven to 275°. The pears should not be overripe. Peel and core the pears and cut them into slices. Place the slices in a saucepan with the wine, vanilla, and half the sugar. Bring to a gentle boil and simmer until the liquid is almost gone. Drain the pears and place in a shallow baking dish and smooth the surface with a spatula.

Beat the egg whites until stiff, adding the remaining sugar as soon as you start beating. Cover the pears with the beaten egg whites, forming peaks with the whites.

Place the baking dish in the preheated oven and bake until whites are set and peaks turn golden: about 15 to 20 minutes.

Serve lukewarm.

NOTE

If you wish to prepare this dish ahead of time, preheat the oven to 350°, place the dish in the oven, then turn off the heat. The pears can stay in the oven for as long as 1 hour without burning.

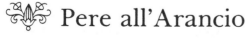

Pere all'Arancio

Pears with orange juice

Serves 6

6 ripe, firm pears (Bosc or Bartlett)
2 cups dry white wine
⅓ cup sugar
Juice of 1 orange
Peel of 1 orange

(continued)

½ *stick cinnamon or a pinch of ground*
  cinnamon
⅓ *cup orange marmalade*
⅓ *cup Aurum, Grand Marnier or Amaretto di*
  Saronno

Peel the pears and halve them. Remove the cores. Place the fruit in a saucepan, add the wine and sugar and bring to a slow boil, uncovered. Add the orange juice. Remove the bitter white flesh of the orange and cut only the outer peel into very thin strips. Add these strips to the pears and simmer until the fruit is tender. The cooking time depends upon the type of pears used. To see if they are done, poke them gently with a fork.

Transfer the pears and orange strips to a bowl or place them in individual serving dishes. Add the cinnamon and orange marmalade to the cooking liquid and simmer for 5 minutes. Add the Aurum or other liqueur, if desired. Simmer a minute longer then pour the liquid over the pears and let stand for at least 1 hour before serving. Chill slightly before serving.

 ## Fragole all'Aceto

Strawberries with vinegar

Serves 4

1 *pint fresh strawberries*
1 *cup wine, either red or white*
2 *teaspoons white vinegar*
Confectioners' sugar

Remove the stems and hulls from the strawberries. Place them in a small bowl and cover with wine. Let the fruit stand for about 5 minutes. Pour off the wine completely; this serves only to wash the berries. If you were to use water instead of wine, the strawberries would lose their taste and get watery. The result justifies the extravagant use of wine.

Fill 2 small bowls with the strawberries and pour 1 teaspoon of vinegar into each bowl. Add sugar according to your taste. Mix well and serve.

NOTE

When I was first served strawberries with vinegar, I couldn't believe it. It sounded preposterous. But the taste of vinegar disappears when it gets overpowered by the taste of

the berries and the acidity brings out the taste of the berries and increases their sweetness. I am told that this is an invention of a famous Italian actor. It has become quite popular and it works.

 # Fragole al Vino

Strawberries with wine

Serves 4

1 pint fresh strawberries
2 cups of wine, either red or white
1 tablespoon sugar (optional)

Remove the hulls from the strawberries, then place them in a shallow bowl. Pour 1 cup of wine over the berries, turn them a couple of times, and then let stand for about 10 minutes. Pour off the wine. All the sand should pour off with it. If there is any left, it will be at the bottom of the dish.

Transfer the berries to a serving bowl, add the sugar, if desired, and pour the second cup of wine over the berries. Refrigerate for about 1 hour before serving.

NOTE

For some reason, the little wild strawberries (Fragole di Bosco in Italian) are usually served with white wine, while the large cultivated ones, common in the United States, are served with red. We feel that either white or red wine goes equally well.

 # Frutta al Rum con Amaretti

Fruit with rum and macaroons

Serves 4 to 6

2 large, ripe pears
2 large, ripe peaches
1 cup fresh pineapple, cut into small chunks

(continued)

2 ripe bananas, sliced
Juice of ½ lemon
6 Amaretti di Saronno Lazzaroni (Italian
   almond macaroons)
½ cup light rum
1 tablespoon sugar
½ cup fresh strawberries

Peel the pears and immediately rub them with lemon to prevent their getting dark. Peel the peaches only if they have dark spots. Otherwise just slice and sprinkle with lemon juice. Slice the pears. Place alongside the pineapple chunks and banana slices.

Amaretti di Saronno Lazzaroni are imported Italian macaroons sold in most groceries around the country. They are wrapped in paper, 2 to a wrapper. When I say 6, I mean 12 halves. Break up 2 halves at a time and crumble them with your hands or, better still, in a mortar. Make a layer of Amaretti crumbs in a shallow bowl and sprinkle the rum over them. Cover the macaroons with a layer of pears. Sprinkle lightly with sugar and cover with another layer of macaroons. Sprinkle with rum, soaking the layer of macaroons and continue alternating layers of fruit with layers of macaroons. The last layer should be of bananas. Garnish with fresh strawberries. If desired, add slivers of dates between the layers. Very little sugar is needed because the macaroons are sweet.

This dish should be prepared well ahead of your serving time. In fact, it is better if refrigerated overnight.

NOTE

If no fresh fruit is available, canned fruit may be used but the result is less satisfactory. If no Amaretti di Saronno Lazzaroni are available, oatmeal cookies may be used rather than American macaroons because the latter are too soft and won't soak up the rum. The result, however, is not the same.

 Sformato di Gelato

Ice cream mold

Serves 6

18 ladyfingers
1 cup rum, light or dark

1 pint vanilla ice cream
1 pint chocolate ice cream
1 pint strawberry ice cream

Line a porcelain or earthenware bowl, 8 inches in diameter and about 5 inches deep, with aluminum foil. Fold the foil carefully so that it clings to the whole inside of the bowl.

Pour the rum into a deep dish and dip the ladyfingers very briefly into the rum. Dip them very briefly because otherwise they will disintegrate. Line the bowl with ladyfingers, pressing them lightly with your hands to the bottom and sides of the bowl. If little spaces form here and there, take a small piece of a ladyfinger and mend the gap. When the whole bowl is lined, the ladyfingers should form a smooth, even surface.

Spoon the ice cream into the hollow, alternating the 3 flavors in 3 layers. You might want to change the flavors but do stick to 3 different colors. Depending upon the size of your bowl, you might have a little ice cream left over or need a little more. It should be completely filled without any empty spaces.

Dip a spoon in hot water and flatten the surface of the ice cream with the back of the spoon.

Place the bowl in the freezer for at least 10 minutes. Remove 30 minutes before serving. Place a round platter on top of the bowl and turn the bowl upside down. Remove the bowl and, very carefully, take off the aluminum foil. If desired, decorate the top of the mold with whipped cram or surround it with a ring of whipped cream, squeezing the cream through a pastry bag.

NOTE

An Italian diplomat's cook taught me this dessert. Her boss frequently gave her very little notice before bringing people to dinner. It has been a reliable dessert for her and for me.

I have prepared the mold with ice milk instead of ice cream in order to make it less rich and fattening. I have also decorated it with fresh berries. It has always made a hit. A small warning: make sure you give it a chance to defrost.

 Sorbetto al Melone

Cantaloupe sherbet

Serves 4 to 5

1 medium-sized ripe cantaloupe
⅓ cup confectioners' sugar
1 ounce light rum (optional)
4 sprigs fresh mint (optional)

Scoop out the pink pulp of the cantaloupe, being careful not to go too close to the rind where the fruit starts to get bitter. Taste the cantaloupe for sweetness and add the sugar accordingly. (In midsummer, cantaloupes are very sweet and might require very little sugar.)

Place the pulp and sugar in a saucepan without water. (The cantaloupe has enough juice; just be careful to collect it all.) Bring the contents to a boil and, as soon as it boils, turn off the heat. Let it cool for a couple of minutes. Place in a blender and run the motor for about 30 seconds (if you have a food processor, 5 seconds will suffice).

Place the mixture in a bowl in the freezer. Remove every ½ hour and whip with an electric mixer. The total freezing time should be about 3 hours. If desired, add rum to the cantaloupe before beating with the mixer.

Serve in small bowls or sherbet glasses, accompanied by ladyfingers. If desired, garnish with sprigs of fresh mint.

Suggested Menus

I have divided the menus into those for luncheons and dinners. Some of the meals can be prepared in advance and need little or no finishing touches. Some of the luncheon suggestions might sound like too much food for our modern way of life. If you feel this is the case, leave out one course.

I have tried to think of the energy problem in planning these menus. If you have to light the oven for a Baked Polenta, you might as well bake apples too. I have tried to put the ingredients that are in season in the same menu. For instance, when green beans are young, strawberries are also in season. You will find both in the same menu.

Readers will find that several meals end with either fruit or cheese (a very common dessert in Italy), or a combination of both, which is equally common. There is, in fact, an Italian proverb that says *"al contadino non far sapere quanto è buono il formaggio con le pere."* This means, don't let the farmer know how good cheese is with pears. The reason is that, if he finds out, he will harvest the pears for himself and eat up the cheese he produces.

Apples are frequently eaten with cheese, but pears are the most popular fruit for that combination. Pears are particularly eaten with Gorgonzola cheese, which is now available in this country.

Richer, more elaborate desserts are reserved for evening meals. This should not prevent a hostess who is planning an elaborate luncheon to take the dessert from a dinner menu and add it to the luncheon menu of her choice. She could also give her guests the choice between fruit and dessert.

A hostess has to be somewhat flexible. I recently gave a luncheon in the country. A guest had warned me on the phone that she was on a diet and would not be eating any starches. Please, I should not be hurt if she refused a course. I gauged my menu accordingly but, as it was a holiday and I wanted the meal to be festive, I did have the Ice Cream Mold as dessert. I also had an enormous bowl of cherries in the center of the table; they were to be both table decoration and her dessert. When the Ice Cream Mold was served she seemed surprised that I was not offering her any. I reminded her of our telephone conversation.

"I said I was on a diet," said she, "I didn't say that I was on a *strict* diet."

As a result, she had both the Ice Cream Mold and the cherries. Remember, a hostess has to be flexible.

Luncheons

Artichokes stuffed with mushrooms
Ham soufflé
*fresh fruit and cheese

Grandmother's little bundles
Scaloppine of veal with lemon
Green beans with oil and lemon
Strawberries with wine

Baked tomatoes
Stuffed fresh anchovies
*Cheese and fruit

Escarole soup with milk
Beef meat loaf
Spinach with oil
Ice cream mold

*(This is a rather rich luncheon but it has the great advantage of
being able to be prepared ahead of time.)*

Spinach and cornmeal soup, Friuli style
Scaloppine of veal with parsley
Salad of mixed cooked vegetables
Fresh figs alla Hotel Gritti, I

*recipe not included in this book

Chicken and corn salad
Ricotta soufflé
*Fruit

Spinach loaf
Poached fish, served with sauce
*Cheese and fruit

Stuffed zucchini
Veal with olives
*Tossed green salad
*Fruit

Baked polenta with white sauce
"Dragged" broccoli with olive oil
Baked apples with rum

Carpaccio
Chicken breasts with cream
Steamed rice
Brussel sprouts and belgian endive salad
*Fruit

Green bean mold, served with tomato sauce
Scaloppine of veal with parsley
Spinach with cream (creamed spinach)
Stuffed peaches

*recipe not included in this book

Asparagus with butter and Parmesan
Lamb stew with eggs
Strawberries with vinegar

Risotto with fresh asparagus
Shrimps with oil and lemon
*Fruit and cheese

Risotto with peas
Fish, sweet and sour
Figs alla Hotel Gritti, II

---

*recipe not included in this book

Dinners

Gnocchi, Roman style
Tasty slices of beef
*Boiled potatoes
Green beans with tomatoes
Chocolate and ladyfingers pudding

Risotto with lemon
Veal shank the Vicenza way
Celery root with butter and Parmesan
Fruit with rum and macaroons

Baked artichokes
Lamb stew with eggs
Pears baked with rum

Minestrone, the Milanese way
Veal cutlet Milanese
Spinach with oil
*Fruit and cheese

Chicken broth with asparagus
Chicken in white wine with mushrooms
*Boiled potatoes
Sautéed zucchini
Ice cream mold

*recipe not included in this book

Beef with lemon
Artichoke hearts in a skillet
Chestnut cake

Tagliatelle with 4 cheeses
Scaloppine of veal with lemon
*Tossed green salad
*Fruit

Asparagus, Milanese style
Maria's veal stew with lemon
Chocolate cake

Crespelle with ricotta and spinach
Roast chicken with rosemary
*Green peas
*Boiled young potatoes
Strawberries in wine

Baked risotto in a mold
Poached fish, served with sauce
*Boiled potatoes
*Tossed green salad
Zabaglione with strawberries

*recipe not included in this book

Baked fish in aluminum foil
*Boiled potatoes
Orange soufflé

*(This might look like a skimpy meal but the fish, baked with shrimps and mussels,
is a meal in itself.)*

Mushroom, celery, and cheese salad with truffles
Boiled chicken with white sauce
*Fresh figs

*(When truffles are in season, figs should be ripe and juicy.
If none are available, serve fresh fruit of various kinds.)*

Rolled smoked salmon
My own roast of veal
*Mashed potatoes
Sautéed zucchini
Green beans sautéed in butter
Coffee brick

Panzanella
Stuffed roast of veal
Grated zucchini
Apples with whipped cream

*recipe not included in this book

Risotto with Champagne
Braised beef the Trento way
Sautéed zucchini
Lemon cream

Ossibuchi with risotto, Milanese style
Salad of mixed cooked vegetables
Pears with currant jelly

A Note on Italian Wines

There was a time when all red wines from Italy were called "Chianti" and were usually mispronounced. White wines (with the exception of Orvieto, Frascati, and Soave) were practically unknown. We have come a long way since then.

Italian law now prohibits wine producers from calling their wine "Chianti Classico" unless it actually is. And Chianti is still popular, but wine drinkers have also become more sophisticated and better informed. Their palates are more sensitive. As Americans have become more interested in drinking wines, Italy has become more interested in exporting them.

You can hear about wines and you can read about wines, but only by drinking them will you learn about them. In this book I have limited myself to the wines that are readily, or in some cases not so readily, available in this country. I have not limited myself to wines from the Veneto or other regions of northern Italy, but have gone as far as Naples and even to Sicily.

It is still true that Italy produces more, and better, red wines than whites. This is the case as far as wines that travel are concerned. Chiantis, from Tuscany, are not only popular and excellent buys, but they are also good everyday wines. I divide them into young Chiantis and aged ones.

As a general rule, only the Chianti Classico ages well. We recently opened an eleven-year-old bottle, let it breathe for a couple of hours, and enjoyed a beautiful soft wine. On the other hand, the non-Classico Chiantis should be drunk at a much earlier age. When a Chianti is young, it is light, fresh, and cheerful. When it has reached a certain age, it can be quite majestic.

My advice is to experiment with Chiantis. They are full of surprises and some of them are most pleasant.

Second in popularity are the wines of the Piedmont. First among these is Barolo, closely followed by Gattinara. Both are made from Nebbiolo grapes and are impressive wines. Personally, I consider these winter wines that do wonderful things with a roast beef or with venison. Either should be about three years old to be at its best.

The Piedmont produces a wealth of lesser wines, like Barbera, Barbaresco, and Freisa, which are readily available in this country. These too are vigorous reds. The white wines of the Piedmont are generally dessert wines and are too sweet to be drunk with a meal.

Relative newcomers to this country (and very successful ones) are the wines of Valtellina. That region, roughly north of Milan, produces some very fine dry reds. They are Sassella, Grumello, and Inferno. Although my guests laugh at the name of the last one, they drink it with pleasure.

Halfway between Milan and Venice is Lake Garda. The slopes surrounding the lake produce some of the best-known wines of Italy. Two of them — Bardolino and Valpolicella — are almost as well known in this country as in the country they come from. Bardolino and Valpolicella are gentle reds, the color of a very fine ruby. This means that they are lighter than the wines of the Piedmont or Valtellina.

Another wine, Chiaretto del Garda, shows up every now and then in the liquor stores. It is what its name implies — a small light red wine with great charm when drunk in its own territory and sometimes a little disappointing when drunk after having traveled a distance.

Continue on your way to Venice and you will come to a village with a familiar name: Soave, with a beautiful old castle overlooking the town. Its pale golden wine is to be tasted wherever you go. Soave should, of course, be drunk chilled.

The whole region between Verona and Padua is glorious wine country. It doesn't produce large amounts of wine but what is produced is very special. For now, only two of the wines of that region come to the United States. They are Durello and Venegazù. Both are available in both red and white. In spite of Italy's reputation for producing better reds, in this case, I prefer the whites.

No grapes are grown in Venice, but to the east of the city in the region of Friuli, grapes grow beautifully. The two most important wines are Tocai (white) and Merlot (red). You will find them mentioned frequently throughout this book; they go particularly well with the food of the region.

Verdicchio is also mentioned a few times in this book. It comes from Ancona, located southeast of Florence. It is a sturdy, slightly bitter white wine. At its best it is very good but I find it difficult to find a Verdicchio in this country that could be considered "at its best."

From Ancona you head toward Naples, or, more precisely, the hills around Sorrento. This is the home of Gragnano, a delicious light red wine when it is at its best. I have been lucky to find some good Gragnano occasionally in the United States, but recently I have been seeing too much of it. Since the region around Sorrento doesn't produce a great deal of wine, I suspect some of this is mislabeled.

One of the recent happy additions to Italian wines in this country comes from Sicily, a land traditionally known for its Marsala. Corvo comes from around Palermo and is available in both red and white. Most people I speak with prefer the red. In my opinion the white Corvo is one of the best Italian wines available.

Illustrated Techniques

Polenta

Polenta is a mush made of coarse cornmeal. The cornmeal is cooked until it gets quite solid. Then it is eaten either instead of bread, or fried on the gridiron, or made into dozens of different dishes, with the addition of cheeses, meats, sausages, mushrooms, or ragouts.

(1) Bring the water to a strong boil, using a large, sturdy pot.

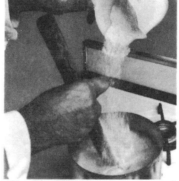

(2) Start pouring the cornmeal into the boiling water, stirring with a long wooden pole.

(3) Slowly add the remainder of the cornmeal, stirring steadily as cornmeal mixes with the water.

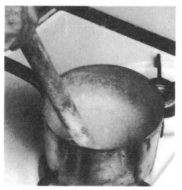

(4) Continue stirring. As the cornmeal mush thickens, stir more slowly.

(5) When the *polenta* is done, lightly moisten a tablecloth and pour the mush onto the cloth. It will form a mound in the center.

(6) Using the wooden pole, spread the *polenta* slightly on the cloth. Allow to cool.

Risotto

Risotto is a creamy mixture of broth, butter, rice, and Parmesan cheese. It is called *"risotto all'onda"* (with waves) because, whereas each grain should be separate, they all should be held together. It is essential to use Italian rice for this dish. The long grain variety doesn't seem to produce that creamy substance that is the basis of a real *risotto*.

(1) Melt the butter in a heavy saucepan. Simmer the broth in a second saucepan nearby.

(2) Add the rice to the hot butter.

(3) Stir the rice while adding the broth, one ladle at a time. As the rice absorbs the broth, add another ladleful so as to just barely cover the kernels.

(4) When the rice is done, the broth will have been absorbed as well.

(5) Add the remaining butter and stir.

Pasta

There are people who feel that making your own pasta is too much trouble. This is certainly true of elbow macaroni and various types of pastina, but when it comes to *tagliatelle, taglierini,* or any of the other forms of thin noodles, people are bound to change their minds, once they have tasted the homemade product. If you are a pasta lover, invest in a pasta-making machine. It simplifies life enormously.

(1)   Place your flour in a mound on a working surface. Make a well in the center of the mound.

(2)   Break the eggs into the well.

(3)   Using a fork, rapidly incorporate the eggs with the flour.

(4)   Protect the sides of the flour mound with your hands so that the loose flour won't spread all over your surface.

(5)   Make sure that the flour and eggs are smoothly blended. Add more flour to the dough by taking it from the sides.

(6)   Begin to knead the dough with your fingers.

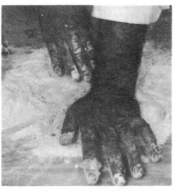

(7) Continue to knead, incorporating the rest of the flour.

(8) Knead the dough until it is smooth.

(9) Run the dough through the pasta machine, using the first setting.

(10) Crank the handle of the machine as you feed the rest of the dough through the machine.

(11) Fold the dough in thirds to prepare to put it through the machine a second time.

(12) Add a little flour to the dough if it seems sticky.

(13) Put the dough through the pasta machine again, using the first setting. Put it through a third time for even thinner dough.

(14) Fold the dough in thirds.

(15) Prepare to send the dough through the machine again, this time using the second setting.

(16) Feed the dough into the machine.

(17) Crank the handle and pull out the long, flat (and thin) dough.

(18) Wrap the dough around your arm as it comes from the machine or gather it in folds at the base.

(19) As you see, the dough emerges as a continuous piece. This is the dough before it has been cut into the desired shapes.

(20) Cut the long piece of dough into small sections that can be fed easily into the machine.

(21) If you decide to make *tagliatelle,* it will look like this.

(22) If you desire *tagliarini,* feed the dough through the machine and you will have pieces like this.

Gnocchi

Gnocchi are dumplings, made of potatoes, cornmeal, spinach, or spinach and cheese. The following photographs show you how to make cornmeal *gnocchi*.

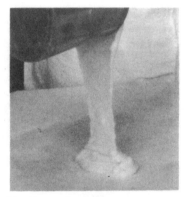

(1) Pour the mixture onto a moistened tablecloth.

(2) It will spread out on the surface.

(3) Flatten the mixture with the back of a wet spoon until you have it the thickness you desire.

(4) Using a cookie cutter, cut rounds of dough.

(5) Place the dough rounds in an ovenproof baking dish that has been greased with butter.

(6) Arrange the rows so that they slightly overlap one another. Continue until you fill the baking dish.

Pie Crust

Pasta Frolla is a Friuli style dough for a basic pie crust. It may be used for meat or vegetable pies as well as for sweet pies. If used for the latter, add sugar to the dough according to the sweetness desired.

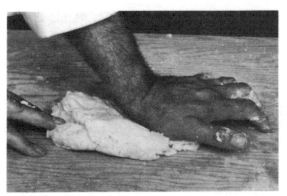

(1)   Press the hard-boiled eggs through a sieve, using your fingers.

(2)   Incorporate the butter, using a knife to cut it into the flour.

(3)   Knead the dough with your hands until all ingredients are blended and dough has a shiny surface.

(4)   Form a ball of the dough, wrap it in wax paper, and let it rest in the refrigerator for at least 30 minutes.

Index